THE GOVERNANCE OF CHINESE CHARITABLE TRUSTS

Legislators in China introduced the charitable trust model in 2016 with the passage of the Chinese Charity Law. They constructed a new legal framework for this model, in order to unlock the potential of trust institutions to further and develop charitable causes. This is the first English-language monograph exploring the governance of Chinese charitable trusts from the perspectives of law and sociology. Through the application of doctrinal analysis and semi-structured qualitative interviews, this book reveals that China's particular political, social, and economic conditions are essential to understanding the legislated governance framework for charitable trusts and its implementation in practice. Embedded in China's unique institutional context, the governance of Chinese charitable trusts can only be fully understood in light of relevant law, administrative practice and private actions taken by charitable trust parties.

HUI JING is an Assistant Professor at the Faculty of Law, University of Hong Kong. He completed his PhD at Melbourne Law School, where his doctoral thesis was awarded the Harold Luntz Graduate Research Prize for Best PhD Thesis. Dr Jing has published in journals including *Legal Studies* and *American Journal of Comparative Law* and he has contributed chapters to several edited collections.

THE GOVERNANCE OF CHINESE CHARITABLE TRUSTS

HUI JING
University of Hong Kong

CAMBRIDGE
UNIVERSITY PRESS

CAMBRIDGE
UNIVERSITY PRESS

Shaftesbury Road, Cambridge CB2 8EA, United Kingdom

One Liberty Plaza, 20th Floor, New York, NY 10006, USA

477 Williamstown Road, Port Melbourne, VIC 3207, Australia

314–321, 3rd Floor, Plot 3, Splendor Forum, Jasola District Centre, New Delhi – 110025, India

103 Penang Road, #05-06/07, Visioncrest Commercial, Singapore 238467

Cambridge University Press is part of Cambridge University Press & Assessment, a department of the University of Cambridge.

We share the University's mission to contribute to society through the pursuit of education, learning and research at the highest international levels of excellence.

www.cambridge.org
Information on this title: www.cambridge.org/9781009327909

DOI: 10.1017/9781009327954

First published 2023

A catalogue record for this publication is available from the British Library.

Library of Congress Cataloging-in-Publication Data
Names: Jing, Hui, 1990- author.
Title: The governance of Chinese charitable Trusts / Hui Jing, The University of Hong Kong.
Description: Cambridge, United Kingdom ; New York, NY : Cambridge University Press, 2023. | Based on author's thesis (doctoral -University of Melbourne Law School, 2020) issued under title: The unique governance structure of Chinese charitable trusts. |
Includes bibliographical references and index.
Identifiers: LCCN 2023003183 (print) | LCCN 2023003184 (ebook) |
ISBN 9781009327909 (hardback) | ISBN 9781009327923 (paperback) |
ISBN 9781009327954 (epub)
Subjects: LCSH: Charitable uses, trusts, and foundation–China. Classification: LCC KNQ526 .J56 2023 (print) | LCC KNQ526 (ebook) | DDC 346.51/0642–dc23/eng/20230209
LC record available at https://lccn.loc.gov/2023003183
LC ebook record available at https://lccn.loc.gov/2023003184

ISBN 978-1-009-32790-9 Hardback

CONTENTS

ACKNOWLEDGEMENTS

This book was developed from my doctoral thesis at Melbourne Law School. I am indebted to a number of people for its completion.

First, I would like to thank my family. They have always been unwavering in their love for me and supportive of the choices I have made. Particular thanks are owed to my mother, Wang Xiuling. Although she did not have the opportunity to enter college, she is still the most brilliant person I have ever known. She taught me that, as a member of society, I must always work hard, keep my feet on the ground, and learn from the exceptional people around me. Her patient, tireless teaching nurtured my resilient character, allowing me to maintain a positive attitude in the face of all the hardships I have encountered.

Second, I would like to thank my supervisors, Professor Matthew Harding and Professor Sarah Biddulph. It was my great fortune to be supervised by them. I feel the deepest gratitude for the encouragement, insight, conscientiousness, and enthusiasm they displayed over the course of my doctoral studies. Without their immense patience and endless support, it would have been impossible for me to have completed my academic training journey in such a smooth way. I also extend my thanks to Professor Eric Descheemaeker, who sat on my advisory committee. His warm-hearted guidance was immeasurably valuable and of great personal importance over the course of my candidature.

Third, I would like to express my sincere gratitude to the following members of Melbourne Law School: Associate Professor Andrew Godwin, Professor Sean Cooney, Professor Chen Jianlin, Professor Ying Khai Liew, Professor Rosemary Langford, Professor Elise Bant, Professor Katy Barnett, and Professor Jason Varuhas. They offered suggestions and comments on my research, allowed me to audit their classes to gain an in-depth understanding of common law subjects, and advised me on how to establish academic connections with members outside of Melbourne Law School. I deeply appreciate their being so accommodating, caring, and considerate.

Fourth, I would like to thank my close friends, Xu Xiaowei, Liu Liyuan, Wang Jiajun, Zhang Yang, Miranda Webster, Lyu Xin, Li Dejian, Lilis Mulyani, Tobias Barkley, Ben Hopper, and Sohidul Islam Riyad. I benefitted tremendously from their kind company and tireless assistance. We shared and discussed ideas on a wide variety of topics, from bridge construction and financial market regulation to animal protection, and from what our favourite chocolates are to which supermarkets we would most like to visit. Their companionship and encouragement made my life in Melbourne deeply memorable and rewarding.

Fifth and last, I would like to extend my thanks to Professor Lusina Ho and Professor Mark Sidel, the two external reviewers for my doctoral thesis. Their recognition of my work gave me a strong sense that my efforts over the past three years were worthy and had borne fruit. Their suggestions on how to develop my thesis into a separate monograph contributed significantly to the publication of this book. I am warmly appreciative of their reviews and generous help.

1

Introduction

I Background

A Development of the Social Welfare System in China over the Past Six Decades

In China, charitable activities played a critical role in social welfare delivery in both the Imperial Era[1] and the Republican Era (1911–49).[2] However, after the establishment of the People's Republic of China (PRC) by the Communist Party of China (CCP or 'party'), due to the socialist ideology held by the leadership at that time, charity was considered part of the capitalist regime and 'an instrument of the ruling class that was used to control, denigrate, and mark off as different the poorer classes of society'.[3] Accordingly, after the establishment of the PRC, in conjunction with the implementation of a planned economy (*jihua jingji* 计划经济), China established a socialist social welfare system for the general public.[4] All independent charities were either prohibited as unlawful organizations or incorporated into the government (for example, the Red Cross Society of China).[5] Since the implementation

1 Karla W. Simon, *Civil Society in China: The Legal Framework from Ancient Times to the 'New Reform Era'* (Oxford University Press, 2013), 77; Yu-Yue Tsu, 'The Spirit of Chinese Philanthropy: A Study in Mutual Aid' (PhD Thesis, The Faculty of Political Science, Columbia University, 1912), 23; Thomas David Dubois, 'Before the NGO: China Charities in Historical Perspective' (2015) 39(4) *Asian Studies Review* 541, 542; Elizabeth Z. Lang, 'Some Reflections on Charity Law in the People's Republic of China' (2003) 15(2) *Bond Law Review* 358, 358.

2 Chung Yan Miu, Huang Xin, Kenneth W. Foster, and Frank Tester, 'Charity Development in China: An Overview' (2007) 17(1) *Asia Pacific Journal of Social Work and Development* 79, 80; Dubois (n 1) 542.

3 Miu et al. (n 2) 80.

4 Deborah Davis, 'Chinese Social Welfare: Policies and Outcomes' (1989) 119 *China Quarterly* 577, 578; Ruby C. M. Chau and Sam W. K. Yu, 'Social Welfare and Economic Development in China and Hong Kong' (1999) 19(1) *Critical Social Policy* 87, 94–5.

5 徐卫 [Xu Wei],《慈善宣言信托制度构建研究》 [Research on the Construction of Charitable Declaration Trusts] (法律出版社 [Law Press], 2012) 16.

of the 'Reform and Opening Up' (*gaige kaifang* 改革开放) policy in 1978, China has faced severe pressure to deliver social welfare services. Hundreds of millions of the needy and disenfranchised remain in dire need of healthcare, education, and financial support. Although China is presently the largest developing country in the world, the Chinese government struggles to satisfy the general welfare needs of the majority of its citizens; the government's public finance expenditure in the foregoing areas is far from sufficient and cannot meet the increasing demand for public welfare.

Confronted with these problems, the Chinese government has gradually realized the necessity of providing a supportive social welfare system while developing a market economy.[6] It believes that this kind of social welfare system cannot be the same as the traditional planned economy model.[7] As a compromise, 'a new multilevel system'[8] involving the government, market, and non-profits was established. In this system, although the government still plays a role in public welfare provision, the non-governmental sector – including markets, NGOs, households, and individuals – is expected to finance and provide the majority of social welfare delivery.[9] In the 2000s, the Chinese government at different levels launched a series of initiatives, clearly identifying NGOs as important partners in their efforts to address pressing social needs.[10] The basic model of public welfare service in China was, thus, established. On the one hand, the state further increased its public expenditure on social welfare to enhance the well-being of its citizens. On the other hand, it gradually promoted the involvement of charities and other social

[6] Qiusha Ma, 'The Governance of NGOs in China since 1978: How Much Autonomy?' (2002) 31(3) *Nonprofit and Voluntary Sector Quarterly* 305, 306; Rebecca Lee, 'Modernize Charity Law in China' (2009) 18 *Pacific Rim Law & Policy Journal* 347, 354; 韩丽欣 [Han Lixin],《中国慈善组织治理法治化研究》 [Research on the Governance of Chinese Charities] (法律出版社 [Law Press], 2015) 4; 徐卫 [Xu Wei] (n 5) 13–16.

[7] 徐卫 [Xu Wei] (n 5) 14–16.

[8] Zhenyao Wang and Yanhui Zhao, 'The Collapse and Reemergence of Private Philanthropy in China, 1949–2012' in Jennifer Ryan, Lincoln C. Chen and Tony Saich (eds.), *Philanthropy for Health in China* (Indiana University Press, 2014) 28–9.

[9] Ying Xu and Ngan-Pun Ngai, 'Moral Resources and Political Capital: Theorizing the Relationship between Voluntary Service Organizations and the Development of Civil Society in China' (2011) 40(2) *Nonprofit and Voluntary Sector Quarterly* 247, 248; Miu et al. (n 2) 83; Lee (n 6) 354.

[10] Adam S. Chodorow, 'Charity with Chinese Characteristics' (2012) 30 *UCLA Pacific Basin Law Journal* 1, 4.

organizations in public welfare provision.[11] This model provided a platform for charities to participate in the provision of social welfare.

B Tight Governmental Control and the Lack of Public Trust

The loosening of control over the charity sector has contributed to the growth and development of charitable organizations. According to the recent official statement on the development of registered social organizations (*shehui zuzhi* 社会组织), there were around 662,000 registered social organizations by the end of 2015, which received donations of about RMB 6.1 billion and mainly conducted activities in areas such as education, social services, health, culture, sports, and environmental protection.[12] However, it is worth noting that, under the legal framework before 2016, the government monopolized charitable resources and controlled the majority of charities recognized by law, and most independent charities could not be registered and were therefore regarded as illegal organizations. The government's tight control over the charitable sector is achieved through the application of a registration procedure (*dengji zhi* 登记制). This procedure is specified in the law regulating charities,[13] which empowers regulators to conduct a substantive examination of the documents submitted by relevant parties seeking to establish a charitable entity. Regulators are empowered to use their administrative discretion to decline the establishment of certain charitable entities whose operations are deemed to pose risks or to require changes to be made to the scope and activities of the proposed charitable entity before granting approval. Approval by regulators is essential to the valid establishment of a charity.

11 Yijia Jing and E. S. Savas, 'Managing Collaborative Service Delivery: Comparing China and the United States' (2009) 69 *Public Administration Review* 101, 102.

12 中国信托业协会 [China Trustee Association] (ed.),《慈善信托研究》 [Research on the Charitable Trust] (中国金融出版社 [China Financial Publishing House], 2016) 74.

13 《社会团体登记管理条例》 [Regulations on Registration Administration of Associations] (People's Republic of China) State Council, 6 February 2016, art 3;《民办非企业单位登记管理暂行条例》 [Interim Regulations on the Administration of the Registration of Privately-Operated Non-Enterprise Organizations] (People's Republic of China) State Council, 25 October 1998, art 5;《基金会管理条例》 [Regulations on Administration of Foundations] (People's Republic of China) State Council, 3 August 2004, art 6. Registration requirement gives the government the power to manipulate what types of charities can be established and what types of public welfare services they can provide, see Xiaoming Feng, 'China's Charitable Foundations: Development and Policy-Related Issues' (2015) 48(2) *Chinese Economy* 130, 144; Anna Jane High, 'Grassroots NGO Regulations and China's Local Legal Culture' (2013) 9 *Socio-Legal Review* 1, 22; Xu and Ngai (n 9) 249; Chodorow (n 10) 10.

Over the past two decades, this legal arrangement has impeded the willingness of private individuals and enterprises to form charities, make charitable donations, and participate in voluntary work carried out by charities. The government's tight legal control over charitable resources has led to public dissatisfaction with the process.

The public is also dissatisfied with the charitable sector in China regarding transparency and accountability. Because of ill-defined governance mechanisms in law and inefficient internal governance rules in charities, scandals involving the misuse of funds have frequently been exposed by the media or the general public. These have greatly damaged the charitable sector's credibility and public trust.[14] For example, in 2013, the Song Qingling Foundation of Henan Province was exposed by the media as having spent more than RMB 120 million (USD 16.99 million) on building a 27-metre tall sculpture, but this sculpture was immediately demolished after construction.[15] Another well-known scandal involving misappropriation of charitable funds was the case of Guo Meimei, a young woman whose social media posts showed her posing in front of a luxury car and wearing expensive gifts of jewellery. The car and the majority of the jewellery were funded by Wang Jun, the former vice chairman of the China Red Cross.[16] A third scandal involved the Red Cross Society of Sichuan Province. Its former executive vice president, Wen Jiabi, was sentenced to 16 years imprisonment for accepting bribes of RMB 550.09 million (USD 77.88 million) and embezzling public funds amounting to

[14] Lin Nie, Helen K. Liu and Wenhao Cheng, 'Exploring Factors That Influence Voluntary Disclosure by Chinese Foundations' (2016) 27(5) *International Journal of Voluntary and Nonprofit Organizations* 2374, 2380; Guosheng Deng, Shuang Lu and Chien-Chung Huang, 'Transparency of Grassroots Human Service Organizations in China: Does Transparency Affect Donation and Grants?' (2015) 39(5) *Human Service Organizations: Management, Leadership & Governance* 475, 476; 韩丽欣 [Han Lixin] (n 6) 1; Jing and Savas (n 11) 105.

[15] Raymond Li, 'Unexplained Destruction of Statue in Henan Raises Suspicion', *South China Morning Post* (7 July 2013), available at: <www.scmp.com/comment/insight-opinion/article/1276973/unexplained-destruction-statue-henan-raises-suspicion> (last accessed 18 June 2020).

[16] 樊小玲 [Fan Xiaoling],《机构形象传播中主体意识的缺失与重建 – "郭美美"事件引发的"红会"危机案例分析》[Absence of Subject Consciousness in the Communication of Institutional Image and Its Reconstruction – A Case Study on the 'Red Cross' Crisis in the 'Guo Meimei Scandal'] (2013) 5 华东师范大学学报 (哲学社会科学版) *Journal of East China Normal University (Humanities and Social Sciences)* 118, 119–20; 陈先红 [Chen Xianhong],《郭美美事件: 微博江湖"真""假"困局》[Guo Meimei Scandal: Dilemmas of 'True' and 'False' in Weibo] (2011) 21 人民论坛 *People's Forum* 60, 60–1.

RMB 295.342 million (USD 41.82 million).[17] These scandals have, to a large extent, discouraged the public from participating in charitable causes. As a result of frequent charity-related scandals, charitable donations in China fell by more than 80 per cent between June and August 2011.[18] Private individuals were especially unlikely to make charitable donations; the majority of donations came from enterprises. There are two main reasons enterprises make charitable donations. The first is that enterprises receive a tax deduction: according to Chinese tax policies, charitable donations are tax-deductible for legal entities but not individuals.[19] The second is that enterprises, in their pursuit of higher financial returns, employ charitable donations to improve their reputations.[20]

C *Establishment of a New Legal Framework for Charity Operation*

In light of the above problems, Chinese legislators and policymakers have held a large number of conferences and forums since the late 1980s to discuss legislative reforms to promote the development of charitable causes. The discussion of legal reform has revolved around two objectives, which are formally articulated in central government policies.[21] The first objective is to strengthen the autonomy of benevolent property

[17] 'Former Executive Vice President of Sichuan Provincial Red Cross Was Sued for Corruption', *Best China News* (20 August 2016), available at: <www.bestchinanews.com/Domestic/7092.html> (last accessed 1 June 2020).

[18] Chodorow (n 10) 49.

[19] 《关于公益性捐赠税前扣除有关问题的通知》 [Notice Concerning the Relevant Issues of Pre-Tax Deduction of Public Welfare Donations] (People's Republic of China) Ministry of Finance; State Administration of Taxation; Ministry of Civil Affairs, 31 December 2018, arts 1–2.

[20] Xiufeng Chen and Li Li, 'The Rise of Corporate Social Responsibility and Charitable Foundations in China' in Chien-Chung Huang, Guosheng Deng, Zhenyao Wang and Richard L. Edwards (eds.), *China's Nonprofit Sector: Progress and Challenges* (Transaction Publishers, 2014) 23–4.

[21] 《中国慈善事业发展指导纲要（2011–2015年）》 [Guidelines for the Development of China's Charitable Causes (2011–2015)] (People's Republic of China) Ministry of Civil Affairs, 15 July 2011, ss 2, 3; 《全国人民代表大会关于国民经济和社会发展第十二个五年规划纲要的决议》 [Resolution of the National People's Congress on the Outline of the Twelfth Five-Year Plan for National Economic and Social Development] (People's Republic of China) National People's Congress, 14 March 2011, ch 33; 《中共中央关于全面深化改革若干重大问题的决定》 [Decision of the Central Committee of the Communist Party of China on Several Major Issues on Comprehensively Deepening Reforms] (People's Republic of China) Central Committee of the Communist Party of China, 12 November 2018, s 13; 《中国农村扶贫开发纲要（2011–2020年）》 [Outline of Poverty Alleviation and Development in China Rural Areas (2011–2020)] (People's

owners and minimize the influence of political forces on the development of the charitable sector. The second objective is to adopt modernized facilitative regimes to buttress the development of the sector and facilitate the management and use of charitable resources generally. From a legal perspective, at the heart of these two objectives is how to strike a balance between the autonomy of private individuals to determine how their resources are used in promoting the state's public welfare goals and the central government's need to ensure that charitable resources are used to benefit the legitimate interests of broader society without facilitating illegal and improper practices. Private individuals are forbidden from using charitable resources for private use: they have the autonomy to determine how to exercise their management rights, but only to the extent that such exercise aligns with the state's public welfare policy.

Alongside the discussion of legislative reforms, a growing number of academics and practitioners have considered the possibility of adopting trusts to develop charitable causes. Over the past two decades, there have been three major institutional forms for establishing charities: foundations (*jijin hui* 基金会), social associations (*shehui tuanti* 社会团体), and privately-operated non-enterprise organizations (*minban feiqiye danwei* 民办非企业单位). They have high establishment thresholds[22] and are subject to the requirement that they do not engage in commercial activities. These forms are generally used by government organs or private companies with large-scale assets. It is financially difficult for an individual to establish a charity through these forms. In contrast, as will be discussed further in Chapter 3, trusts are seen as having three main institutional advantages over foundations, social associations, and privately-operated non-enterprise organizations. First, trust creation has no threshold for initial start-up funds. Second, the cy pres doctrine can be applied in certain situations to save a trust from failure and thus preserve the trust assets in the public domain on an ongoing basis. Third, trusts can carry out commercial activities if the profits obtained are exclusively used for charitable purposes.

Republic of China) Central Committee of the Communist Party of China and State Council, 27 May 2011, ss 6, 8.

22 For example, for the purpose of establishment, a foundation should have initial capital of not less than RMB 8 million in the case of a national public foundation, not less than RMB 4 million in the case of a local public foundation, and not less than RMB 2 million in the case of a non-public foundation. The initial capital should be currency capital deposited in a bank account. See《基金会管理条例》 [Regulations on Administration of Foundations] (People's Republic of China) State Council, 3 August 2004 (n 13) art 8.

To encourage the general public to play a proactive role in developing charitable undertakings, legislators, drawing on the experience of public welfare trusts in Japan[23] and South Korea,[24] introduced public welfare trusts to the Chinese legal system in 2001 with the promulgation of the Chinese Trust Law.[25] However, public welfare trusts have been unsuccessful over the last twenty years: no more than twenty public welfare trusts have been successfully established.[26] There are two reasons for this failure. The first is the difficulty that benevolent property owners have in identifying public welfare administration authorities (regulators). The law makes no mention of who the regulators of public welfare trusts are and how they can be identified. The parties to public welfare trusts find it difficult to determine to whom a registration application can be submitted.[27] The second reason relates to the conservative attitude taken by regulators towards registration.[28] In practice, regulators have been unwilling to approve the establishment of public welfare trusts due to the concern that their supervision of public welfare trusts might attract public scrutiny and that any regulatory failure or scandal will result in irrevocable reputational damage.[29] For these two reasons, a gap has opened up between the advantages that public welfare trusts were supposed to have in developing charities and the limited role they play in practice.

Drawing on the failure of public welfare trusts, Chinese legislators introduced the charitable trust in 2016 with a view to unlocking the

[23] Makoto Arai, 'Trust Law in Japan: Inspiring Changes in Asia, 1922 and 2006' in Lusina Ho and Rebecca Lee (eds.), *Trust Law in Asian Civil Law Jurisdiction: A Comparative Analysis* (Cambridge University Press, 2013) 44–5.

[24] Ying-Chieh Wu, 'Trust Law in South Korea: Developments and Challenges' in Lusina Ho and Rebecca Lee (eds.), *Trust Law in Asian Civil Law Jurisdiction: A Comparative Analysis* (Cambridge University Press, 2013) 47; 王建军 [Wang Jianjun], 燕翀 [Yan Chong], and 张时飞 [Zhang Shifei],《慈善信托法律制度运行机理及其在我国发展的障碍》[The Operational Mechanism and Theories Related to the Charitable Trust and Its Development Obstacles in Mainland China] (2011) 4 环球法律评论 *Global Law Review* 108, 109.

[25] 《中华人民共和国信托法》 [Trust Law of the People's Republic of China] (People's Republic of China) National People's Congress, 28 April 2001, ch 6.

[26] For details on these established public welfare trusts, see 赵廉慧 [Zhao Lianhui],《信托法解释论》 [Interpretative Theory of Trust Law] (中国法制出版社 [China Legal Publishing House], 2015) 526–9.

[27] See analysis in Section II of Chapter 3.

[28] 中国信托业协会 [China Trustee Association] (n 12) 65; 赵廉慧 [Zhao Lianhui] (n 26) 542.

[29] See analysis in Section III of Chapter 4.

potential of trust institutions to promote charitable causes. They constructed a new legal framework for this model. In this framework, greater scope was given to the civil capacity of legal actors,[30] and special regulators (i.e., civil affairs departments and banking regulatory authorities)[31] were introduced to supervise charitable trust affairs. The 2016 legislative reforms facilitated the use of charitable trusts and made their establishment and regulation easier than for public welfare trusts. However, it is unclear to what extent and in what ways charitable trusts relate to the old model of public welfare trusts. Do legislators expect charitable trusts to replace public welfare trusts in the furtherance of charitable causes? Or do legislators expect the two models to operate in parallel? The law makes no mention of these issues. Rather, it uses the expression 'trusts belong to (*shuyu* 属于) public welfare trusts'[32] to describe the relationship between the two models. This legislative language has given rise to intense debate. Some opine that the two models are identical and thus share the same legal meaning.[33] Others propose that public welfare trusts are in nature distinguishable from charitable trusts.[34] As the charitable trust model has only recently been established, there is a great deal of uncertainty in its operation, and the design of the laws and regulations to promote and regulate it is likewise continually developing.

[30] Siyi Lin, 'China's New Charity Law: A New Era of Charitable Trusts' (2018) 24(8) *Trusts & Trustees* 768, 770–1.

[31] 《慈善信托管理办法》[Administrative Measures for Charitable Trusts] (People's Republic of China) China Banking Regulatory Commission and Ministry of Civil Affairs, 10 July 2017, arts 47–51.

[32] 《中华人民共和国慈善法》 [Charity Law of the People's Republic of China] (People's Republic of China) National People's Congress, 16 March 2016, art 44;《慈善信托管理办法》[Administrative Measures for Charitable Trusts] (People's Republic of China) China Banking Regulatory Commission and Ministry of Civil Affairs, 10 July 2017 (n 31) art 2.

[33] 倪受彬 [Ni Shoubin],《现代慈善信托的组织法特征及其功能优势 – 与慈善基金会法人的比较》[The Advantage and Character of Modern Charitable Trusts as Organizations: Compared to Charity Foundations] (2014) 46(7) 学术月刊 *Academic Monthly* 86, 87; 王建军 [Wang Jianjun], 燕翀 [Yan Chong], and 张时飞 [Zhang Shifei] (n 24) 110.

[34] 中国信托业协会 [China Trustee Association] (n 12) 62–6; 李文华 [Li Wenhua],《完善我国慈善信托制度若干问题的思考》 [Thoughts on Several Issues of Perfecting the Charitable Trust System in China] (2017) 7 法学杂志 *Law Science Magazine* 89, 91; 刘迎霜 [Liu Yingshuang],《我国公益信托法律移植及其本土化: 一种正本清源与直面当下的思考》[The Transplantation and Localization of Charitable Trusts in China: A Thought of Radical Reform and Facing up to the Present] (2015) 27(1) 中外法学 *Peking University Law Journal* 151, 154–5.

In this context, important questions remain about how charitable trusts function in China. This book focuses on one central question: How are charitable trusts governed in both law and practice? The charitable trust model was introduced when public welfare trusts had failed, with legislators seeking to use this new model to encourage public participation in charitable undertakings. This book examines the similarities and differences between charitable trusts and public welfare trusts to identify the legislative changes that the new charity law has made to the governance framework for charitable trusts. This analysis elucidates the role that legislators expect charitable trusts to play in the Chinese legal system, as well as the changes in the relationship between the state and private individuals in the provision of social welfare goods.

In addition to the law, this book will also critically examine the practical implementation of the legislated governance framework. The Chinese bureaucratic system indicates that government control over charitable trusts and the charitable sector is not going to change any time soon.[35] The establishment and development of charitable trusts bear the mark of China's political and social norms. In this context, this book will study the ways in which trust parties and regulators engage with the law, evaluating the strengths and weaknesses of the current legal governance framework and identifying the factors that influence the behavioural patterns of each actor.

II Literature Review

This section provides an overview of the existing literature on Chinese charitable trusts, especially works relating to two pertinent aspects of the governance of charitable trusts: first, the policy and social contexts in which Chinese charitable trusts operate; and second, the legal rules governing Chinese charitable trusts. After examining these two aspects, this book will be located relative to the existing literature.

A The Policy and Social Context for Charitable Trusts

The institutional context in which the charitable trust model has evolved and is evolving has been extensively explored by Chinese legal scholars, economists, and social scientists, as well as their English-speaking

[35] Dejian Li, 'Reform of Charity Governance in China: From Economic and Comparative Perspectives' (PhD Thesis, Faculty of Law, The University of Liverpool, 2017) 270.

counterparts. In substance, the two bodies of literature overlap considerably with each other, both touching upon the development and reform of Chinese charity laws.

The literature on the relevance of China's social, political, legal, and economic conditions to the evolution of Chinese charities and the laws governing them is extensive and diverse, both in Chinese and in English. This literature essentially reflects the insights of legal realists, for whom the application of law is not simply 'a mechanical exercise in deductive reasoning'.[36] To better understand the practical implementation of written laws, one must attend to the 'reactions of [relevant actors] to [specific] facts and to the life around them'.[37] As Ḥanoch Dagan suggests in *Reconstructing American Legal Realism and Rethinking Private Law Theory*: '[L]aw cannot be understood merely by reference to its static elements (its existing rules); understanding the doctrinal materials at any given moment as the things to be classified misses the inherent dynamism of the law'.[38] Such realist thinking is prevalent in the literature relating to Chinese charities. The application of realist thinking in the

[36] Brian Leiter, 'Legal Formalism and Legal Realism: What Is the Issue' (2010) 16(2) *Legal Theory* 111, 122. See also Oliver Wendell Holmes, 'The Path of the Law' (1997) 110(5) *Harvard Law Review* 991, 998; Kristen Rundle, *Forms Liberate: Reclaiming the Jurisprudence of Lon L Fuller* (Hart, 2012) 48; Kristen Rundle, 'Opening the Doors of Inquiry: Lon Fuller and the Natural Law Tradition' in George Duke and Robert P. George (eds.), *The Cambridge Companion to Natural Law Jurisprudence* (Cambridge University Press, 2017) 452; Charles C. Goetsch, 'The Future of Legal Formalism' (1980) 24(3) *American Journal of Legal History* 221, 222–3; Jude Wallace and John Fiocco, 'Recent Criticisms of Formalism in Legal Theory and Legal Education' (1980) 7(3) *Adelaide Law Review* 309, 311; Gerard McMeel, 'What Kind of Jurist Was Peter Binks' (2011) 19 *Restitution Law Review* 15, 33; Christine B. Harrington and Barbara Yngvesson, 'Interpretive Sociolegal Research' (1990) 15(1) *Law & Social Inquiry* 135, 140–1; G. Edward White, 'From Sociological Jurisprudence to Realism: Jurisprudence and Social Change in Early Twentieth-Century America' (1972) 58(6) *Virginia Law Review* 999, 1004; Grant Gilmore, 'Legal Realism: Its Cause and Cure' (1961) 70(7) *Yale Law Journal* 1037, 1038.

[37] Brian Z. Tamanaha, *Beyond the Formalist-Realist Divide: The Role of Politics in Judging* (Princeton University Press, 2010) 80.

[38] Ḥanoch Dagan, *Reconstructing American Legal Realism & Rethinking Private Law Theory* (Oxford University Press, 2013) 131. See also Hanoch Dagan, 'Doctrinal Categories, Legal Realism, and the Rule of Law' (2015) 163 *University of Pennsylvania Law Review* 1889, 1916; Brian Leiter, 'Rethinking Legal Realism: Toward a Naturalized Jurisprudence' (1997) 76(2) *Texas Law Review* 267, 267; Brian Leiter, 'Legal Realism and Legal Positivism Reconsidered' (2001) 111(2) *Ethics* 278, 281; Allan Beever and Charles Rickett, 'Interpretive Legal Theory and the Academic Lawyer' (2005) 68(2) *Modern Law Review* 320, 336; Carlos E. Gonzalez, 'Statutory Interpretation: Looking Back – Looking Forward' (2006) 58(3) *Rutgers Law Review* 703, 717; Ilene H. Nagel, 'The

Chinese context requires consideration of the Chinese political and economic environment, government developmental policies, and important party policies. According to Ying Xu and Ngan-Pun Ngai, 'As the government wants to maintain political stability, the current administrative rules and regulations that concern these [charities] do not aim to expand their social rights and freedoms, but rather give various officials the legal right to intervene in, interfere with, or control [charitable] activities'.[39] In contrast to the Western democratic model, China's party and state make political and social stability their policy priority: '[M]aintaining economic growth with social stability has been and will continue to be the central leadership's political priority.'[40] China's party and state prohibit any action directly threatening political or social stability or challenging the authority of the political system.[41] On the other hand, so long as a new institution does not adversely affect, but rather contributes to, political stability and societal control, the CCP and state often allow for, and even promote, its development, taking initiatives to remove obstacles created by their previous policies.[42] The current charity-promoting policy is a good example. As Lincoln Chen, Jennifer Ryan, and Tony Saich state, '[A]s China continues to allow nonprofits to expand their role, the government has begun to shift the balance, opening space for [charities] to solve social problems while maintaining control over the growth and development of civil organizations that could become a threat to [political and social] stability'.[43]

Over the last three decades, the government's tight political control of the charitable sector has significantly impeded the development of civil organizations in China. There have been intense discussions of legislative reforms to empower and encourage charities to develop charitable undertakings. The suggested legislative reforms can be divided into two categories. The first is based on micro-analysis, focusing on identifying the challenges facing the charity law system and its possible solutions. For

Legal/Extra-Legal Controversy: Judicial Decisions in Pretrial Release' (1983) 17(3) *Law & Society Review* 481, 512.

39 Xu and Ngai (n 9) 248.

40 Xian Huang, 'The Politics of Social Welfare Reform in Urban China: Social Welfare Preferences and Reform Policies' (2013) 18 *Journal of Chinese Political Science* 61, 79.

41 Xu and Ngai (n 9) 253; High (n 13) 29; Li (n 35) 265.

42 Li (n 35) 265.

43 Lincoln C. Chen, Jennifer Ryan and Tony Saich, 'Introduction: Philanthropy for Health in China: Distinctive Roots and Future Prospects' in Jennifer Ryan, Lincoln C. Chen and Tony Saich (eds.), *Philanthropy for Health in China* (Indiana University Press, 2014) 8.

example, Feng Xiaoming suggests that there should be a clear legal definition of the relationship between government, enterprises, and civil society, and that the registration procedures for charities should be simplified and the dual management requirement (whereby charities are required to have a sponsor organization to assist the civil affair departments in the creation and oversight of all charities) should be dismantled.[44] Similarly, Rebecca Lee opines that modernizing the facilitative regimes for charity operation depends on 'minimizing government influence over the establishment and management of charitable organization[s]; developing a coherent legal definition of charity to standardize charitable operation; providing more support to small, grassroots charitable organizations so as to promote diversity in charity operation; and enhancing fiscal incentives for charitable organizations to buttress development of the sector generally'.[45] The second category of legislative reforms is based on macro-analysis, focusing on how to coordinate the relationship between civil society and government and how to foster a vibrant and autonomous civil society in light of China's political and social culture. For instance, Pitman Potter argues that, to create an environment favourable to the growth and prosperity of charities, the government should minimize its bureaucratic control over the charitable sector and secure the autonomy of charities in delivering public welfare.[46] Recognizing the importance of China's policy and social traditions, Adam Chodorow argues that legal reform alone is not enough to create an autonomous civil society; rather, policymakers and legislators should change both China's legal rules and its social and political conditions.[47]

Studying the links between China's social and policy conditions and its law-making process and law enforcement is not exclusive to the charity sector. The English and Chinese literatures have also engaged extensively with these links when examining corporate governance, Chinese judges' decision-making, and enforcement campaigns in China.[48] Regarding

44 Feng (n 13) 152.

45 Lee, 'Modernize Charity Law in China' (n 6) 353.

46 Pitman B. Potter, 'Belief in Control: Regulation of Religion in China' (2003) 174 *China Quarterly* 317, 337.

47 Chodorow (n 10) 54. See also C. David Lee, 'Legal Reform in China: A Role for Nongovernmental Organizations' (2000) 25 *Yale Journal of International Law* 363, 429.

48 See, e.g., Virginia E. Harper Ho, 'Beyond Regulation: A Comparative Look at State-Centric Corporate Social Responsibility and the Law in China' (2013) 46 *Vanderbilt Journal of Transnational Law* 375; Xin He and Kwai Hang Ng, 'In the Name of Harmony: The Erasure of Domestic Violence in China's Judicial Mediation' (2013) 27(1)

corporate governance, one view is that, due to the increasing forces of economic competition and globalization, it is difficult for national governments to maintain their own policies or regulatory systems.[49] Many scholars have argued that economic globalization will lead to convergence across nations in corporate governance practice.[50] Chenxia Shi rejects this argument. By identifying political factors as the key determinants of corporate governance development in China, she states that market globalization and China's integration into the world economy will not lead to the convergence of its corporate governance with international models. China's social, political, and legal traditions are essential to shaping its corporate governance model. Significant factors include China's longstanding preoccupation with state ownership of property, its top-down regulatory system and weak enforcement, and its distinctive business regulatory culture.[51]

This social and policy context also plays a vital role in influencing the decision-making of Chinese judges. Xin He and Kwai Hang Ng, in *Embedded Courts: Judicial Decision-Making in China*, suggest that the behaviours of Chinese courts are shaped by different social forces, including administrative embeddedness, political embeddedness, social embeddedness, and economic embeddedness.[52] Because of these social forces, Chinese judges' behaviour often differs from what one might

International Journal of Law, Policy and the Family 97; Xin He and Kwai Hang Ng, 'Inquisitorial Adjudication and Institutional Constraints in Chinese Civil Justice' (2013) 35(4) *Law & Policy* 290; Sarah Biddulph, Sean Cooney and Ying Zhu, 'Rule of Law with Chinese Characteristics: The Role of Campaigns in Lawmaking' (2012) 34(4) *Law & Policy* 373; Carlos Wing-Hung Lo, Gerald E. Fryxell, Benjamin van Rooij, Wei Wang and Pansy Honying Li, 'Explaining the Enforcement Gap in China: Local Government Support and Internal Agency Obstacles as Predictors of Enforcement Actions in Guangzhou' (2012) 111 *Journal of Environmental Management* 227; Jie Gao, 'Governing by Goals and Numbers: A Case Study in the Use of Performance Measurement to Build State Capacity in China' (2009) 29(1) *Public Administration and Development* 21.

49 David Brady, Jason Beckfield and Wei Zhao, 'The Consequences of Economic Globalization for Affluent Democracies' (2007) 33 *Annual Review of Sociology* 313, 318; William Sites, 'Primitive Globalization? State and Locale in Neoliberal Global Engagement' (2000) 18(1) *Sociological Theory* 121, 121–2.

50 Brady, Beckfield and Zhao (n 49) 313, 318.

51 Chenxia Shi, *Political Determinants of Corporate Governance in China* (Routledge, 2012) 18. See also Virginia E. Harper Ho, 'Corporate Governance as Risk Regulation in China: A Comparative View of Risk Oversight, Risk Management, and Accountability' (2012) 3 (4) *European Journal of Risk Regulation* 463, 475; Ho (n 48) 427.

52 Kwai Hang Ng and Xin He, *Embedded Courts: Judicial Decision-Making in China* (Cambridge University Press, 2017) 191. The policy goals of the central government have

expect from a strict reading of the law. The conclusion drawn by Xin He and Kwai Hang Ng is consistent with Brian Tamanaha's observation in *Beyond the Formalist–Realist Divide: The Role of Politics in Judging* that judges do not strictly follow legal rules and precedents; rather, they make choices in consideration of practice-related social and institutional factors, as well as their moral views and personal biases.[53] A similar process is at work in China's enforcement campaign. China responds to enforcement failures in areas such as food safety, environmental pollution, and working conditions differently from other nations, demonstrating a strong preference for 'extralegal forms of political intervention'[54] in law enforcement. As Sarah Biddulph, Sean Cooney, and Ying Zhu argue, 'It is the strong planned nature of the campaign and its emphasis on state leadership of [law-making] and enforcement that continues to shape the development of China's particular version of the rule of law'.[55]

been internalized into the institutional constraints of the courts. Extra-legal factors permeate the decision-making process of Chinese courts. See Yuqing Feng and Xin He, 'From Law to Politics: Petitioners' Framing of Disputes in Chinese Courts' (2018) 80 *China Journal* 130, 131; Kwai Hang Ng and Xin He, 'The Institutional and Cultural Logics of Legal Commensuration: Blood Money and Negotiated Justice in China' (2017) 122(4) *American Journal of Sociology* 1104, 1138; Xin He and Fen Lin, 'The Losing Media? An Empirical Study of Defamation Litigation in China' (2017) 230 *China Quarterly* 371, 373; Xin He, 'No Malicious Incidents: The Concern for Stability in China's Divorce Law Practice' (2017) 26(4) *Social & Legal Studies* 467, 467–8; Xin He, 'Administrative Reconsideration's Erosion of Administrative Litigation in China' (2014) 2(2) *Chinese Journal of Comparative Law* 252, 252; He and Ng, 'Inquisitorial Adjudication and Institutional Constraints in Chinese Civil Justice' (n 48) 290; He and Ng, 'In the Name of Harmony: The Erasure of Domestic Violence in China's Judicial Mediation' (n 48) 113.

53 Tamanaha (n 37) 6. See also Alexander Green, 'Expanding Law's Empire: Interpretivism, Morality and the Value of Legality' (2011) 4(1) *European Journal of Legal Studies* 122, 132; McMeel (n 36) 33; White (n 36) 1004; Gilmore (n 36) 1038; Leiter, 'Rethinking Legal Realism: Toward a Naturalized Jurisprudence' (n 38) 267; Leiter, 'Legal Realism and Legal Positivism Reconsidered' (n 38) 281.

54 Biddulph, Cooney and Zhu (n 48) 374.

55 Ibid. 373. See also Sarah Biddulph, 'The Production of Legal Norms: A Case Study of Administrative Detention in China' (2003) 20 *UCLA Pacific Basin Law Journal* 217, 240; Benjamin van Rooij, 'China's War on Graft: Politico-Legal Campaigns against Corruption in China and Their Similarities to the Legal Reactions to Crisis in the US' (2005) 14(2) *Pacific Rim Law & Political Journal* 289, 289; Benjamin van Rooij, Rachel E. Stern and Kathinka Fürst, 'The Authoritarian Logic of Regulatory Pluralism: Understanding China's New Environmental Actors' (2016) 10(1) *Regulation & Governance* 1, 4–5; Virginia E. Harper Ho, 'From Contracts to Compliance: An Early Look at Implementation under China's New Labor Legislation' (2009) 23 *Columbia Journal of Asian Law* 35, 45; Young Nam Cho, 'The Politics of Lawmaking in Chinese Local People's Congresses' (2006) 187 *China Quarterly* 592, 594; Benjamin van Rooij,

Although the literature examined so far is not directly linked to Chinese charitable trusts, it is still pertinent for two reasons. First, it identifies and explores the social, economic, political, and legal factors relevant to law-making and law enforcement in China more generally. These factors can help identify the factors related to the governance of charitable trusts and how they interact in the design and development of legislative governance rules for charitable trusts. Second, the hypothesis of this book is that the governance framework of Chinese charitable trusts can only be understood in light of China's particular circumstances and the relevant laws, administrative practices, and private actions of trust parties. Notwithstanding the rich literature on the institutional context within which charitable trusts operate, the various policy and social factors are often identified and discussed in a highly abstract and generalized manner. Furthermore, the current literature does not provide a detailed analysis of whether these policy and social factors are related to the governance of charitable trusts and, if so, how they impact the creation and administration of charitable trusts. In this regard, this literature review helps one understand the challenges and complexities confronted in the governance of charitable trusts. Two lines of inquiry are particularly relevant in this regard: (a) how the Chinese institutional setting affects the ways in which trust parties and regulatory officials behave and (b) to what extent legislated governance goals are implemented in practice.

B Legal Rules Governing Chinese Charitable Trusts

There is a substantial body of literature in Chinese analysing specific questions on the legal rules governing Chinese charitable trusts. These rules and the related literature are explored in detail in Chapters 3 and 4. The Chinese literature mainly concentrates on a textual analysis of the law, with a focus on three aspects of the governance of charitable trusts: (a) the dominant role of settlors in the administration of charitable trust affairs; (b) the negative role that regulators play in supervising charitable trusts; and (c) the under-determined legal nature of beneficiaries.

Gerald E. Fryxell, Carlos Wing-Hung Lo and Wei Wang, 'From Support to Pressure: The Dynamics of Social and Governmental Influences on Environmental Law Enforcement in Guangzhou City, China' (2013) 7(3) *Regulation & Governance* 321, 341; Ho (n 48) 427; Lo et al. (n 48) 235; Gao (n 48) 21.

The works dealing with the first aspect recognize that a tension between settlors and trustees plays a central role in the governance structure of Chinese charitable trusts. This tension has three aspects: (a) the legal title of charitable trust assets; (b) the allocation of powers between settlors and trustees; and (c) the legal character of the Chinese charitable trust; that is, whether it is more like an agency relationship than a trust. These three aspects are inter-related. First, the Chinese Trust Law stipulates that, to create a trust, the settlor needs to entrust their property rights to the trustee and allow the trustee to administer or dispose of such property rights in the interests of a beneficiary or for any intended purposes.[56] The legal term 'entrust' suggests that settlors are entitled to retain the legal title to charitable trust assets.[57] This legislative approach illustrates that protecting the autonomous interests of settlors is critical to the creation and ongoing operation of charitable

[56] 《中华人民共和国信托法》 [Trust Law of the People's Republic of China] (People's Republic of China) National People's Congress, 28 April 2001 (n 25) art 2.

[57] Lusina Ho, *Trust Law in China* (Sweet & Maxell Asia, 2003) 41; Lusina Ho, Rebecca Lee and Jinping Jin, 'Trust Law in China: A Critical Evaluation of Its Conceptual Foundation' in Lusina Ho and Rebecca Lee (eds.), *Trust Law in Asian Civil Law Jurisdiction: A Comparative Analysis* (Cambridge University Press, 2013) 86; Lusina Ho, 'Trust Laws in China: History, Ambiguity and Beneficiary's Rights' in Lionel Smith (ed.), *Re-Imaging the Trust: Trusts in Civil Law* (Cambridge University Press, 2012) 195–6; Rebecca Lee, 'Conceptualizing the Chinese Trust' (2009) 58(3) *International & Comparative Law Quarterly* 655, 660; 何宝玉 [He Baoyu], 《信托法原理研究》 [Research on the Jurisprudence of Trust Law] (中国政法大学出版社 [China University of Political Science and Law Press], 2005) 10–11. The term 'entrust' contemplates the transfer of legal title for the creation of a valid Chinese trust. See Charles Zhen Qu, 'The Doctrinal Basis of the Trust Principles in China's Trust Law' (2003) 38 *Real Property, Probate and Trust Journal* 345, 357–8; Kai Lyu, 'Re-Clarifying China's Trust Law: Characteristics and New Conceptual Basis' (2015) 36 *Loyola of Los Angeles International and Comparative Law Review* 447, 455; 周小明 [Zhou Xiaoming], 《信托制度: 法理与实务》 [Trust System: Theory and Practice] (中国法制出版社 [China Legal Publishing House], 2012) 41–2; 陈向聪 [Chen Xiangcong], 《信托法律制度研究》 [Research on Trust Law System] (中国检察出版社 [China People's Procuratorate Press], 2007) 6; 谭振亭 [Tan Zhenting], 《信托法》 [Trust Law] (中国政法大学出版社 [China University of Political Science and Law Press], 2010) 7; 赵廉慧 [Zhao Lianhui] (n 26) 183–5. The Chinese Trust Law is modelled on the Trust Act of Taiwan, of Japan, and of South Korea, but in the three jurisdictions the transfer of legal title is required for the creation of a valid trust. See Wen-Yeu Wang, Chih-Cheng Wang and Shieh Jer-Shenq, 'Trust Law in Taiwan: History, Current Features and Future Prospects' in Lusina Ho and Rebecca Lee (eds.), *Trust Law in Asian Civil Law Jurisdiction: A Comparative Analysis* (Cambridge University Press, 2013) 70–1; Masayuki Tamaruya, 'Japanese Law and the Global Diffusion of Trust and Fiduciary Law' (2017) 103 *Iowa Law Review* 2229, 2238; 谢哲胜 [Xie Zhesheng], 《信托法》 [Trust Law] (元照出版公司 [Angle Publishing], 2009) 45, 110–11; Arai (n 23) 29; Wu (n 24) 48–9.

trusts. Second, under the existing legal framework, settlors are endowed by law with extensive powers while trustees are burdened by law with broad duties. This legislative approach is deeply rooted in the background against which the Chinese Trust Law was enacted.[58] Moreover, due to the silence of the law regarding what these powers and duties entail, some scholars have argued that this approach makes it easy for the settlor to intervene and creates significant uncertainty around the performance of the trustee's duties.[59] Third, when (a) and (b) are viewed together, it becomes clear that charitable trusts closely resemble agency relationships.[60] But in what ways and to what extent are Chinese charitable trusts similar to and different from Chinese agency relationships? This question has not yet been thoroughly investigated in the existing literature. What is more, the literature does not consider the significance of the answer to this question for understanding the governance of Chinese charitable trusts.

The literature in Chinese also engages extensively with the narrow issue of the significance of the government regulator's changing roles and powers in the establishment of Chinese charitable trusts, from registration (*dengji* 登记) to recording (*bei'an* 备案).[61] Many works argue that,

58 Ruiqiao Zhang, 'Trust Law of China and Its Uncertainties: Examination of the Rights and Obligations of Trust and Ownership of Trust Property' (2015) 10 *National Taiwan University Law Review* 45, 69; 何宝玉 [He Baoyu],《信托法原理研究（第二版）》[Research on the Jurisprudence of Trust Law (2nd ed.)] (中国法制出版社 [China Legal Publishing House], 2015) 171;《关于<中华人民共和国信托法（草案）>的说明》 [Explanations on the Trust Law of the People's Republic of China (Draft)] (People's Republic of China) Standing Committee of the People's Congress, 24 December 1996, ss 1–3;《全国人大法律委员会关于<中华人民共和国信托法(草案)>修改情况的汇报》 [Report of the Law Committee of the National People's Congress on the Revision of Trust Law of the People's Republic of China (Draft)] (People's Republic of China) National People's Congress, 3 July 2000, ss 1–3; 赵廉慧 [Zhao Lianhui] (n 26) 268; 何宝玉 [He Baoyu] (n 57) 11; Lyu (n 57) 456.

59 何宝玉 [He Baoyu] (n 58) 171–2; 赵廉慧 [Zhao Lianhui] (n 26) 266.

60 高凌云 [Gao Lingyun],《被误读的信托 – 信托法原论》 [A Misreading of Trust: Discussion on the Origin of Trust] (复旦大学出版社 [Fudan University Press], 2010) 261; 王众 [Wang Zhong],《中国信托法原理与实例精要》 [Principles and Examples of the Chinese Trust Law] (中国政法大学出版社 [China University of Political Science and Law Press], 2017) 8; Lee (n 57) 660; Ho, *Trust Law in China* (n 57) 41–2; 何宝玉 [He Baoyu] (n 58) 15–19.

61 《慈善信托管理办法》[Administrative Measures for Charitable Trusts] (People's Republic of China) China Banking Regulatory Commission and Ministry of Civil Affairs, 10 July 2017 (n 31) ch 3;《中华人民共和国慈善法》 [Charity Law of the People's Republic of China] (People's Republic of China) National People's Congress, 16 March 2016 (n 32) art 47.

through recording as opposed to registration, regulators are legally entitled to engage in only a formal[62] examination of the trust documents and have no discretion to decline recording applications where the trust documents meet the formal requirements of the law. Consistent with the textual interpretation of the term 'recording', some scholars have observed that policymakers have given more scope to the civil capacity of legal actors.[63] Furthermore, regulators for charitable trusts are clearly tasked with educating and supporting charity participants on best practices in the carrying out of charitable activities.[64] The law has also adopted numerous collaborative measures to encourage the public to play an active role in raising awareness of charitable trusts. Many scholars suggest that the current favourable regulatory environment reflects the increasing level of autonomy and capacity of private parties and reflects the fact that regulators have attributed great value to the role of individuals in the advancement of state–society relationships.[65] While this conclusion is drawn from an analysis of the changed legal provisions, the literature has not explored whether this textual change has been

[62] 吕鑫 [Lyu Xin],《从公益信托到慈善信托: 跨国移植及其本土建构》[From Public Welfare Trusts to Charitable Trusts: Transnational Transplantation and Local Construction] (2019) 10 社会科学战线 *Social Science Front* 199, 203; 魏艳 [Wei Yan],《慈善信托政府监管权配置研究》[Research on Allocation of Administrative Regulatory Powers for Charitable Trusts] (2018) 6 国家行政学院学报 *Journal of Chinese Academy of Governance* 103, 104; 楼秋然 [Lou Qiuran],《理解慈善信托中的"近似原则": 美国经验与中国借鉴》[Understanding Cy Pres in Charitable Trusts: American Experience and Its Adoption in China] (2019) 3 中国政法大学学报 *Journal of China University of Political Science and Law* 49, 61; 王涛 [Wang Tao],《慈善法的立法理念、制度创新和完善路径》 [Research on the Legislative Idea, System Innovation and Development Path of the Chinese Charity Law] (2018) 33(1) 法学论坛 *Legal Forum* 143, 146.

[63] Lin (n 30) 770–2.

[64] See《国务院关于促进慈善事业健康发展的指导意见》 [Guiding Opinions of the State Council on Promoting Healthy Development of Charitable Causes] (People's Republic of China) State Council, 24 November 2014, chs 4–5;《中国慈善事业发展指导纲要（2011–2015年）》 [Guidelines for the Development of China's Charitable Causes (2011–2015)] (People's Republic of China) Ministry of Civil Affairs, 15 July 2011 (n 21) s 3;《中共中央关于全面深化改革若干重大问题的决定》[Decision of the Central Committee of the Communist Party of China on Several Major Issues on Comprehensively Deepening Reforms] (People's Republic of China) Central Committee of the Communist Party of China, 12 November 2018 (n 21) s 13;《慈善信托管理办法》[Administrative Measures for Charitable Trusts] (People's Republic of China) China Banking Regulatory Commission and Ministry of Civil Affairs, 10 July 2017 (n 31) ch 6;《中华人民共和国慈善法》 [Charity Law of the People's Republic of China] (People's Republic of China) National People's Congress, 16 March 2016 (n 32) ch 9.

[65] 楼秋然 [Lou Qiuran] (n 62) 62; 王涛 [Wang Tao] (n 62) 144.

reflected in regulatory practice, nor has it considered the factors in addition to law that may influence regulatory practice.

There is also an extensive Chinese literature on the legal nature and role of beneficiaries in Chinese charitable trusts. A striking debate prevails among legal scholars regarding the legal nature of the object. Are the objects who receive benefits from charitable trusts beneficiaries or merely recipients? The distinction between beneficiaries and recipients is not theoretically significant in the context of common law charitable trusts. However, this distinction is particularly meaningful in understanding the nature of Chinese charitable trusts and the role of objects receiving charitable trust benefits. If these objects are beneficiaries, it means they have an interest in the proper distribution of charitable assets and are therefore entitled to claim distribution. If these objects are only recipients, it means they have no interest in the proper distribution of charitable assets and therefore play no role in the governance structure of charitable trusts. The distinction between 'beneficiary' and 'recipient' is not clear in the area of Chinese charitable trusts. In law, the term 'beneficiary' is used extensively, suggesting that the objects who receive benefits are beneficiaries in the trust law sense.[66] In contrast, many academic papers and commentaries have regarded the term 'beneficiary' as speculative, arguing that it can be interpreted as meaning either beneficiary or recipient.[67]

Current academic debates have mainly focused on the conceptual distinction between beneficiary and recipient. While scholars have recognized that the interpretation of an object's nature has an important bearing on our understanding of its capacity to exercise supervisory roles,[68] they have fallen short of pointing out the relevance of the distinction between 'beneficiary' and 'recipient' to the rights or powers that the objects may have in the governance of charitable trusts. In the

[66] See《慈善信托管理办法》[Administrative Measures for Charitable Trusts] (People's Republic of China) China Banking Regulatory Commission and Ministry of Civil Affairs, 10 July 2017 (n 31) arts 10–11;《民政部、中国银行业监督管理委员会关于做好慈善信托备案有关工作的通知》 [Notice of Civil Affairs Department and China Banking Regulatory Commission on the Recordation Work for Charitable Trusts] (People's Republic of China) Civil Affairs Department and China Banking Regulatory Commission, 25 August 2016, s 2.

[67] 中国信托业协会 [China Trustee Association] (n 12) 62, 84; 赵廉慧 [Zhao Lianhui] (n 26) 555; 陈向聪 [Chen Xiangcong] (n 57) 278–9; 谭振亭 [Tan Zhenting] (n 57) 199–200; 谢哲胜 [Xie Zhesheng] (n 57) 219.

[68] 赵廉慧 [Zhao Lianhui] (n 26) 554–5.

current literature, the answer to the question of which term, 'beneficiary' or 'recipient', best describes the objects receiving trust benefits has not been directly related to the analysis of the governance of charitable trusts. The real question that needs to be explored is what powers or rights the objects of a charitable trust may have.

Current literature concerning the unique features of Chinese charitable trusts has identified the efforts that lawmakers have made towards the construction of a legal framework for charitable trusts; it has also contributed to the discussion of the underlying objectives of charitable trusts to promote charitable undertakings and strengthen settlor autonomy. However, this literature has not considered the relevance of each objective to the design of the governance structure of charitable trusts, the ways in which the two objectives interact, and the implications of this for understanding the legal nature of charitable trusts.

In the area of charitable trusts, the current literature has examined the legislative provisions governing the internal relationship between trust parties and the role of regulators; however, it has not considered how trust parties interact with regulators in the day-to-day governance of charitable trusts, what uncertainties trust parties and regulators may encounter when performing their legal roles, and what strategies they have adopted to mitigate the risks that may arise out of the implementation of the law. Legal realists have argued that, because the application of law is not an 'exercise in mechanical deduction',[69] it is possible that actual practices may differ from what one might expect to arise from a strict interpretation of the law.[70]

In terms of the ambiguities in the current legal framework and the legal uncertainties that arise from these ambiguities, much of the Chinese literature has recited the problems and has proposed solutions based on textual interpretation of legal rules without undertaking a comprehensive analysis of the broader social and policy contexts within which the rules were developed and operate. In particular, the literature does not consider what specific ambiguities the current legal framework has created and how policy and social factors affect the ways in which trust parties and regulators address these ambiguities. This is anomalous, as there is little point in proposing reforms to the challenges and legal uncertainties of today without understanding how charitable trust laws are practically

[69] Leiter (n 36) 116.

[70] Tarunabh Khaitan, *A Theory of Discrimination Law* (Oxford University Press, 2015) 13.

implemented and the extra-legal factors affecting the governance and administration of charitable trusts.

In contrast to the abundant Chinese literature on charitable trusts, there is very little literature in English examining their introduction and development in mainland China. An exception is Lin Siyi's analysis of the advantages and disadvantages of the Chinese charitable trust system.[71] The dearth of English literature is scarcely surprising given that the charitable trust model was only recently introduced into the Chinese legal system in 2016. However, although the public welfare trust – an institution serving the same function of encouraging charitable causes – has been present in the Chinese legal system for two decades, there nonetheless remains a dearth of English literature on this topic. This is surprising, suggesting either that the topic has been discounted or discussed without exhaustive analysis or that its significance has not been fully appreciated by writers in English.

C *Locating This Book in Relation to Existing Literature*

The current study of the governance of charitable trusts contributes to the literature by locating charitable trusts within the Chinese legal, policy, and social contexts and by examining the ways in which the legislated governance rules regarding charitable trusts are implemented in practice. It engages with both the Chinese and English language literatures in three ways.

First, it engages in a detailed analysis of the legal regulatory framework, identifying gaps in the current laws governing charitable trusts. This analysis reveals the continuities and discontinuities between public welfare trusts and charitable trusts regarding the checks-and-balances mechanisms between trust parties; it also identifies the ways in which regulators interact with trust parties in the governance of charitable trusts. At the macro-level, this analysis identifies the progress that legislators have made to strengthen the autonomy of private individuals in charitable undertakings.

Second, this book analyses the regulation of charitable trusts in practice. The comparison between law and practice reveals the social and policy norms that underpin the traditional legal system for charities and that continue to inform the regulatory system of charitable trusts today.

[71] Lin (n 30) 771–5.

To carry out this comparison, semi-structured qualitative interviews with regulatory officials were conducted in both eastern developed areas and western undeveloped areas in China. Regional differences[72] in the regulatory practices of charitable trusts – a supportive regulatory environment in the east and a conservative one in the west – suggest that the policy and social context is relevant to the performance of regulators' roles in practice. The law and its institutional context should be examined together to identify how legal actors engage with the law and how the law is carried out in practice.[73] In this light, this book explores the social and policy factors that regulators have taken into account when implementing the law.

Third, this book extends the literature examining the checks-and-balances mechanisms between settlors and trustees by exploring how

[72] See analysis in Section III of Chapter 4.

[73] Sally Falk Moore, 'Law and Social Change: The Semi-Autonomous Social Field as an Appropriate Subject of Study' (1973) 4(4) *Law & Society Review* 719, 719. There is a vast literature examining the correlation between law and its institutional context. Cotterell and Sarat suggest that 'far from community dissolving as law becomes more prominent, the growing complexity and bulk of law reflects the increasing complexity, intricacy and richness of communal social relationships in their various networks'. See Roger Cotterell and Austin D Sarat, *Law, Culture and Society: Legal Ideas in the Mirror of Social Theory* (Ashgate Publishing Ltd, 2006) 161. Friedman states that 'legal institutions are responsive to social change; moreover, they have a definite role, rather poorly understood, as instruments that set off, monitor, or otherwise regulate the fact or pace of social change'. See Lawrence M. Friedman, 'Legal Culture and Social Development' (1969) 4(1) *Law & Society Review* 29, 29. Reimann holds that 'comparative law has come to look at the world in terms of coexisting legal cultures, i.e., as parts of large social structures consisting of economies, religions, and social habits'. See Mathias Reimann, 'The Progress and Failure of Comparative Law in the Second Half of the Twentieth Century' (2002) 50(4) *American Journal of Comparative Law* 671, 677. For works devoted exclusively to the correlation between law and its institutional context, see Roger Cotterell, 'Seeking Similarity, Appreciating Difference: Comparative Law and Communities' in Andrew Harding and Esin Örücü (eds.), *Comparative Law in the 21st Century* (Kluwer Academic Publishers, 2002) 35–54; David Nelken, 'Legal Transplants and Beyond: Of Disciplines and Metaphors' in Andrew Harding and Esin Örücü (eds.), *Comparative Law in the 21st Century* (Kluwer Academic Publishers, 2002) 19–34; 杜健荣 [Du Jianrong],《法律与社会的共同演化 – 基于卢曼的社会系统理论反思转型时期法律与社会的关系》 [Co-Evolution of Law and Society Reflection – On the Relationship between Law and Society in Transition Period by Luhmann's Social System Theory] (2009) 2 法制与社会发展 *Law and Social Development* 109, 109–17; 范愉 [Fan Yu],《新法律现实主义的勃兴与当代中国法学反思》 [The Rise of New Legal Realism and Reflections on Current Chinese Law] (2006) 4 中国法学 *China Legal Science* 38, 38–51; 季卫东 [Ji Weidong],《法律议论的社会科学研究新范式》 [New Method of Social Scientific Study in Legal Discussion] (2015) 6 中国法学 *China Legal Science* 25, 25–41.

contracts are used to redistribute each party's powers and duties. The settlor is endowed by law with extensive powers while the trustee is burdened by law with onerous duties. Charity law does not clearly define what these powers or duties entail and how the role of each party is to be discharged. This book examines real-world contracts and interviews with relevant actors (i.e., trustee managers and settlors) to identify how trust parties use contracts in the governance of charitable trusts and the reasons behind these uses.[74] Contract theorists acknowledge that contracts are widely used as tools to allocate risks between relevant parties.[75] In the Chinese charitable trust setting, trust parties tend to use contractual tools to vary the legal framework of charitable trusts to mitigate the risks posed by regulatory practice and the vagueness of the law. The present book enriches contract law scholarship and legal realist scholarship by examining how trust parties use contracts to distribute their powers and duties and what role extra-legal factors have played in the planning and development of relevant contract clauses. It shows that the vagueness of the law creates risk for trust parties, motivating them to use contractual tools to guide the management of charitable trusts. This observation, along with the analysis of regulatory practice, provides insights for trust practitioners and academics seeking to understand how newly-recorded charitable trusts are actually governed in China.

This book examines charitable trusts with reference to the legal rules governing them, locates their governance practices within policy and social contexts, and synthesizes the three perspectives outlined. In doing so, this book seeks to make an original contribution to scholarship on the governance of Chinese charitable trusts.

[74] See analysis in Section III of Chapter 5.

[75] See, e.g., Stephen A. Smith, *Contract Theory* (Oxford University Press, 2004) 308; Jeannie Marie Paterson, Andrew Robertson and Arlen Duke, *Contract: Cases and Materials* (Thomson Reuters, 2016) 540; John Cartwright, *Contract Law: An Introduction to the English Law of Contract for the Civil Lawyer* (Hart, 3rd ed., 2016) 131; Stewart Macaulay, 'Non-Contractual Relations in Business: A Preliminary Study' (1963) 28(1) *American Sociological Review* 55, 63; Lisa Bernstein, 'Opting out of the Legal System: Extralegal Contractual Relations in the Diamond Industry' (1992) 21(1) *Journal of Legal Studies* 115, 130; Stewart Macaulay, 'An Empirical View of Contract Law' (1985) 1985 *Wisconsin Law Review* 465, 475; Albert Choi and George Triantis, 'The Effect of Bargaining Power on Contract Design' (2012) 98(8) *Virginia Law Review* 1665, 1670; Alan Schwartz and Robert E. Scott, 'Contract Theory and the Limits of Contract Law' (2003) 113(3) *Yale Law Journal* 541, 555.

III Legal Definition of Charitable Trust Governance

A Semantic Meaning of Governance

This book examines the governance of Chinese charitable trusts. As such, the analysis of this book depends on how one defines the term 'charitable trust governance'. Semantically, there is no uniform interpretation of 'governance'.[76] Context plays a vital role in unravelling its meaning.[77] Etymologically, it derives from the Latin words *gubernare* and *gubernator*, which refer to 'steering a ship and to the steerer or captain of a ship'.[78] 'Governance' originates from the old French word *gouvernance*, which means 'control and the state of being governed'.[79] The term is not a 'precise one and its meaning is affected by cultural variables'.[80] As David Renz and Fredrik Andersson observe, '[T]he concept of governance has been defined less clearly than is necessary to advance research in this field'.[81] Legal words, in essence, 'are best understood and investigated by reference to the content of the doctrines that create the concepts rather than by reference to dictionary definitions'.[82] Nevertheless, dictionary definitions are a good starting point. Examining how 'governance' is defined in dictionaries can shed light on subsequent discussions of charitable trust governance in China. In authoritative dictionaries such as the *Modern Chinese Dictionary*, the *Oxford English Dictionary*, and the *New Shorter Oxford English Dictionary on Historical*

[76] The term 'governance' refers to the 'set of practices and procedures in place to ensure that an entity operates to achieve its objectives in an effective and transparent manner'. See The Treasury, The Australian Government, *Development of Governance Standards-Consultation Paper* (December 2012) 5. The term 'governance' refers to 'the systems and processes concerned with ensuring the overall direction, control, and accountability of an organization'. See David O. Renz and Fredrik O. Andersson, 'Nonprofit Governance: A Review of the Field' in Chris Cornforth and William A. Brown (eds.), *Nonprofit Governance: Innovative Perspectives and Approaches* (Routledge, 2014) 18.

[77] See analysis in Section II-A.

[78] John H. Farrar, *Corporate Governance in Australia and New Zealand* (Oxford University Press, 2001) 3; 韩丽欣 [Han Lixin] (n 6) 105; Shi (n 51) 26.

[79] 韩丽欣 [Han Lixin] (n 6) 105; Shi (n 51) 26; Farrar (n 78) 3.

[80] Roman Tomasic, 'Good Corporate Governance: The International Challenge' (2000) 12 *Australian Journal of Corporate Law* 142, 143.

[81] Renz and Andersson (n 76) 18.

[82] Matthew Conaglen, *Fiduciary Loyalty: Protecting the Due Performance of Non-Fiduciary Duties* (Hart, 2010) 77.

Principles, 'governance' is generally understood as a set of procedures, methods, or rules by which something is regulated,[83] or as a method of management.[84]

B Governance in Context

Existing scholarship has extensively analysed the meanings of 'corporate governance' and 'charity governance'. Exploring how these terms have been understood can illuminate how the dictionary meaning of governance is implemented in particular contexts. This analysis can then contribute to the understanding of governance in the Chinese charitable trust setting. Although the meaning of governance varies in these three legal contexts, comparisons between charity governance and corporate governance shed light on the interpretation of charitable trust governance – particularly given that the language used to describe charitable trust governance suggests similar conceptual characteristics and origins as those for corporate governance and charity governance.

1 Corporate Governance and Charity Governance

Critical writings and commentaries from a wide range of disciplines have studied the meaning of 'corporate governance'.[85] Examination of these

[83] The term 'regulate' means 'to control, govern, or direct by rules or regulations'. See J. A. Simpson and E. S. C. Weiner (eds.), *The Oxford English Dictionary (XIII)* (Clarendon Press, 2nd ed., 1989) 524; Lesley Brown (ed.), *The New Shorter Oxford English Dictionary on Historical Principles (Volume 2 N-Z)* (Clarendon Press, 4th ed., 1993) 2530. See also 汉语大字典编纂处 [Office of Chinese Dictionary Compilation],《现代汉语词典》 [Modern Chinese Dictionary] (四川辞书出版社 Sichuan Dictionary Press, 2014) 276; 中国社会科学院语言研究所 [Institute of Language Studies, Chinese Academy of Social Sciences],《现代汉语词典》 [Modern Chinese Dictionary] (商务印书馆 The Commercial Press, 7th ed., 2016) 482.

[84] J. A. Simpson and E. S. C. Weiner (eds.), *The Oxford English Dictionary (VI)* (Clarendon Press, 2nd ed., 1989) 710; Lesley Brown (ed.), *The New Shorter Oxford English Dictionary on Historical Principles (Volume 1 A-M)*, vol 2 (Clarendon Press, 4th ed., 1993) 1123. See also Susan Butler (ed.), *Macquarie Dictionary* (Macquarie Dictionary Publishers, 5th ed., 2009) 722; Ray Finkelstein, P. J. Butt, Rod Howie and David Hamer (eds.), *LexisNexis Concise Australian Legal Dictionary* (LexisNexis Butterworths, 5th ed., 2015) 285; Raymond Finkelstein, David Hamer, R. N. Howie, Margaret Allars, R. CD. McCallum and J. C. Gibson (eds.), *LexisNexis Australian Legal Dictionary* (LexisNexis Butterworths, 2nd ed., 2016) 689; 中国社会科学院语言研究所 [Institute of Language Studies, Chinese Academy of Social Sciences] (n 83) 1690; 汉语大字典编纂处 [Office of Chinese Dictionary Compilation] (n 83) 1021.

[85] In the field of financial economics, corporate governance relates to the methods by which suppliers of finance to corporations assure themselves of getting a return on their

scholarly works yields no standard definition. According to some scholars, 'corporate governance' relates to the set of procedures and practices by which companies are regulated, managed, or controlled;[86] others emphasize the fulfilment of institutional objectives.[87] For example, the China Security Regulatory Commission's *Governance Codes for Listed Companies in China*[88] states that 'corporate governance' deals with the methods by which a corporation is controlled and directed and the ways in which its objective is achieved by way of internal management.

Likewise, the term 'charity governance' is also open to interpretation. In some scholarly writings, it is defined according to the internal management of charities. In *Fundamental Issues of the Non-Profit Organization Law in China*, 'charity governance' is defined as a set of rules, standards, and procedures through which a charitable organization is managed, controlled, or regulated.[89] Other works have incorporated the values underlying the creation and operation of charities into the

investments. See Andrei Shleifer and Robert W. Vishny, 'A Survey of Corporate Governance' (1997) 52(2) *Journal of Finance* 737, 737; Oliver E. Williamson, 'Corporate Finance and Corporate Governance' (1988) 43(3) *Journal of Finance* 567, 588–9; Lucian Bebchuk, Alma Cohen and Allen Ferrell, 'What Matters in Corporate Governance?' (2009) 22(2) *The Review of Financial Studies* 783, 823–4. In accounting theory, corporate governance mainly focuses on ensuring the quality of the company's financial information and determining how to use this information to evaluate assets and reward performance. See Philip Brown, Wendy Beekes and Peter Verhoeven, 'Corporate Governance, Accounting and Finance: A Review' (2011) 51(1) *Accounting & Finance* 96, 153; Richard G. Sloan, 'Financial Accounting and Corporate Governance: A Discussion' (2001) 32(1) *Journal of Accounting and Economics* 335, 340–1.

86 See Shi (n 51) 25; John H. Farrar, 'Developing Corporate Governance in Greater China' (2002) 25(2) *University of New South Wales Law Journal* 462, 463. See also Ian M. Ramsay, 'The Corporate Governance Debate and the Role of Directors' Duties' in Ian M Ramsay (ed.), *Corporate Governance and the Duties of Company Directors* (Centre for Corporate Law and Securities Regulation, 1997) 2; Daniel Greenberg (ed.), *Jowitt's Dictionary of English Law (Volume 1: A–I)* (Sweet & Maxwell, 4th ed., 2015) 586; Trischa Mann (ed.), *Australian Law Dictionary* (Oxford University Press, 2nd ed, 2013) 188.

87 There is no agreement on what a company's objective is. The objective of a company can be classified into three types: prioritizing the shareholders' interests, prioritizing the shareholders' interests while simultaneously considering the interests of other stakeholders, and prioritizing the stakeholders' interests. See Reegan Grayson-Morison and Ian Ramsay, 'An Analysis of Companies' Business Objectives' (2014) 32(6) *Company and Security Law Journal* 438, 438; Donald C. Clarke, 'Corporate Governance in China: An Overview' (2003) 14(4) *China Economic Review* 494, 498–9.

88 《上市公司治理准则》 [Governance Codes for Listed Companies in China] (People's Republic of China) China Security Regulatory Commission, 30 September 2018, art 3.

89 北京大学非营利法组织研究中心 [Peking University Law School Nonprofit Organization Law Research Center], 《中国非营利组织法的基本问题》 [Fundamental Issues of the Non-Profit Organization Law in China] (中国方正出版社 [China

definition of 'charity governance'. An illustrative example is the definition given in *Research on the Governance of Chinese Charities*: 'charity governance' refers to a set of principles or rules that enable charities to be managed in a way that achieves their public benefit objectives in an effective and transparent manner.[90]

2 Charitable Trust Governance

In contrast to the abundant discussions of the definitions of 'corporate governance' and 'charity governance', the literature examining how the governance of charitable trusts should be understood is sparse.[91] The dearth of literature is hardly surprising because the charitable trust model was only introduced into the Chinese legal system in 2016. Based on the understanding of corporate governance and charity governance

Fangzheng Press], 2006) 126. For scholarly writings that endorse this definition, see, e.g., 王涛 [Wang Tao] (n 62) 145; 李德健 [Li Dejian],《公共利益与法人自治的平衡 – 中国慈善法人制度变革的进路选择》[The Balance of Public Interest and Legal Person Autonomy – Selection of Approaches for Reform of the Chinese Charity Legal Person System] (2016) 31(163) 法学论坛 *Legal Forum* 54, 58; 董蕾红 [Dong Leihong] and 李宝军 [Li Baojun],《论慈善组织的政府监管》[On the Government Supervision over Charitable Organizations] (2015) 6 山东大学学报(哲学社会科学版) *Journal of Shandong University (Philosophy and Social Sciences)* 77, 78–9.

90 韩丽欣 [Han Lixin] (n 6) 122. For other works that endorse this definition, see, e.g., 马金芳 [Ma Jinfang],《我国社会组织立法的困境与出路》[The Dilemma and Outlet of the Social Organization Legislation in China] (2016) 6 法商研究 *Study of Law and Business* 3, 10; 高静华 [Gao Jinghua],《慈善透明的困境与治理策略》[Dilemmas of the Transparency of Charities and Governance Strategies] (2018) 15 中国社会组织 *China Social Organization* 53, 55; 谢琼 [Xie Qiong],《立体监管: 我国慈善事业发展的理性选择》[Stereoscopic Supervision: Rational Choice for the Development of Charitable Causes in China] (2015) 4 国家行政学院学报 *Journal of Chinese Academy of Governance* 73, 75. In Australia, the consultation paper *Review of Not-for-Profit Governance Arrangements*, issued by the Department of the Treasury (Australia) in 2011, is important in understanding the meaning of governance. This paper provides charities with a wide range of suggestions for the practice of good governance. In this paper, charity governance is defined as the practices and procedures within and by which the charity is run to achieve its objectives in a transparent and effective manner. See The Treasury, The Australian Government, *Review of Not-for-Profit Governance Arrangement-Consultation Paper* (2011) 5. See also The Treasury, The Australian Government (n 76) 5. This definition has been endorsed by the governance guide (*Governance for Good: The ACNC's Guide for Charity Board Members*) issued by the Australian Charities and Not-for-profits Commission in 2013. See Australian Charities and Not-for-profits Commission, *Governance for Good: The ACNC's Guide for Charity Board Members* (July 2013) 3.

91 Evelyn Brody observed that charitable trust governance is focused on the governing of trustees. See Evelyn Brody, 'Charity Governance: What's Trust Law Got to Do with It?' (2005) 80 *Chicago-Kent Law Review* 641, 686.

previously discussed, one can identify two elements that are most relevant to the definition of 'governance'. The first deals with the rules or procedures by which an entity (corporation or charity) is managed or administered. The second relates to the purpose of governance: namely, an entity is governed to achieve its institutional objectives in an effective and transparent manner. When these two elements are viewed together, it can be said that governance is concerned with the rules or practices by which the objective of an entity is achieved through management. In this light, this book defines the governance of charitable trusts as a set of mechanisms that ensure the trustee of a charitable trust complies with their duties in order to effectively realize the charitable purpose or public benefit that the charitable trust pursues. This definition of charitable trust governance focuses on the control of trustees' power and on the mechanisms available to ensure their accountability for exercising that power.

IV Hypothesis and Research Questions

A Hypothesis

This book focuses on the governance structure of Chinese charitable trusts, assessing it from the perspective of China's particular political, social, and economic conditions. It tests the hypothesis that the governance framework for Chinese charitable trusts can only be fully understood in light of relevant law, administrative practice, and private actions taken by trust parties. This hypothesis comprises three inter-related aspects. First, the law sets up a governance framework for charitable trusts but is vague and under-determined in various respects. Second, administrative practice is a significant component of the governance framework because regulators in China are subject to intense administrative and policy pressures and are thus highly responsive to extra-legal concerns. Third, private action is essential in the governance framework because trust parties vary the framework of the law to mitigate risks posed by administrative practice and the vagueness of the law.

As discussed in Section III, 'charitable trust governance' denotes any governance mechanism ensuring that the trustee of a charitable trust complies with their duties in order to effectively realize the charitable purpose or the public benefit pursued by the charitable trust. This definition indicates that the focus of charitable trust governance is on how a trustee's exercise of power should be controlled. Based on this understanding, there are four types of actors relevant to the governance of charitable trusts, each of whom exerts pressure on trustees to ensure they comply with their duties. Settlors can exercise their statutory or contractual powers to supervise the trustee's administration of charitable trust affairs. Beneficiaries might have standing to bring proceedings to remedy the misuse of charitable trust assets where they have particularized (or individualized) interests in the proper distribution of trust assets after receiving notice. Regulators can exercise their regulatory powers to interfere with the management of charitable trusts and to punish trustees for non-compliant behaviours. Finally, the general public can access information disclosed by trustees and report the misuse of charitable funds to the relevant regulators. The subsequent discussions of charitable trust governance in this book will focus on the roles of these four actors and the ways in which they interact both in law and in practice.

This book identifies the factors that shape the governance framework for charitable trusts – legal, administrative, and contractual. It examines the realization of these factors in the creation and ongoing administration of charitable trusts. It also examines the rules governing the creation and administration of charitable trusts and how these rules are implemented in practice. A closer scrutiny of the Chinese Charity Law suggests that, in contrast to public welfare trusts, legislators have constructed a public law–private law hybrid model for charitable trusts. On the one hand, the state has given greater scope to the civil capacity of legal actors. Private actors are permitted to define the ways in which their private funds are used for charitable purposes as defined by the state. On the other hand, the state is unwilling to relinquish its control over the use of charitable trusts, granting regulators extensive powers to monitor whether charitable assets are being used in alignment with the state's social welfare goals.[92] This public law–private law hybrid is reflected in the vagueness of the legal rules governing charitable trusts, which has created risks for both trust parties and regulators. Furthermore, the social and policy environment in which charitable trusts are established and operate plays a vital role in determining how the legal governance framework is implemented in practice. Regulators have long been subject to intense policy and administrative pressures and have greater incentives to consider extra-legal factors when implementing the law. Trust parties

[92] See analysis in Section II of Chapter 4.

are willing to take private action to define the ways in which they interact so as to mitigate risks posed by regulatory practice and the vagueness of the law.[93]

The literature reviewed in Section II indicates that political objectives largely dictate the development of the charitable sector in China. Although the Chinese Charity Law was implemented to mediate the relationship between civil society and the state, the balance leans more in favour of the state's public welfare goals. In fact, the state uses the new charity law to guide the public's charitable activities in order to advance its own public welfare goals. The government has exercised strict control over the charitable sector for a long time; therefore, it will be difficult to change its traditional methods and ideas within a short time.[94] Given this, one may ask the following question: In what way does this policy and social context influence the implementation of the legislated governance framework? The answer can shed light on how trust parties engage with the law in practice and further illuminate the continuities and discontinuities between regulators' behavioural patterns before and after the new charity law was introduced.

To test the above hypothesis, the book takes the following steps. First, the legal governance framework for Chinese charitable trusts is examined across a range of issues. To this end, Chapter 2 discusses the public law–private law hybrid model that legislators have created for charitable trusts. Chapter 3 traces the legislative process of the Chinese Charity Law and the Measures for Charitable Trusts, investigating what legal rules have been constructed for the governance of charitable trusts.[95] This examination compares charitable trusts and public welfare trusts, as well as the rules underpinning both. Chapter 3 explores the nature and scope of the autonomy of parties to determine what types of benefits the trust will create and which sectors of the community can receive such benefits. Chapter 4 analyses the ways in which regulators control the establishment and development of trusts for the purpose of promoting public benefit.

Second, by examining charitable trust contracts and interviewing persons with charitable trust experience, Chapters 4 and 5 analyse the ways in which trust parties and regulators perform their roles in practice. This analysis locates the governance of Chinese charitable trusts in their

[93] See analysis in Section III of Chapter 5.
[94] Li (n 35) 270.
[95] See analysis in Chapter 3.

institutional context. In doing so, it identifies the political and social factors relevant to governance practice and their influence on the implementation of legislated governance rules.[96]

B Research Questions

The analyses in Section IV-A raise three questions to be answered in this book. The first question is, How has the charity law shaped the governance structure of charitable trusts? To answer this, Chapters 2 and 3 study the laws and regulations relevant to public welfare trusts and charitable trusts, respectively; practice in respect of public welfare trusts over the last two decades; and legislative changes that the new charity law has made to the governance framework for charitable trusts. It is revealed that, while charitable trusts are tasked with a similar legislated objective to public welfare trusts (i.e., promoting charitable undertakings), there are fundamental differences regarding the legislated governance rules. The rules governing charitable trusts have elevated the scope of autonomy of private parties and, in theory, limited the extent to which the creation and ongoing operation of a charitable trust is subject to state intervention.[97] These differences incline towards the conclusion that, in contrast to the public law model of public welfare trusts, legislators have constructed a public law–private law hybrid model for Chinese charitable trusts.

While the hybrid model demonstrates the state's desire to promote private philanthropy, it also shows its unwillingness to relinquish control over charitable undertakings.[98] Chapter 2 explores the particular mixture of public law and private law norms that co-exist in the Chinese charitable trust, as well as the implications of this hybrid model for the governance of charitable trusts. Based on the analysis of the charitable trust's hybrid nature, Chapter 3 discusses the legal regulation of trust parties; it covers the assignment of statutory powers and duties to settlors and trustees, the ways in which the checks-and-balances mechanisms between them are established, and the roles that beneficiaries under a charitable trust might play in the governance framework. Chapter 4 explores the new regulatory framework for charitable trusts, providing a textual analysis of the law relevant to the assignment of statutory

96 See analysis in Chapters 4 and 5.
97 See analysis in Section III of Chapter 3.
98 See analysis in Section II of Chapter 2.

powers to each regulator (i.e., civil affairs departments and banking regulatory authorities), how the two regulators interact in law, and what regulatory measures they can undertake.

The second question is, How have regulators implemented the legal regulatory regime in practice? Chapter 4 explores this question by drawing upon empirical findings from the regulatory practice of charitable trusts. Under the legal framework, regulators are granted broad powers to oversee whether trust assets are being managed in compliance with the state's broader interests. However, the regulatory framework is vague and incomplete regarding what these regulatory powers and duties entail in substance and how they should be exercised. This vagueness in the law has created substantive risks for regulators, motivating them to adopt strategies to protect their interests from being adversely affected when engaging with the law.[99] Chapter 4 identifies the deficiencies of the current regulatory framework, the legal uncertainties that these deficiencies have created, and the strategies that regulators have taken in the exercise of their powers and responsibilities.

Apart from the law, China's social and political circumstances, within which charitable trusts are introduced and operate, play a vital role in shaping the decision-making of regulatory officials.[100] In the Chinese bureaucratic system, regulators are highly responsive to extra-legal factors in their implementation of the law.[101] This approach helps regulators strictly control the use of charitable trusts for public welfare purposes and minimizes the risks that may arise from the performance of their responsibilities.[102] Drawing on the empirical findings from regulatory practice, Chapter 4 identifies the extra-legal factors shaping the regulatory framework and the ways in which these factors are realized in the administration and supervision of charitable trusts.

The two questions already mentioned lead to a third: What private actions have trust parties taken when engaging with the law? Chapter 5 explores this question through an examination of charitable contracts collected for this research. In the public law–private law hybrid model, trust parties are granted greater autonomy to determine the distribution of rights and responsibilities between them in the day-to-day management of

[99] See analysis in Section II of Chapter 4.
[100] See analysis in Section III of Chapter 4.
[101] Ibid.
[102] Ibid.

charitable trusts.[103] The law establishes checks-and-balances mechanisms between trust parties. However, it does not clearly define how these mechanisms should operate and what measures can be taken by trust parties when these mechanisms are inadequate to regulating their relationship.[104] In view of the risk posed by regulatory practice and the vagueness of the law, the parties to charitable trusts are strongly motivated to use contracts to clarify their powers and duties and to define the ways in which they interact with regulators. Similar to regulators, practice shows that trust parties consider a wide range of extra-legal factors in the planning and development of contract clauses, seeking to use these clauses to mitigate risks in the performance of their legal roles.[105]

To explore how contractual tools are used by trust parties, Chapter 5 examines three subsidiary questions. In what ways are contracts used in the management of charitable trusts? What types of relationships are regulated by charitable trust contracts? And how do extra-legal factors affect the planning of contract terms between trust parties? To address these questions, Chapter 5 considers areas where the law governing the relationship between trust parties is vague, the risks that trust parties may confront when implementing the law, and the policy and social norms underlying the creation and ongoing administration of charitable trusts.

C *Questions beyond the Scope of This Book*

Although this book examines the governance structure of charitable trusts both in law and in practice, it focuses on how legislated rules are implemented in practice in the governance of charitable trusts. Examination of such governance practices can help to identify problems or deficiencies in the current legislative framework. For example, the current law makes no mention of the role beneficiaries might play in the governance of charitable trusts,[106] and it does not evaluate the extent to which a more restrictive approach regarding the settlor's role in charitable trust governance might adversely affect their willingness to make donations.[107] It fails to detail the rules governing information disclosure, and it does not require trustees to explain in their financial and annual

[103] See analysis in Section III of Chapter 3.
[104] Ibid.
[105] See analysis in Section III of Chapter 5.
[106] See analysis in Section IV of Chapter 3.
[107] See analysis in Section III of Chapter 3.

work reports how well they have realized the public benefit goals the trust was set up to deliver.[108] This makes it more difficult for settlors, regulators, and the general public to understand and evaluate the performance of charitable trusts and their trustees. This book discusses these problems alongside its analysis of the governance of charitable trusts. However, it does not articulate a detailed pathway for the reform of the governance rules of Chinese charitable trusts: this would require an examination of these problems from a more comprehensive perspective, encompassing law, sociology, and politics.

Furthermore, this book does not provide an in-depth analysis of the different theories concerning the governance of charitable trusts or issues relating to how an appropriate balance might be struck between the needs of the state in using trusts to promote charitable undertakings and the needs of benevolent owners to have more autonomy to deal with their properties. Rather, it focuses on the legal construction of the current system and the challenges it has created. It also evaluates the legislated governance structure of charitable trusts in light of the policy and social contexts in which they operate, identifying the factors influencing how each actor engages with the law.

V Research Methods

This book is an in-depth study of the legal rules governing Chinese charitable trusts and how the legislated governance goals are implemented in practice. It adopts three methods: textual analysis of the legal rules and other legal mechanisms, such as charitable trust contracts; semi-structured qualitative interviews with individuals with charitable trust experience; and translation of Chinese sources.

A Textual Analysis

Documentary sources include legislation, explanatory memoranda, official speeches, public information on recorded charitable trusts, academic treatises, and comparative works. These sources relate to the book's analysis in different ways. Legislation and explanatory memoranda provide information on legal rules that have been constructed for the governance of charitable trusts and the core values that charitable trusts

[108] See analysis in Section II of Chapter 4.

exist to pursue. Official speeches provide information for policy reasons underlying the legislative reform of charitable trusts and the interaction between the state and the general public in promoting charitable undertakings. Public information on recorded charitable trusts provides information on charitable trust practice, including what types of charitable trusts have been created, what their charitable purposes are, and how they have been administered and regulated. Academic treatises provide information on areas where current research can be continued or expanded and on areas where this book can make further contributions. Comparative works provide information on continuities and discontinuities between charitable trusts and public welfare trusts regarding governance and measures that lawmakers have taken to unlock the potential of trusts to develop and further charitable causes.

The textual analysis is divided into two parts. The first part is an interpretation of Chinese charitable trusts; it includes a critical analysis of legislative provisions, the nature and function of Chinese charitable trusts, and the threshold for establishing Chinese charitable trusts. In contrast to the deep historical roots of charitable trusts in common law, charitable trusts are new to the Chinese legal system. The successful establishment of Chinese charitable trusts still faces many problems. In this regard, the textual analysis here clarifies and compares[109] analogous domestic institutions, such as Chinese public welfare trusts and Chinese agency systems. Comparing these two institutions provides a framework for understanding how Chinese charitable trusts operate and helps identify three issues in the model of governance set out by legislation: (a) the ways in which settlors and trustees perform their roles in law, (b) the relationship between Chinese charitable trusts and Chinese agency

[109] At present there is no uniform agreement on the nature of comparative law. Some scholars opine that comparative law is a research method, while others suggest that comparative law is a research methodology, a discipline, or a science. For works devoted exclusively to the nature of comparative law, see J. Michael Rainer, *Introduction to Comparative Law* (Manz, 2010) 19–25; H. Patrick Glenn, 'Against Method' in Maurice Adams and Dirk Heirbaut (eds.), *The Method and Culture of Comparative Law: Essays in Honour of Mark Van Hoecke* (Oxford University Press, 2014) 177; Jaakko Husa, 'Research Designs of Comparative Law: Methodology or Heuristics?' in Maurice Adams and Dirk Heirbaut (eds.), *The Method and Culture of Comparative Law: Essays in Honour of Mark Van Hoecke* (Oxford University Press, 2014) 53–5; Jaap Hage, 'Comparative Law as Method and the Method of Comparative Law' in Maurice Adams and Dirk Heirbaut (eds.), *The Method and Culture of Comparative Law: Essays in Honor of Mark Van Hoecke* (Hart, 2014) 44–5; A. Kh Saidov, *Comparative Law*, tr William Elliott Butler (Wildy, Simmonds & Hill, 2003) 28–31; Reimann (n 73) 683–7.

systems, and (c) the role and function of the regulatory authority in the governance of Chinese charitable trusts.

The second part is an examination of the legal nature of Chinese charitable trusts. As already noted in Section I, because of the onerous requirement to obtain regulatory approval, only twenty public welfare trusts have been successfully established over the last twenty years. Drawing on the failure of public welfare trusts, lawmakers have established a new governance model for charitable trusts, imbuing this newly established institution with its public law–private law nature. Studying the ways in which public law norms interact with private law norms can help explain why lawmakers chose to legislate a whole new regime (the charitable trust) rather than reform the model of public welfare trusts. Furthermore, this study sheds light on how the checks-and-balances mechanisms between trust parties are established. At the macro level, it also assesses the efforts of lawmakers to advance 'state–society relationships'.[110] Legislative history offers an explanation of the development of the law.[111] Charitable trusts are introduced in a context in which large numbers of poor, disabled, and unemployed people have created a huge social demand for charitable causes. As such, to explore the legal nature of charitable trusts, this book will also examine the policy and social contexts within which charitable trust rules operate and develop.

B Semi-structured Qualitative Interviews

The governance model of the Chinese charitable trust has not been studied at all by Chinese scholars, let alone using empirical research methods. An analysis of the law suggests a tension between settlors and trustees, both of whom are given wide discretionary powers, implying that regulatory agencies play a passive role in supervising the administration of Chinese charitable trusts. The law concerning Chinese charitable trusts has only been in place since 2016; as such, many aspects of the practice of governance are still in their formative stages, with the extant literature not

[110] Lee, 'Modernize Charity Law in China' (n 6) 372.

[111] Esin Örücü, 'Unde Venit, Quo Tendit Comparative Law' in Andrew Harding and Esin Örücü (eds.), *Comparative Law in the 21st Century* (Kluwer Academic Publishers, 2002) 3; Michael Salter and Julie Mason, *Writing Law Dissertations: An Introduction and Guide to the Conduct of Legal Research* (Pearson Education Limited, 2007) 193; Martin Löhnig, 'Comparative Law and Legal History: A Few Words about Comparative Legal History' in *The Method and Culture of Comparative Law: Essays in Honour of Mark Van Hoecke* (Oxford University Press, 2014) 114.

offering any in-depth analysis of the questions noted in Section IV-B. Given this, gaining insights into the ways in which the legislative scheme of the charitable trust has been practically implemented is significant for evaluating the strengths and weaknesses of the current governance structure for Chinese charitable trusts. Law is an aspect of broader society; as such, it is necessary to examine the law and its institutional context together to identify the ways in which the law is implemented in practice. This book engages in direct contact with human participants through the method of semi-structured qualitative interviews to explore how each of these powerful actors interacts in the day-to-day governance of charitable trusts and to clarify the ways in which regulators exercise their roles and responsibilities of oversight of charitable trusts.

Thirty-one interviews were conducted in Beijing, Shanghai, Shenzhen, Hangzhou, and Guangzhou from October 2018 to January 2019, where most of the charitable trusts are established and where the main regulators and legislators are located. Additional later interviews and more informal discussions with trustee managers and lawyers working in the charitable sector continued into early 2020. Ethics approval was granted before the commencement of this empirical study. Interviews were carried out to obtain insights from participants on the basis that their responses would be anonymous. Two categories of interviewees were involved, and all interviewees had expertise and experience in Chinese charitable trusts. The first category of interviewees comprised private actors, including lawyers, academics, and trustee managers. Interviews with this category of actor elicited their opinions on the ways in which the settlor and the trustee perform their roles, issues of day-to-day governance, and measures taken to comply with legislated governance goals. The second category of interviewees comprised public actors: namely, officials working in regulatory agencies. Interviews with these actors enabled the author to investigate the interaction between the two institutional objectives – promoting charitable undertakings and securing the autonomy of trust parties – of Chinese charitable trusts, the standing of the beneficiary, and the attitude of regulatory authorities to the regulation of Chinese charitable trusts. To ensure anonymity, the identifying information of the interviewees has been replaced with codes: L for lawyers, A for academics, T for trustee managers, and R for regulatory officials.

The qualitative analysis of empirical data gathered through interviews enriches the understanding of the governance practice of Chinese charitable trusts. The qualitative analysis in this book yields two significant findings. First, there is a considerable gap between theoretical analysis and practice regarding the governance of Chinese charitable trusts. Second, the policy and social contexts play an important role in realizing the governance goals set out by legislation: regulators and trust parties do not respond to the legal governance model perfectly, and their behaviours are significantly affected by factors transcending the law.

C Translation of Chinese Sources

This book draws on both English and Chinese sources. As such, the author's translations of relevant legal rules and concepts into English are essential to the analysis. The translation of Chinese legal concepts into English can be problematic when there are no close equivalents in English. This is particularly true in the case of Chinese charitable trusts. Accordingly, each chapter that examines the governance of Chinese charitable trusts – for example, Chapter 2 in the case of public welfare trusts (*gongyi xintuo* 公益信托) and Chapter 4 in the case of recording (*bei'an* 备案) and supervisory conversation (*jianguan tanhua* 监管谈话) – provides an explanation of the Chinese terms and how to understand them in English. Unless otherwise indicated, all English translations of Chinese text and materials are the author's own and are based on the following four principles. First, regarding Chinese to English translations, accuracy in meaning has been preferred over literal translation. Take the concept *jing zhun fu pin* (精准扶贫). This concept often occurs in connection with policy documents or official speeches. While its literal meaning is 'precise poverty alleviation', it has been translated here as 'targeted poverty alleviation'. Second, regarding the interview data, accuracy in meaning has also been preferred over literal translation. By focusing on the precise meaning of individual words and terms, a literal or technical translation cannot accurately convey the actual meaning of the interview respondents. Third, semi-official English translations – namely, English translations available on websites, such as those of PKU law or Westlaw China, which do not have any official status – have been modified where the translation is considered suboptimal or deficient. Fourth, where it assists in understanding, the original Chinese text has been included in parentheses after the English translation to identify the relevant concepts. Illustrative examples are the three major institutional forms for establishing charities in China: foundations (*jijin hui* 基金会), social associations (*shehui tuanti* 社会团体), and privately-operated non-enterprise organizations (*minban feiqiye danwei* 民办非企业单位).

2

Chinese Charitable Trusts as Public Law–Private Law Hybrids

I Introduction

This chapter analyses the legal nature of the charitable trust model and the implications of this analysis for the governance of charitable trusts. The charitable trust model was introduced when public welfare trusts had failed, with legislators seeking to use this new model to encourage public participation in charitable undertakings. Drawing on lessons from the failure of public welfare trusts, legislators created a public law–private law hybrid model for charitable trusts. In this model, the state gives trust parties greater autonomy over the types of benefit the charitable trust can create and which sectors of society can receive those benefits. However, the state still reserves a high degree of control over charitable trusts to ensure they conform with the state's public welfare goals. This hybrid nature demonstrates how the state understands the role and function of charitable trusts and the core values legislators expect charitable trusts to pursue.

Section II analyses the hybrid nature of the charitable trust model by examining its legislative provisions. This analysis serves two aims: first, to identify the conflicts and contradictions that may arise between the autonomy of trust parties and the broader interests of the state in the implementation of policies pertaining to charitable trusts; and second, to explore how these conflicts and contradictions are addressed in light of the hybrid nature of charitable trusts.

After considering the hybrid nature of charitable trusts, Section III uses the analysis of the public law–private law hybrid model to discuss the implications for the governance of charitable trusts. The hybrid nature of charitable trusts was intentionally created by legislators. It permeates and informs the design of the governance framework for charitable trusts. In Chapter 1, the governance of charitable trusts was defined as a set of mechanisms that ensure the trustee of a charitable trust complies with its duties in order to effectively realize the charitable purpose or the public benefit pursued by the charitable trust. This definition suggests that charitable trust governance focuses on how trustees should exercise their powers and what measures can be taken to ensure their accountability for that exercise.

Adopting this definition, Section III-A identifies the actors relevant to the control of trustees' exercise of power in light of the hybrid nature of charitable trusts and how they are connected to the analysis of charitable trust governance. Because the implementation of the law is influenced by legal and extra-legal factors, it is possible that actual practice may diverge from the law. The past practice has shown that trust parties and regulators proactively engage with the law and are also strongly responsive to extra-legal concerns when performing their legal roles. Section III-B analyses the implications of this practice for the governance of charitable trusts.

II The Nature of the Public Law–Private Law Hybrid

As analysed in Chapter 1, with the mass transfer of wealth into private hands, China now possesses enormous socioeconomic resources that can be mobilized to develop charitable undertakings. However, the channels by which private actors can participate in charitable causes are extremely limited.[1] Still worse are the obstacles facing the establishment of foundations, social groups, and private non-enterprise units, the three major legal forms for establishing charities. It was in this context that legislators introduced the model of public welfare trusts to the Chinese domestic legal system in 2001. The public welfare trust model has not been successful, however: no more than twenty public welfare trusts have been

[1] Siyi Lin, 'China's New Charity Law: A New Era of Charitable Trusts' (2018) 24(8) *Trusts & Trustees* 768, 768–9; 徐卫 [Xu Wei],《慈善宣言信托制度构建研究》 [*Research on the Construction of Charitable Declaration Trusts*] (法律出版社 [Law Press], 2012) 52; 朱志峰 [Zhu Zhifeng],《公益信托的法律特征及我国模式的探索》[Legal Nature of the Charitable Trust and Exploration of a Chinese Model] (2008) 22(6) 当代法学 *Contemporary Law Review* 112, 112; 薛智胜 [Xue Zhisheng] and 王海涛 [Wang Haitao],《论我国公益信托监察人法律制度的完善》 [Perfecting the Institution of the Trust Supervisor in the Chinese Charitable Trust System] (2009) 11(2) 天津大学学报（社会科学版）*Journal of Tianjin University (Social Science)* 123, 123; 王建军 [Wang Jianjun], 燕翀 [Yan Chong] and 张时飞 [Zhang Shifei],《慈善信托法律制度运行机理及其在我国发展的障碍》[The Operational Mechanism and Theories Related to the Charitable Trusts and Its Development Obstacles in Mainland China] (2011) 4 环球法律评论 *Global Law Review* 108, 111.

established over the last two decades.[2] To unlock the potential of the trust institution to develop charitable causes, legislators introduced the charitable trust model in 2016.

In contrast to public welfare trusts – a model located entirely within the sphere of public law[3] – the charitable trust model is a mixture of both public law and private law norms. Private law deals with actions in which legal actors protect their autonomous interests; public law deals with approaches to the administration and governance of society as a whole.[4] In light of this distinction, in the charitable trust setting, private law norms indicate that the state has granted trust parties greater control over the exercise of their management rights. For example, settlors have the autonomy to determine how to dispose of their private funds for charitable purposes as defined by the state. In comparison, public law norms indicate that the state is reluctant to relinquish its control over charitable trusts, seeking to guide the public to use trusts to serve its own public welfare goals. For example, the state defines the scope of charitable purposes, and trust parties are not allowed to consider different purposes, such as promoting political causes in areas not welcomed by the state or considering ancillary or subsidiary private benefits when disposing of charitable assets. There is a tension between these two types of norms in both the substantial and procedural aspects of charitable trusts. Take the role of settlors. The granting of broad powers to settlors enables them to proactively engage with the management of charitable trusts. However, a

[2] For details on these established public welfare trusts, see 赵廉慧 [Zhao Lianhui],《信托法解释论》 [*Interpretative Theory of Trust Law*] (中国法制出版社 [China Legal Publishing House], 2015) 526–9.

[3] 金锦萍 [Jin Jinping],《论公益信托之界定及其规范意义》 [Research on the Definition of the Public Welfare Trust and Its Normative Significance] (2015) 6 北京大学学报(哲学社会科学版) *Journal of Peking University (Philosophy & Social Sciences)* 72, 83; 李子顺 [Li Zishun],《公益信托的性质与税收优惠》 [The Nature of the Public Welfare Trust and Its Tax Privileges] (2009) 2 法律适用 *Journal of Law Application* 91, 92; 朱志峰 [Zhu Zhifeng] (n 1) 112; 赵廉慧 [Zhao Lianhui] (n 2) 523.

[4] Jody Freeman, 'Extending Public Law Norms through Privatization' (2003) 116(5) *Harvard Law Review* 1285, 1303–4; Janet McLean, 'Convergence in Public and Private Law Doctrines: The Case of Public Contracts' (2016) 2016(1) *New Zealand Law Review* 5, 9; Justin Friedrich Krahe, 'The Impact of Public Law Norms on Private Law Relationships' (2015) 2 *European Journal of Comparative Law and Governance* 124, 126; 张家慧 [Zhang Jiahui],《诉权意义的回复 — 诉讼法与实体法关系的理论基点》[Responses to the Meaning of Appealing Right: Theoretical Basis of the Relationship between Procedural Law and Substantive Law] (2000) 2 法律评论 *Law Review* 58, 60; 王锡三 [Wang Xisan],《近代诉权理论的探讨》[On the Theory of Modern Appealing Right] (1989) 6 现代法学 *Modern Law Science* 16, 17.

settlor's autonomy is also strictly constrained in that their power can only be exercised in conformity with the state's public welfare policies.

The charitable trust at common law has a rich history and can also be characterized as a public law–private law hybrid. However, the ways in which its public law and private law norms interact differ considerably from Chinese charitable trusts. This divergence is due to the particular Chinese institutional context in which charitable trusts are introduced and operate. Through comparison with charitable trusts at common law, this section explores questions about the public law–private law nature of Chinese charitable trusts and the unique characteristics of this hybrid model. This model is examined in two steps. First, Chinese public welfare trusts are compared with Chinese charitable trusts to identify how legislators understand their relationship and the extent to which the public law nature of public welfare trusts might illuminate the nature of charitable trusts. Second, Chinese charitable trusts are compared with charitable trusts at common law to identify their differences and to find the unique attributes of the Chinese charitable trust's hybrid model.

A The Relationship between Public Welfare Trusts and Charitable Trusts

The public welfare trust is clearly understood to be a matter of public law, although one may draw on private law concepts of personhood to give it substance. The consensus among scholars and practitioners is that the public welfare trust primarily belongs to the sphere of public law.[5] Given the historical background against which charitable trusts were introduced, it is undisputed that charitable trusts were constructed by drawing on the experiences and lessons of public welfare trusts over the past twenty years. Nonetheless, it is unclear to what extent and in what ways the two institutions relate to each other. Clarifying their relationship can shed critical light on the legal nature of charitable trusts.

Let us first consider what the law says about the relation between the two institutions. Pursuant to article 44 of the Chinese Charity Law and article 2 of the Measures for Charitable Trusts, 'charitable trusts belong to (*shuyu* 属于) public welfare trusts'.[6] This legislative language has given

[5] 赵廉慧 [Zhao Lianhui] (n 2) 523; 金锦萍 [Jin Jinping] (n 3) 83; 李子顺 [Li Zishun] (n 3) 92.

[6] 《中华人民共和国慈善法》 [Charity Law of the People's Republic of China] (People's Republic of China) National People's Congress, 16 March 2016, art 44;《慈善信托管理办法》[Administrative Measures for Charitable Trusts] (People's Republic of China) China Banking Regulatory Commission and Ministry of Civil Affairs, 10 July 2017, art 2.

rise to intense debate over the relationship between the two institutions. Some scholarly writings and commentaries have opined that the two institutions are identical and thus share the same legal meaning;[7] others have proposed that public welfare trusts are in nature distinguishable from charitable trusts.[8] Aside from the semantic difference between the terms 'charitable'[9] and 'public welfare',[10] examining what 'belong to' means in the context of charitable trusts is key. This examination involves a textual interpretation of the legal term and offers useful insights for further constructive discussion of the relationship between the two institutions.

7 倪受彬 [Ni Shoubin],《现代慈善信托的组织法特征及其功能优势 — 与慈善基金会法人的比较》[The Advantage and Character of Modern Charitable Trusts as Organizations: Compared to Charity Foundations] (2014) 46(7) 学术月刊 *Academic Monthly* 86, 87; 朱志峰 [Zhu Zhifeng] (n 1) 112; 王建军 [Wang Jianjun], 燕翀 [Yan Chong] and 张时飞 [Zhang Shifei] (n 1) 110.

8 中国信托业协会 [China Trustee Association] (ed.),《慈善信托研究》 [*Research on the Charitable Trust*] (中国金融出版社 [China Financial Publishing House], 2016) 62–6; 吕鑫 [Lyu Xin],《从公益信托到慈善信托: 跨国移植及其本土建构》[From Public Welfare Trusts to Charitable Trusts: Transnational Transplantation and Local Construction] (2019) 10 社会科学战线 *Social Science Front* 199, 200; 李文华 [Li Wenhua],《完善我国慈善信托制度若干问题的思考》 [Thoughts on Several Issues of Perfecting the Charitable Trust System in China] (2017) 7 法学杂志 *Law Science Magazine* 89, 91; 刘迎霜 [Liu Yingshuang],《我国公益信托法律移植及其本土化: 一种正本清源与直面当下的思考》[The Transplantation and Localization of Charitable Trusts in China: A Thought of Radical Reform and Facing up to the Present] (2015) 27(1) 中外法学 *Peking University Law Journal* 151, 154–5.

9 In the Chinese language, the concept of charity represents benevolence, sympathy, and compassion, which offer relief to the destitute. See 马剑银 [Ma Jianyin],《中国慈善法立法观察》 [Legislative Observations on the Chinese Charity Law] in 杨团 [Yang Tuan] (ed.), 《中国慈善发展报告（2016）》 [*Annual Report on China's Philanthropy Development (2016)*] (社会科学文献出版社 [Social Science Academic Press], 2016) 28–30; 薛宁兰 [Xue Ninglan] and 邓丽 [Deng Li],《中国慈善法研究与立法建议稿》 [*Research on Chinese Charity Law and Relevant Legislative Proposals*] (中国社会科学出版社 [China Social Science Press], 2014) 125; 阮建芳 [Ruan Jianfang],《慈善与公益》 [*Charity and Public Welfare*] (同心出版社 [Tongxin Publishing House], 2013) 53; 金锦萍 [Jin Jinping] (n 3) 74; 刘迎霜 [Liu Yingshuang] (n 8) 155; 李文华 [Li Wenhua] (n 8) 91.

10 In the Chinese language, the concept of public welfare relates to providing benefits for the whole community or solving fundamental problems in relation to human beings, such as fairness, justice, and equality. See 王建军 [Wang Jianjun], 燕翀 [Yan Chong], and 张时飞 [Zhang Shifei] (n 1) 109; 金锦萍 [Jin Jinping] (n 3) 74–5; 刘迎霜 [Liu Yingshuang] (n 8) 155; 李文华 [Li Wenhua] (n 8) 91.

In Chinese dictionaries, 'belong to' has two meanings: 'be part of the ownership of' and 'fall under the category of'.[11] How do the dictionary meanings of 'belong to' relate to its legal meaning? Since the laws relevant to charitable trusts make no mention of the meaning of 'belong to', it is helpful to look at the usage of 'belong to' in related areas of law. Considering the kinds of relationships regulated by the charitable trust, trust laws, contract laws, and property laws have been chosen for the purpose of demonstration. Examination of how 'belong to' has been used in these three legal areas reveals two distinct legal meanings, each consistent with one of the dictionary meanings. First, to say that A belongs to B means that B has ownership of A. This kind of meaning is evident in article 242 of the Chinese Civil Code[12] and article 16 of the Chinese Trust Law.[13] Second, to say that A belongs to B means that A falls under the scope or category of B. Two examples are article 980 of the Chinese Civil Code[14] and article 60 of the Chinese Trust Law.[15] Given the results of this analysis, the next question is, To what extent can one refer to these three areas of law when investigating the legal meaning of 'belong to' for charitable trusts?

[11] 汉语大字典编纂处 [Office of Chinese Dictionary Compilation],《现代汉语词典》[*Modern Chinese Dictionary*] (四川辞书出版社 Sichuan Dictionary Press, 2014) 723; 中国社会科学院语言研究所 [Institute of Language Studies, Chinese Academy of Social Sciences], 《现代汉语词典》 [*Modern Chinese Dictionary*] (商务印书馆 [The Commercial Press], 7th ed., 2016) 1215.

[12] 《中华人民共和国民法典》第二百四十二条: 法律规定专属于国家所有的不动产和动产,任何单位和个人不能取得所有权。 The author's English translation is: 'No units or individuals shall be allowed to acquire ownership of the immovables and movables which are exclusively owned by the State as are provided for by law'.

[13] 《中华人民共和国信托法》第十六条: 信托财产与属于受托人所有的财产相区别，不得归入受托人的固有财产或者成为固有财产的一部分。 The author's English translation is: 'The trust property is different from the property belonging to the trustee, and may not be included in, or made part of the trustee's own property'.

[14] 《中华人民共和国民法典》第九百八十条: 管理人管理事务不属于前条规定的情形，但是受益人享有管理利益的，受益人应当在其获得的利益范围内向管理人承担前条第一款规定的义务。 The author's English translation is: 'Where the management affairs of the administrator do not fall under the circumstances specified in the preceding article, but the beneficiary possesses the benefits of the management, the beneficiary shall assume the obligations specified in the first paragraph of the preceding article to the administrator within the scope of the benefits obtained'.

[15] 《中华人民共和国信托法》第六十条: 为了下列公共利益目的之一而设立的信托，属于公益信托... （7）发展其他社会公益事业。 The author's English translation is: 'A trust created for one of the following public welfare purposes belongs to the scope of public welfare trusts ... (7) developing other public welfare causes'.

Two observations may be made here. First, it is clear that the legal usages of 'belong to' in trust, contract, and property law do not entail the meaning that A is the same as B in terms of its nature or scope. Does this conclusion also apply to charitable trusts? The answer is unclear. Since each law has unique characteristics and concerns, the experience of related areas of law cannot be applied directly without closely reviewing the unique characteristics of charitable trusts and the extent to which these unique characteristics distinguish charitable trusts from contracts or private trusts. Before analysing the characteristics of charitable trusts in Section II-B, it is at least safe to conclude the following: while the legal meanings of 'belong to' in contract, property, and trust law have a certain guiding significance, it is unclear to what extent this guiding significance illuminates the relation between charitable trusts and public welfare trusts. The second observation derives from the first. Based on the institutional similarities between charitable trusts, property, and contracts, as well as the applicability of trust laws to charitable trusts, the legal meaning of 'belong to' in these three areas of law can be referenced in the study of the relationship between charitable trusts and public welfare trusts. If this approach is valid, one possible conclusion is that charitable trusts fall under the scope of public welfare trusts, meaning that public welfare trust doctrines may be applicable to charitable trusts. In this sense, the legal structure of charitable trusts may also contain a considerable public element.

B The Legislative Arrangement of Chinese Charitable Trusts

As discussed in Section II-A, the effectiveness of the semantic analysis of 'belong to' is limited when examining how charitable trusts interact with public welfare trusts. The semantic interpretation shows that charitable trusts might relate to public welfare trusts to a certain degree. However, it cannot illustrate how public law thinking takes effect in charitable trusts, or whether private law norms exist in the structure of the charitable trust, and, if so, in what ways the two norms interact with each other. Based on the analysis in Section II-A, this section examines the legal nature of charitable trusts according to their legislative arrangements.

The legislative arrangements of charitable trusts provide information about the roles of trust parties and regulators in the governance structure of charitable trusts and the ways in which they interact. This examination can shed light on how the state understands the institutional nature of charitable trusts. Where appropriate, comparisons will be made with charitable trusts at common law to delineate the unique characteristics of the governance framework of Chinese charitable trusts. Although the development of charitable trusts varies in China and common law jurisdictions, comparisons with charitable trusts in common law jurisdictions may shed light on the interpretation of Chinese charitable trusts – particularly given that the language describing Chinese charitable trusts suggests similar conceptual characteristics and origins to charitable trusts at common law.

1 The Mixture of Public Law and Private Law Norms

In contrast to the flourishing development of charitable trusts at common law,[16] almost 95 per cent of trusts created in China over the last two decades have been commercial trusts: namely, trusts established for commercial purposes.[17] In line with the experiences of commercial trust businesses, a large number of regulations (*guizhang* 规章) stipulate that the key objective of commercial trusts is to protect the rights and interests of parties to commercial trusts.[18] Despite the rapid development of commercial trust businesses in post-reform China, the large numbers of poor, disabled, and unemployed people have created a huge social demand for developing charitable causes.[19] Regulators and legislators

[16] Alison Dunn, 'As Cold as Charity: Poverty, Equity and the Charitable Trust' (2000) 20 *Legal Studies* 222, 223; Allan D. Vestal, 'Critical Evaluation of the Charitable Trust as a Giving Device' (1957) 1957(3) *Washington University Law Review* 195, 195–6; John H. Langbein, 'The Secret Life of the Trust: The Trust as an Instrument of Commerce' (1997) 107 *Yale Law Journal* 165, 188.

[17] 中国人民大学信托与基金研究所 [Institute of Trust and Fund of Renmin University of China],《中国信托业发展报告（2018）》 [*The Development Report of Chinese Trust Business (2018)*] (中国经济出版社 [China Economic Publishing House], 2018) 112–3; 中国人民大学信托与基金研究所 [Institute of Trust and Fund of Renmin University of China],《中国信托业发展报告（2016）》 [*The Development Report of Chinese Trust Business (2016)*] (中国经济出版社 [China Economic Publishing House], 2018) 106–7.

[18] See, e.g.,《信托公司集合资金信托计划管理办法》 [*Administrative Measures for Collective Investment Trust Schemes of Trust Companies*] (People's Republic of China) China Banking Regulatory Commission, 4 February 2009, art 1;《信托投资公司信息披露管理暂行办法》 [*Interim Measures for the Administration of Information Disclosure by Trust Companies*] (People's Republic of China) China Banking Regulatory Commission, 18 January 2015, s 1.

[19] Adam S. Chodorow, 'Charity with Chinese Characteristics' (2012) 30 *UCLA Pacific Basin Law Journal* 1, 34–5; Chung Yan Miu, Huang Xin, Kenneth W. Foster and Frank Tester, 'Charity Development in China: An Overview' (2007) 17(1) *Asia Pacific Journal of Social Work and Development* 79, 80–1; Anthony J. Spires, 'Contingent Symbiosis and Civil Society in an Authoritarian State: Understanding the Survival of China's Grassroots NGOs' (2011) 117(1) *American Journal of Sociology* 1, 12; Qiusha Ma, 'The

have held a wide range of conferences and forums to discuss legislative reforms to empower trusts to develop charities. Considering the gap between the advantages that public welfare trusts supposedly have for developing charities and the limited role that they have played in practice; legislators introduced the charitable trust model in 2016 with the enactment of the Chinese Charity Law. The reason charitable trusts were introduced reveals the main role that legislators expected this new model to play: namely, to encourage the public to use trusts to further the public welfare goals of the state.[20] This role is implied in the legislative arrangements of charitable trusts, indicating that this model is a public law–private law hybrid.

(a) **Public Law Norms** The charitable trust model was introduced when charity development was a crucial concern of the state. As such, one of the core roles of this model is to encourage the general public to participate in the promotion of charitable undertakings. This is illustrated in article 1 of the Measures for Charitable Trusts. It stipulates that the primary purpose of the Measures for Charitable Trusts is to provide guidelines for the creation and administration of charitable trusts so as to unlock the potential of this new model to further and develop charitable causes in China. This new model's public law role is apparent in three types of legislative arrangements: the requirement of public benefit, the rule of all charitable use, and the granting of wide supervisory powers to regulators.

(i) The Public Benefit Doctrine The public benefit doctrine is stipulated in article 7 of the Measures for Charitable Trusts. Pursuant to this article, a trust established for the purpose of carrying out public benefit activities (*gongyi huodong* 公益活动) is considered to be a charitable trust. The 'public benefit test' is also crucial to the creation of charitable trusts in common law jurisdictions. It is in the public benefit, not in the

Governance of NGOs in China since 1978: How Much Autonomy?' (2002) 31(3) *Nonprofit and Voluntary Sector Quarterly* 305, 318; 王振耀 [Wang Zhenyao],《现代慈善与社会治理： 2013 年度中国公益事业发展报告》 [*Modern Charity and Social Governance: 2013 Annual Report of the Charitable Sector in China*] (社会科学文献出版社 [Social Science Academic Press], 2014) 9–10; 徐卫 [Xu Wei] (n 1) 27–8, 33–5.

20 《关于<中华人民共和国慈善法（草案）>的说明》 [*Explanations on the Charity Law of the People's Republic of China* (Draft)] (People's Republic of China) Standing Committee of the People's Congress, 9 March 2016, pt 1; 中国信托业协会 [China Trustee Association] (n 8) 73–4.

interests of private individuals, that the valid status of a common law charitable trust is acknowledged.[21] There is considerable divergence between common law charitable trusts and Chinese charitable trusts over the meaning of 'public benefit'. In Chinese law, charitable trusts are required to serve the interests of the whole political community. Article 7 of the Measures for Charitable Trusts provides a list of legitimate charitable purposes in China, including alleviating poverty, protecting and improving the ecological environment, and providing relief for the damage caused by natural disasters. These purposes are consistent with the state's public welfare goals and they show that legislators expect charitable trusts to further and develop the broader interests of the state. Trust purposes outside the scope of 'legitimate charitable purposes' are not 'charitable' under Chinese law. Article 7's list of legitimate purposes evidences the state's control over the use of charitable resources. Following from this understanding, private actors have the autonomy to define the types of public benefits created by the charitable trust and what sectors of the public can receive those benefits. However, their autonomy is highly constrained; it can only be exercised to the extent that charitable resources are used in compliance with the state's public welfare policy.[22]

The public benefit doctrine in common law jurisdictions operates differently. Take the charity law in England and Wales ('English charity law') for instance. In English charity law, the public benefit doctrine does not require charitable trusts to benefit the whole political community[23] or to consider the interests of the state as a whole.[24] The general rule is that trusts for political purposes are not of a charitable nature.[25] To be in

[21] Jonathan Garton, *Public Benefit in Charity Law* (Oxford University Press, 2013) [6.05].

[22] 朱志峰 [Zhu Zhifeng] (n 1) 113; 赵廉慧 [Zhao Lianhui] (n 2) 533–4; 金锦萍 [Jin Jinping] (n 3) 82; 刘迎霜 [Liu Yingshuang] (n 8) 155;《关于<中华人民共和国慈善法（草案）>的说明》 [Explanations on the Charity Law of the People's Republic of China (Draft)] (People's Republic of China) Standing Committee of the People's Congress, 9 March 2016 (n 20) s 1.

[23] Hubert Picarda, *The Law and Practice Relating to Charities* (Bloomsbury Professional, 4th ed., 2010) 225.

[24] Kathryn Chan, *The Public–Private Nature of Charity Law* (Hart, 2016) 62.

[25] *National Anti-vivisection Society* v *Inland Revenue Commissioners* [1948] AC 31, 49–52; Garton (n 21) [8.03]–[8.05]; Picarda (n 23) 225. In Australia, there is no general rule against trusts for political purposes. It is debatable whether a political purpose is charitable or not and this question should be assessed on a case-by-case basis. See *Charities Act 2013* (Cth) ss 11, 12(1)(1) and (2); *Aid/Watch Inc* v *Federal Commissioner of Taxation* (2010) 272 ALR 417, 429–30; *Public Trustee* v *Attorney-General (NSW)* (1997) 42 NSWLR 600, 608; Joyce Chia, Matthew Harding and Ann

the public benefit, a charitable trust is not required to further the state's public goals; it need only further an altruistic or other-regarding interest defined by the charitable trust with some constraints.[26] The public benefit doctrine under English charity law normally requires charitable trusts to be public in 'only the altruistic, and not the public-welfare-compliant sense'.[27] As such, key elements of this doctrine – the numerical negligibility test, the personal nexus rule, and the concern with the exclusion of the poor – are primarily intended to preserve the altruistic quality of charitable trusts[28] rather than to promote the state's public welfare goals.

(ii) The Rule of All Charitable Use The second aspect demonstrating the charitable trust's public law role is the legislative requirement of 'all charitable use'. Article 23 of the Measures for Charitable Trusts stipulates that charitable trust assets and the proceeds thereof shall all be used for charitable purposes. The effect is to prevent charitable trusts from becoming vehicles for corruption or the unregulated flow of funds. The rule's rationale can be understood in two dimensions. The first relates to the charity-promoting goal of charitable trusts. Because the charitable trust model is designed to further the state's public welfare goals, any use of charitable trusts for private purposes is not permitted. The second dimension relates to legislators' concerns that charitable assets may be misused by trust parties.[29] Over the last two decades, the media have exposed a series of scandals involving the misuse of charity funds. Legislators are therefore fully aware of the misappropriation risk arising from the trustees' management and use of charitable trusts. Moreover,

O'Connell, 'Navigating the Politics of Charity: Reflections on Aid/Watch Inc v Federal Commissioner of Taxation' (2011) 35 *Melbourne University Law Review* 353, 383–4.

26 Matthew Harding, *Charity Law and the Liberal State* (Cambridge University Press, 2014) 88–9; Juliet Chevalier-Watts, *Charity Law: International Perspectives* (Routledge, 2018) 73; Mary Synge, *The 'New' Public Benefit Requirement: Making Sense of Charity Law?* (Hart, 2015) 79; F. H. Newark, 'Public Benefit and Religious Trusts' (1946) 62(3) *Law Quarterly Review* 284, 240; Paul Harpur, 'Charity Law's Public Benefit Test: Is Legislative Reform in the Public Interest' (2003) 3(2) *Queensland University of Technology Law and Justice Journal* 1, 12.

27 Chan (n 24) 80.

28 Hilary Delany, 'The Law Relating to Charitable Trusts: Judicial Guidance and Statutory Intervention' (2011) 33 *Dublin University Law Journal* 196, 208; Linda Sugin, 'Rhetoric and Reality in the Tax Law of Charity' (2016) 84(6) *Fordham Law Review* 2607, 2632; Garton (n 21) [5.25]; Harpur (n 26) 433.

29 See also analysis in Section III of Chapter 5.

because the establishment of charitable trusts is in its formative stage, it is not yet clear how this institution's legislative framework will be practically implemented and what challenges it may face. To minimize the misappropriation risk associated with charitable assets, the law strictly requires that charitable trusts be operated solely for the furtherance of charitable purposes. Any use of charitable assets for non-charitable purposes will be invalid and attract legal liabilities on the part of the trustees directly in charge.[30] Similar to the public benefit doctrine, this rule is consistent with the idea that charitable trusts should be used in alignment with the public welfare goals of the state.

In common law, charitable trusts must also be exclusively charitable. Charitable status will be lost if there exist any purposes that are not charitable on their own.[31] In a long line of cases, English and Australian courts have upheld two exceptions to the rule of exclusivity: ancillary purposes and severance.[32] A charitable trust will not fail where the non-charitable purpose authorized by the trust instrument is merely incidental or subsidiary to a charitable purpose.[33] Moreover, charitable status can be upheld where charitable purposes can be severed from non-charitable purposes.[34] In contrast to Chinese charitable trusts, these exceptions have two implications. First, the common law approach avoids the risk of striking down the validity of the whole trust and allows charitable elements to take effect, thereby retaining charitable resources in the public domain to the largest possible extent. Second, the common law approach gives more weight to the autonomy of private actors in determining to what extent and in what ways their private funds can be used for charitable purposes.

(iii) The Regulator's Wide Powers In both Chinese law and common law, regulators are granted broad powers to supervise the administration

[30] 《慈善信托管理办法》 [Administrative Measures for Charitable Trusts] (People's Republic of China) China Banking Regulatory Commission and Ministry of Civil Affairs, 10 July 2017 (n 6) art 59.

[31] G. E. Dal Pont and Stefan Petrow, *Law of Charity* (LexisNexis Butterworths, 2010) [13.2]; *Ofrex (George Drexler) Foundation (Trustees)* v *IRC* (1965) 3 All ER 529, 530.

[32] See, e.g., *Trustees Executors & Agency Co Ltd* v *Zelman Memorial Symphony Orchestra Ltd* [1958] VR 523, 526; *Radmanovich* v *Nedeljkovic* [2001] NSWSC 492, [189]; *Bath and North East Somerset Council* v *HM Attorney General* [2002] EWHC 1623(Ch), [25]; *Public Trustee* v *Attorney-General (NSW)* (n 25) 621. See also Garton (n 21) [2.19].

[33] Pont and Petrow (n 31) [3.29].

[34] G. E. Dal Pont, *Charity Law in Australia and New Zealand* (Oxford University Press, 1999) 223.

of charitable trusts. For example, in Australia, the Australian Charities and Not-for-profits Commission (ACNC) has powers to suspend and remove the trustee of a charitable trust and to direct application of charitable trust assets.[35] In England and Wales, the Charity Commission has powers to restrict the transactions a charity trustee may enter into, appoint trustees, and freeze a charitable trust's bank account.[36] In Chinese law, regulators also have broad powers to supervise a trustee's performance of their duties. For example, they have powers to revoke the trustee's registration license and to conduct supervisory conversations (*jianguan tanhua* 监管谈话).[37] These two powers enable regulators to easily intervene in the trustee's ongoing management of charitable trusts.

The power to revoke in the Chinese charitable trust is a type of ex post supervision. Regulators may exercise this power when trust parties severely contravene charitable trust laws or regulations. The legal consequences of the exercise of this power have a strong deterrent effect, as the revocation of a registration license effectively bans trustees from engaging in trust businesses for a long period of time.[38] In comparison, the application of supervisory conversations is a type of ex ante supervision. It is a phase in the ongoing administrative decision-making process.[39] The application of supervisory conversations includes educative and disciplinary elements.[40] The power to revoke and the application of supervisory conversations align with the objectives of deterring the wrongful conduct of trustees and protecting the public interest in the proper administration of charitable assets.

The procedure for exercising these two regulatory powers provides insights into the public law norms of the regulatory framework for charitable trusts. The charity law imposes very few restrictions on the

35 *Australian Charities and Not-for-Profits Commission Act 2012* (Cth) ch 4 pt 4-2 div 100.

36 *Charities Act 2011* (England and Wales) pt 6. See also Picarda (n 23) 768–9.

37 《信托公司管理办法》 [Measures for Administration of Trust Companies] (People's Republic of China) China Banking Regulatory Commission, 23 January 2007, art 53;《慈善信托管理办法》[Administrative Measures for Charitable Trusts] (People's Republic of China) China Banking Regulatory Commission and Ministry of Civil Affairs, 10 July 2017 (n 6) art 51.

38 On detailed account of this power, see analysis in Section II of Chapter 4.

39 孟强龙 [Meng Qianglong],《行政约谈法治化研究》 [Study on Legalization of Administrative Interviews] (2015) 6 行政法学研究 *Administrative Law Review* 99, 105–6; 王虎 [Wang Hu],《风险社会中的行政约谈制度: 因应、反思与完善》 [The System of Administrative Interviews in Risk Society: Response, Reflection, and Improvement] (2018) 1 法商研究 *Study of Law and Business* 22, 26.

40 See analysis in Section II of Chapter 4.

exercise of these two powers. As such, the process by which regulators intervene in the management of charitable trust affairs is largely relaxed. The law does not specify the procedure by which the power to revoke registration licenses can be exercised and makes no mention of the factors relevant to revoking the registration license of a trustee.[41] Likewise, there are massive ambiguities regarding the nature of the supervisory conversation and its scope of application.[42] The vagueness of the law grants regulators a high degree of discretion in the performance of their responsibilities. Regulators can easily intervene in the management of charitable trusts to meet the dual purpose of satisfying the public's demand for accountability and preventing dishonest trustees from committing fraud. This creates a great deal of uncertainty for trustees' management of charitable trusts.

(b) Private Law Norms The legal structure of charitable trusts contains a number of private law norms in addition to the public law norms analysed in Section II-B-1(a). Article 44 of the Chinese Charity Law and article 2 of the Measures for Charitable Trusts prescribe that charitable activities should be carried out in conformity with settlors' wishes. What does the phrase 'in conformity with settlors' wishes' mean? Questions relating to the understanding of this phrase include, How do the settlors' wishes manifest in the administration of charitable trust affairs? In what ways are the settlors' wishes given effect? Is there scope for conflict to arise between the furtherance of charitable purposes and the protection of settlors' wishes? Although the law does not address these questions, the phrase *prima facie* embodies a strong private law tendency as it provides scope for settlors to exercise their management rights. It is the settlor who places a certain amount of assets in a charitable trust. Therefore, the settlor may have a strong desire to see how their assets will be used.

[41] Section 35-10(2) of the *ACNC Act* prescribes the factors that the commissioner should consider when determining whether the registration of a charity should be revoked. These factors include the nature, significance, and persistence of any contravention of the *ACNC Act* and the extent to which the charity conducts its affairs in a way that may cause harm to public trust and confidence. See *Waubra Foundation and Commissioner of Australian Charities and Not-for-profits Commission* [2017] AATA 2424, [27]; *Australian Charities and Not-for-Profits Commission Act* (n 35) s 35-10(2).

[42] 朱新力 [Zhu Xinli] and 李芹 [Li Qin],《行政约谈的功能定位与制度建构》 [The Functional Orientation and Institutional Design of Administrative Interviews] (2018) 4 国家行政学院学报 *Journal of Chinese Academy of Governance* 91, 92; 王虎 [Wang Hu] (n 39) 26–7.

In view of the experience of public welfare trusts, legislators chose to establish a public law–private law hybrid model for charitable trusts in which private actors are granted greater control over the use of their private funds. Section II-B-1(b) explores the private law norms of charitable trusts. This analysis serves two purposes: (a) to identify these private law norms and the ways in which they take effect and (b) to provide a basis for discussions about the interaction between public law norms and private law norms in the legal structure of charitable trusts.

(i) The Settlor's Wide Powers The default rules for common law trusts entail 'divestment instead of retention':[43] settlors drop out of the picture[44] once charitable trusts are validly established. Due to tax concerns, settlors tend to adopt two mechanisms to maintain their roles in the day-to-day management of charitable trusts: the letter of wishes[45] and the trust protector.[46] In contrast, settlors under Chinese charitable trusts

[43] Ying Khai Liew, 'Justifying Anglo-American Trusts Law' (2021) 12 *William & Mary Business Law Review* 685, 714.

[44] Kai Lyu, 'Re-Clarifying China's Trust Law: Characteristics and New Conceptual Basis' (2015) 36 *Loyola of Los Angeles International and Comparative Law Review* 447, 458; Tsun Hang Tey, 'Reservation of Settlor's Powers' (2009) 21(2) *Singapore Academy of Law Journal* 517, 524.

[45] For an account of the letter of wishes, see Arthur Underhill, David J. Hayton, Paul Matthews and Charles Mitchell, *Underhill and Hayton Law Relating to Trusts and Trustees* (LexisNexis Butterworths, 17th ed., 2007) 835, 943; Alexander A. Bove Jr, 'The Letter of Wishes: Can We Influence Discretion in Discretionary Trusts' (2009) 35 *ACTEC Journal* 38, 39; Deborah S. Gordon, 'Letters Non-Testamentary' (2013) 62 *University of Kansas Law Review* 585, 629; Tsun Hang Tey, 'Letters of Wishes' (2009) 21 *Singapore Academy of Law Journal* 193, 194–5; David Hayton, 'English Fiduciary Standards and Trust Law' (1999) 32 *Vanderbilt Journal of Transnational Law* 555, 574–5; *Investors Compensation Scheme Ltd* v *West Bromwich Building Society* (1998) 1 WLR 896, 903; *Hartigan Nominees Pty Ltd* v *Rydge* (1992) 29 NSWLR 405, 420, 424; *Re Rabaiott's Settlement* [2000] WTLR 953, 968; *Breakspear* v *Ackland* (2008) 3 WLR 698, 711; *Re Londonderry's Settlement* [1965] Ch 918, 936.

[46] For a detailed analysis of the trust protector, see Richard C. Ausness, 'The Role of Trust Protectors in American Trust Law' (2010) 45(2) *Real Property, Trust and Estate Law Journal* 319, 321–2, 348; Stewart E. Sterk, 'Trust Protectors, Agency Costs, and Fiduciary Duty' (2005) 27 *Cardozo Law Review* 2761, 2763, 2768; Philip J. Ruce, 'The Trustee and the Trust Protector: A Question of Fiduciary Power: Should a Trust Protector Be Held to a Fiduciary Standard?' (2011) 59 *Drake Law Review* 67, 68. The courts in common law jurisdictions have the power to remove a protector in accordance with their inherent jurisdiction of facilitating and supervising the administration of a trust. See Lynton Tucker, Nicholas Le Poidevin, James Brightwell, Thomas Fletcher and Aidan Briggs (eds.), *Lewin on Trusts (Volume I)* (Sweet & Maxwell, 20th ed., 2020) 1266; *Pope* v *Drp Nominees Pty Ltd* (1999) 337 SASC [26], [34], [45]; *Blenkinsop* v *Blenkinsop Nominees*

are endowed by law with extensive powers. This legislative approach enables settlors not only to define the ways in which charitable assets are managed but also to be proactive in supervising the performance of trustees' duties. Unlike their common law counterparts, settlors under Chinese law are legally allowed to thoroughly and consistently intervene in the management of trust affairs. Two examples are the settlor's powers to consent and to appoint trust supervisors.

Article 38 of the Measures for Charitable Trusts prescribes that settlors are empowered to grant or withhold consent on certain matters, such as adding new settlors, increasing trust assets, and changing the scope of beneficiaries. The granting of the power to consent derives from the notion that owners have maximal freedom in disposing of their assets.[47] The goal of protecting settlor autonomy is also evident in the protection provided by statute when settlors exercise this power. For example, settlors can issue consent to relieve trustees from fiduciary liabilities in transactions involving conflicts of duty (or of duty and interest). Aside from the granting of fully informed consent by settlors, there still exists one strict requirement before a trustee's no conflict liabilities can be exempted: that the transactions concerned be carried out at a fair market price. In substance, this requirement is consistent with the protection of the will and autonomous interest of the settlor. After all, without truly understanding the risks that such transactions might carry, settlors cannot be allowed to freely determine whether to take the risk of waiving that protection. Relaxing the no conflict principle can help balance its protective function and the value of ensuring the autonomy of settlors. Autonomous decisions still outweigh that protective function but only if settlors fully understand the consequences of their decisions.

Besides the power to consent, the settlor under a charitable trust also has the power to appoint trust supervisors. By appointing a trust supervisor, the settlor can keep a close eye on the performance of the trustee's

Pty Ltd (as trustee for Blenkinsop Family Trust (No 2)) [2016] WASC 61, [47]; *Blenkinsop v Herbert* [2017] WASCA 87, [72]–[74], [76].

47 Simon Gardner, *An Introduction to The Law of Trusts* (Oxford University Press, 3rd ed., 2011) 296; John D. Morley and Robert H. Sitkoff, 'Making Directed Trusts Work: The Uniform Directed Trust Act' (2019) 44(1) *ACTEC Law Journal* 3, 8; Robert H. Sitkoff, 'Trusts and Estates: Implementing Freedom of Disposition' (2014) 58 *Saint Louis University Law Journal* 643, 651; John H. Langbein, 'Mandatory Rules in the Law of Trusts' (2004) 98(3) *Northwestern University Law Review* 1105, 1121; Matthew Conaglen, 'The Nature and Function of Fiduciary Loyalty' (2005) 121 *Law Quarterly Review* 452, 164.

duties.[48] In contrast to public welfare trusts, the appointment of trust supervisors is not mandatory for charitable trusts.[49] Whether a trust supervisor is appointed depends primarily on the settlor's wishes. Furthermore, the law does not specify the trust supervisor's powers and their obligations in the exercise of these powers. Accordingly, the extent to which trust supervisors play a supervisory role might vary significantly depending on the contractual arrangements between settlors, trustees, and trust supervisors. The vesting of wide discretion in trust parties suggests that giving effect to settlor autonomy is an important goal of charitable trusts.[50]

(ii) The Rule of Standing The rule of standing also reflects the private law norms in the legal structure of charitable trusts. There is a distinction between public law and private law regarding who can sue. Private law integrates the question of standing into its causes of action, while public law considers standing separately. Private law grants standing as a matter of right on the basis of the plaintiff's personal interests. Public law considers the determination of standing to be a discretionary judicial task involving the weighing or balancing of multiple concerns.[51] This divergence is primarily attributable to the different types of relationships regulated by private law and public law outlined at the outset of Section II.

This procedural dimension offers a number of critical insights into the substantive dimension of Chinese charitable trusts. The rule of standing illuminates the private law aspects of Chinese charitable trusts. In the legal framework, regulators cannot bring proceedings to remedy the

[48] 张淳 [Zhang Chun],《<中华人民共和国信托法>中的创造性规定及其评析》 [The Creative Provisions in the Trust Law of the People's Republic of China and Its Evaluation] (2002) 2 法律科学 *Law Science* 110, 119; Frances H. Foster, 'American Trust Law in a Chinese Mirror' (2010) 94 *Minnesota Law Review* 602, 645; 中国信托业协会 [China Trustee Association] (n 8) 85–6; Sterk (n 46) 2763.

[49] 《中华人民共和国信托法》 [Trust Law of the People's Republic of China] (People's Republic of China) National People's Congress, 28 April 2001, art 64;《慈善信托管理办法》 [Administrative Measures for Charitable Trusts] (People's Republic of China) China Banking Regulatory Commission and Ministry of Civil Affairs, 10 July 2017 (n 6) art 11.

[50] Hui Jing, 'The Legal Nature of the Chinese Charitable Trust' in Matthew Harding and Ying Khai Liew (eds.), *Asia-Pacific Trusts Law: Theory and Practice in Context* (Hart, 2021) 271, 280.

[51] 相庆梅 [Xiang Qingmei],《民事诉权论》 [Research on the Right of Civil Suits] (PhD Thesis, China University of Political Science and Law, 2006) 9–10; Chan (n 24) 98; 王锡三 [Wang Xisan] (n 4) 16–7; 张家慧 [Zhang Jiahui] (n 4) 59–60.

misuse of charitable assets on behalf of the public.[52] Although promoting charitable undertakings is one of the objectives of charitable trusts, the rule of standing limits courts' jurisdiction to adjudicate charitable trust lawsuits initiated by regulators. Limiting the parties entitled to file lawsuits against defaulting trustees to only settlors and trust supervisors indirectly promotes the autonomy of private actors. Trustees can follow settlors' instructions without worrying that these instructions violate what a regulator determines to be the best interest of the trust's charitable purpose. This legislative approach aligns with the private law tendency of charitable trusts and is responsive to the goal of facilitating settlors' wishes.

In contrast, charitable trust laws in common law jurisdictions show a strong public law tendency regarding who can sue and the scope of standing. Charitable trusts are trusts for purposes and not for persons;[53] therefore, they have no beneficiaries as understood in express private trust law. The Attorney-General, acting as the guardian and protector of the public interest,[54] is granted standing to supervise whether a trust is administered in alignment with its charitable purposes.[55] Aside from the Attorney-General, any person who has a 'greater-than-public'[56] interest may also be entitled to launch charitable trust lawsuits. In Australia and

[52] 《慈善信托管理办法》 [Administrative Measures for Charitable Trusts] (People's Republic of China) China Banking Regulatory Commission and Ministry of Civil Affairs, 10 July 2017 (n 6) art 49; 《中华人民共和国信托法》 [Trust Law of the People's Republic of China] (People's Republic of China) National People's Congress, 28 April 2001 (n 49) art 22.

[53] *BSH Holding Pty Ltd* v *Commissioner of State Revenue* [2000] VSC 302, [9].

[54] Fiona Hanlon, 'An Analysis of the Office of Attorney General in Australia and Directions for the Future' (PhD Thesis, Faculty of Law, The University of Melbourne, 2007) 23; *Perpetual Trustees Victoria Limited* v *Barns & Anor* [2012] VSCA 77, [42]; Luis Kutner and Henry H. Koven, 'Charitable Trust Legislation in the Several States' (1966) 61 *Northwestern University Law Review* 411, 422; Picarda (n 23) 727–9; Pont (n 34) 266–7.

[55] As Lord Macnaghten observed in *Wills* v *Solicitor-General for New Zealand*, '[i]t is the province of the Crown as parens patriae to enforce the execution of charitable trusts, and it has been always recognized as the duty of the [Attorney-General] to intervene for the purpose of protecting charities and affording advice and assistance to the court in the administration of charitable trusts'. See *Wills* v *Solicitor-General for New Zealand* [1903] AC 173, 181–2. See also *Bathurst City Council* v *PWC Properties Pty Ltd* (1998) 157 ALR 414, [39], [54], [67]; *Ngarluma Aboriginal Corp RNTBC* v *Attorney General (WA)* [2014] WASC 245, [55]; *Laura & Alfred West Cottage Homes Inc* v *Attorney-General (SA)* [2018] SASA 19, [4]; *Attorney General (NSW)* v *Homeland Community Ltd* [2015] NSWCA 15, [3]; *Radmanovich v Nedeljkovic* (n 32) [14]; *Perpetual Trustees Victoria Limited v Barns & Anor* (n 54) [42].

[56] Chan (n 24) 100.

England, statutes and common law show that 'any person interested in the charity' can be granted standing to bring charity proceedings.[57] The 'person interested' rule is a 'practical rule of justice'[58] endowing the courts with a measure of discretion in determining how to deal with charitable trust disputes. This rule substantively expands the scope of persons who have standing to sue and facilitates the role of the courts in controlling trustees' exercise of power.

2 The Relationship between Public Law Norms and Private Law Norms

The analysis in Section II-B-1 illustrates how the norms of public law and private law manifest themselves in different dimensions of charitable trusts. The following question arises: How do the two types of norms interact with each other? The answer will illuminate the relationship between the autonomy interest of settlors and the public interest in the proper management of charitable assets. Examination of the charitable trust's legislative arrangements suggests that public law norms prevail as the hybrid model continues to privilege state control over the autonomy of private parties.

Although the law does not explicitly answer this question, a closer look at article 59 of the Measures for Charitable Trusts and article 105 of the Chinese Charity Law provides insights. Both articles stipulate that any use of charitable trust assets for non-charitable purposes will attract administrative liabilities on the part of the trustee. A textual interpretation of these articles leads to two observations. First, settlors have the autonomy to determine what types of benefits the charitable trust will create and how charitable assets should be distributed.[59] It is the settlor who places a certain amount of assets in a charitable trust. Therefore, the settlor is entitled to decide how their assets should be used for the

[57] On Australian statutes, see *Trustee Act 1925* (ACT) s 94A(3)(g); *Trustee Act 1936* (SA) s 36(1c)(e); *Trusts Act 1973* (Qld) s 106(2)(c); *Supreme Court Civil Procedure Act 1932* (Tas) s 57(2). On Australian case law, see, e.g., *Thorn v Bettens* [2006] SASC 59, [12]; *Metropolitan Petar v Mitreski* [2001] NSWSC 976, [16]; *Ngarluma Aboriginal Corp RNTBC* v *Attorney General (WA)* (n 55) [47], [52]. On statutes in England and Wales, see *Charities Act 2011* (n 36) s 115. On English case law, see, e.g., *Haslemere Estates Ltd* v *Baker* (1982) 1 WLR 1109, 1122D; *Bradshaw* v *University College of Wales* (1988) 1 WLR 190, 194E; *Re Hampton Fuel Allotment Charity* (1988) 3 WLR 513, 520.

[58] Chan (n 24) 100.

[59] 《慈善信托管理办法》 [Administrative Measures for Charitable Trusts] (People's Republic of China) China Banking Regulatory Commission and Ministry of Civil Affairs, 10 July 2017 (n 6) arts 14, 38.

furtherance of charitable causes. Moreover, the state is also willing to uphold a settlor's decision regarding the management of charitable assets. This approach encourages the wide use of charitable trusts by the public and reflects the idea that benevolent property owners have maximal liberty to use their assets.[60]

Second, where a charitable trust is validly established, the relevant parties are prohibited by law from advancing their private interests when disposing of charitable assets. Charitable resources can only be used to further and promote the state's public welfare goals. Settlors may exercise greater control over the use of charitable assets on the condition that this use complies with the legitimate interests of the state as a whole. Regulators represent the interests of the state. They are granted broad powers by law to control the use of charitable trusts in alignment with the state's requirements.[61] Given this analysis, it can be reasonably asserted that, in the Chinese charitable trust setting, private law norms are subordinated to public law norms in that a settlor's exercise of autonomy must conform to the state's public welfare goals.

C Observations on the Hybrid Nature of Chinese Charitable Trusts

Analysis of the charitable trust's legislative arrangements illuminates its public law–private law hybrid nature. Three observations are relevant here. First, public law norms predominate in the legal structure of Chinese charitable trusts. In contrast to charitable trusts at common law, charitable trusts in China must further the state's legitimate interests. The charitable trust model was tasked to develop and promote the state's public welfare goals from its very inception. The state clearly defines the scope of 'charitable purposes' to guide the use of charitable resources by the public. The state's strict control over the use of charitable trusts is secured by granting wide supervisory powers to regulators. These powers allow regulators to easily intervene in the trustee's management of charitable trusts. For example, they can advise trust parties on how charitable trusts should be administered and issue notices or letters to trustees to direct the use of charitable assets.[62]

Second, in view of the experience of public welfare trusts, legislators have incorporated the norms of private law in both substantial and

[60] See also analysis in Section II-B-1(b).

[61] See analysis in Section II-B-1(a).

[62] See analysis in Section II-B of Chapter 4.

procedural aspects of the legal framework of charitable trusts. The law grants private parties greater autonomy in determining the scope of charitable trusts and the allocation of rights and responsibilities between settlor and trustee in the day-to-day operations of charitable trusts.[63] The charity law enables settlors not only to define the ways in which charitable trusts are managed but also to be proactive in supervising trustees' performance of their responsibilities. This approach is in stark contrast to that of common law charitable trusts, where settlors tend to use the letter of wishes or trust protectors to secure some role in the ongoing management of charitable assets. Article 2 of the Measures for Charitable Trusts and article 44 of the Chinese Charity Law require a trustee to manage and dispose of charitable assets in alignment with the settlor's wishes. The scope of the 'wishes' here is strictly limited. Settlors can choose the method by which charitable trusts are managed and select how charitable assets are distributed to selected beneficiaries. A trustee is obliged to follow the settlor's wishes but only to the extent that such wishes facilitate the use of charitable resources for public welfare goals defined by the state. Settlors are not allowed to use charitable trusts to further their personal interests or to advance private goals.

Third, the interactions of these two types of norms are conditioned by China's particular policy and social context. The charitable trust model has been introduced in an environment where China faces profound charity needs and where the public welfare trust has proven inadequate. The state seeks to use charitable trusts to encourage the public to participate in the development of charitable undertakings. To achieve this, the state gives private actors autonomy over the use of private funds for charitable purposes. However, the state also grants regulators broad powers to ensure that charitable trusts are used in compliance with its public welfare goals. The allocation of rights and obligations between trust parties and regulators in the creation and ongoing administration of charitable trusts shows that the private interests of trust parties continue to be subordinated to the interests of the broad community and, ultimately, to the interests of the state.

[63] 楼秋然 [Lou Qiuran], 《理解慈善信托中的"近似原则"：美国经验与中国借鉴》 [Understanding Cy Pres in Charitable Trusts: American Experience and Its Adoption in China] (2019) 3 中国政法大学学报 *Journal of CUPL* 49, 62; 王涛 [Wang Tao], 《慈善法的立法理念、制度创新和完善路径》 [Research on the Legislative Idea, System Innovation and Development Path of the Chinese Charity Law] (2018) 33(1) 法学论坛 *Legal Forum* 143, 144.

The hybrid nature of charitable trusts connects us back to the relationship between charitable trusts and public welfare trusts. As analysed previously,[64] while the semantic interpretation of 'belong to' suggests that charitable trusts may relate to public welfare trusts to a certain extent, it cannot illustrate how the two institutions interact. To fill this analytical gap, a closer review of the legal nature of charitable trusts is undertaken in this section. By offering an interpretation and examination of the legislative arrangements relevant to charitable trusts, this analysis demonstrates that charitable trusts are distinguishable from public welfare trusts. Specifically, in contrast to the public law nature of public welfare trusts, the legal nature of charitable trusts is a hybrid in which a certain amount of weight has been given to the promotion of the autonomy interest of benevolent property owners. The legal nature of a particular institution informs how its legislative framework should be put into effect. Given the private law norms of charitable trusts, it follows that the extent to which the experiences of public welfare trusts apply to charitable trusts may be strictly limited and that charitable trusts and public welfare trust are in nature not synonymous.

III Implications for Charitable Trust Governance

Examination of the legislative provisions of charitable trusts demonstrates that the hybrid nature of charitable trusts is distinctive because of China's particular political, economic, and social conditions. In view of the failure of public welfare trusts, legislators introduced the hybrid model for charitable trusts to encourage public participation in charitable undertakings. In the Chinese charitable trust setting, the tension between public law and private law is seen through the tension between the social welfare goals of charitable trusts and the autonomy of private parties to decide how to use their private funds for charitable purposes. The charitable trust's hybrid nature was intentionally created by legislators, and it permeates the governance framework for charitable trusts. Based on the analysis of the hybrid nature of charitable trusts in Section II, this section discusses the implications of that analysis for the governance of charitable trusts.

[64] See analysis in Section II-A.

A Parties Relevant to Charitable Trust Governance

Building upon the dictionary definition of governance and the understanding of governance in specific contexts such as charities and corporations, the analysis in Chapter 1 defined the governance of Chinese charitable trusts as a set of mechanisms ensuring the trustee of a charitable trust complies with their duties in order to effectively realize the charitable purpose or the public benefit pursued by the charitable trust. On this definition, the focus of charitable trust governance lies in how charitable trusts should be administered, and the focus of how charitable trusts should be administered in turn lies in how a trustee's exercise of power should be supervised and controlled and what measures can be taken to ensure their accountability for that exercise.

There are four types of parties relevant to charitable trust governance. Their role is to exert pressure on trustees to comply with their duties. The first are settlors: they exercise their statutory or contractual powers to oversee whether charitable trusts are being administered according to their charitable purposes. The second are beneficiaries: they have an incentive to supervise whether trust properties are being distributed according to the notice of distribution of charitable assets issued by the trustee; they may have standing to bring proceedings to remedy the misuse of charitable trust assets. The third are regulators: they exercise their regulatory powers to oversee whether charitable trusts are being administered according to the public welfare policy of the state and to punish trustees when their management of charitable trusts contravenes the law or is incompliant with regulatory measures. The fourth party is the general public: they can access the information disclosed by charity trustees, report the misuse of charity funds to the relevant regulators, and participate in charity-promoting activities to improve public awareness of charitable trusts. The definition of 'charitable trust governance' sheds light on what types of parties may be relevant to the governance of charitable trusts and what potential roles they may play. However, this definition cannot explain how these four parties interact and to what extent they can in fact hold trustees accountable for their exercise of power.

The hybrid nature of the charitable trust model is the foundation of its governance framework. Analysis of the public law–private law hybrid not only explains how these four parties influence the trustee's exercise of power; it also clarifies how they interact in the governance structure of charitable trusts. The norms of private law in the legal structure of charitable trusts mainly relate to the internal relationship between the parties to charitable trusts (i.e., settlors, trustees, and beneficiaries). The ways in which these parties interact clarifies how trustees exercise their powers in the management of charitable trust affairs. Two types of questions arise. The first relates to the tension between settlors and trustees: What are the mechanisms by which checks and balances between settlors and trustees are established? What are the powers and duties that the law has assigned to settlors and trustees? How are these powers and duties performed by each party?[65] The second type of question relates to the role of beneficiaries: Are beneficiaries entitled to file lawsuits in respect of trustees' maladministration of charitable trusts? If so, how could the scope and nature of their standing be defined? Is their standing limited to the individualized interest they have in the trust assets? Or can their standing extend to the general administration of charitable trusts, irrespective of how much and what kind of interest they have in the trust assets?[66]

The norms of public law in the legal structure of charitable trusts mainly relate to the role of regulators. In the legal framework of charitable trusts, regulators are granted wide supervisory powers by law, such as the powers to assess (*pinggu* 评估) whether charitable trusts are being administered in alignment with their charitable purposes,[67] to conduct supervisory conversations to compel trustees to explain the charitable trust business,[68] and to revoke the registration license of a trustee.[69] The granting of broad powers to regulators enables them to play a proactive role in the administration of charitable trust affairs. For example, they can issue letters or notices to inspect whether the information required by law has been disclosed in a timely and adequate manner, and they can

[65] See analysis in Section III of Chapter 3.

[66] See analysis in Section IV-B of Chapter 3.

[67] 《慈善信托管理办法》[Administrative Measures for Charitable Trusts] (People's Republic of China) China Banking Regulatory Commission and Ministry of Civil Affairs, 10 July 2017 (n 6) art 50. See also analysis in Section II of Chapter 4.

[68] 《慈善信托管理办法》[Administrative Measures for Charitable Trusts] (People's Republic of China) China Banking Regulatory Commission and Ministry of Civil Affairs, 10 July 2017 (n 6) art 51;《信托公司管理办法》 [Measures for Administration of Trust Companies] (People's Republic of China) China Banking Regulatory Commission, 23 January 2007 (n 37) art 53. See also analysis in Section II of Chapter 4.

[69] 《中华人民共和国慈善法》 [Charity Law of the People's Republic of China] (People's Republic of China) National People's Congress, 16 March 2016 (n 6) art 98;《信托公司管理办法》 [Measures for Administration of Trust Companies] (People's Republic of China) China Banking Regulatory Commission, 23 January 2007 (n 37) art 59. See also analysis in Section II of Chapter 4.

take charity-promoting measures (e.g., educational and training programmes) to encourage the public to play a supervisory role in trustees' performance of their duties. The manner in which regulators oversee the operation of charitable trusts may impact heavily on the ways in which trustees discharge their management roles. These public law norms connect the analysis of charitable trust governance to the role of regulators and the interaction between regulators and trust parties.

B Governance in Practice

Because the application of law is not an 'exercise in mechanical deduction',[70] the practice of charitable trusts may differ from their legislative framework.[71] The law concerning charitable trusts is vague and underdetermined. This vagueness motivates trust parties and regulators to adopt strategies to protect their interests from being adversely affected in the implementation of the law.[72] The implementation of the policies pertaining to charitable trusts involves contradictions and conflicts between the autonomy of trust parties and the broader interests of the state. These include giving trust parties greater control over the exercise of their management rights and ensuring that charitable resources are used to benefit the legitimate interests of broader society.[73] Regulatory practice and the allocation of powers between regulators and trust parties show that these conflicts are dealt with in a manner favouring the public interest: that is, the interests of the broader community and the interests of the state itself as interpreted and enforced by the regulator are prioritized over the private interests of trust parties.[74] The way in which these contradictions and conflicts are addressed demonstrates how the state understands the public law–private law nature of charitable trusts, which in turn influences how trust parties and regulators engage with the law in practice.

In practice, regulators and trust parties engage proactively with the law and are responsive to extra-legal considerations when performing their

[70] Brian Leiter, 'Legal Formalism and Legal Realism: What Is the Issue' (2010) 16(2) *Legal Theory* 111, 116.

[71] All jurisdictions have some gap between aspirational rules and their practical enforcement. See Tarunabh Khaitan, *A Theory of Discrimination Law* (Oxford University Press, 2015) 13.

[72] See analysis in Chapters 4 and 5.

[73] See analysis in Section I of Chapter 1.

[74] See analysis in Section II-C.

legal roles.[75] As noted in Section II-B, regulators are granted broad supervisory powers by law. How should these powers be exercised? To what extent may regulators play a supervisory role? Regulators often consider these questions in light of the state's social needs and the policy challenges articulated by the state.[76] The critical social and policy environment in which charitable trusts are established and operate is essential to determining how regulators discharge their supervisory roles. The willingness of regulators to consider extra-legal factors exhibits public law tendencies and facilitates state control over the use of charitable resources. These issues are explored in more detail in Chapter 4.

Regarding the role of settlors, Section II-B showed that the law endows settlors with broad powers in the management of charitable trusts. Settlors have the power to determine in what ways charitable assets are distributed and how trust affairs should be administered. This legislative approach reveals the state's desire to motivate private philanthropy and demonstrates the private law norms in the legal structure of Chinese charitable trusts. However, the law does not clearly define how settlors' powers should be exercised and in what ways settlors should interact with trustees in the day-to-day governance of charitable trusts. This vagueness introduces a great deal of uncertainty into trustees' management of charitable trusts and produces legal uncertainty in some aspects of the relationship between settlors and trustees.[77] To mitigate the risks posed by the vagueness of the law, the parties to charitable trusts are strongly motivated to use contractual tools to vary the framework of the law.[78] These issues are explored in more detail in Chapter 5.

That trust parties and regulators adopt strategies to guide the performance of their legal roles underlines the importance of examining the governance of charitable trusts from the perspectives of both law and practice. In relation to law, analysis of charitable trust governance includes the relationship between trust parties, the nature and scope of the powers of regulators, and the interaction between trustees and regulators. In relation to practice, analysis of charitable trust governance includes the private actions taken by trust parties and the ways in which regulators perform their responsibilities. From the perspective of the public law–private law divide, public law norms indicate that analysis

[75] See analysis in Chapters 4 and 5.
[76] See analysis in Section III of Chapter 4.
[77] See analysis in Section III of Chapter 3.
[78] See analysis in Section III of Chapter 5.

of charitable trust governance should include the role of regulators and the ways in which they interact with trust parties. Private law norms indicate that analysis of charitable trust governance should engage with the roles of trustees, settlors, and beneficiaries and the ways in which these parties interact. In light of the hybrid nature of the charitable trust model and the ways in which its legal governance framework is implemented, this book proposes three perspectives from which the governance structure of charitable trusts can be analysed: legal regulation, administrative regulation, and contractual regulation.

IV Conclusion

As with all charitable trusts, Chinese charitable trusts are a type of public law–private law hybrid. This chapter explored the Chinese charitable trust's particular mixture of public law and private law norms. Regardless of the weight assigned to each norm, in Chinese charitable trusts, private law norms are always subordinated to public law norms insofar as the operation of charitable trusts must conform to the state's public welfare policy. This chapter explored how this hybrid nature permeates and informs the governance structure of charitable trusts and the relationships it establishes between the parties interested in trust governance: settlors, trustees, beneficiaries, regulators, and the general public.

Legislators have sought to use charitable trusts to encourage public participation in the development of charitable undertakings. However, by creating this particular public law–private law hybrid, the legislative regime governing charitable trusts has created a number of ambiguities in the governance framework. These ambiguities have motivated trust parties and regulators to adopt strategies to guide the performance of their legal roles.

In light of the ways in which trust parties and regulators engage with the law and the public law–private law nature of charitable trusts, this chapter highlights three perspectives relevant to understanding the governance structure of charitable trusts: legal regulation, administrative regulation, and contractual regulation. Chapter 3 examines the legal regulation of trust parties. Chapter 4 examines regulatory practice. Chapter 5 examines the use of contractual tools in shaping governance. Together, they provide an in-depth analysis of the different perspectives required to identify the particular governance structure of Chinese charitable trusts and to elucidate its distinctive characteristics.

3

Legal Regulation

I Introduction

Chapter 2 analysed the public law–private law nature of China's charitable trust model. It showed that the Chinese charitable trust's hybrid nature permeates and informs the design of its governance structure and constitutes the foundation on which the analysis of charitable trust governance rests. Based on this analysis, the author proposes three perspectives from which governance of charitable trusts may be understood: the legal regulation of trust parties in law, the regulatory practice of charitable trusts, and the use of contractual tools between trust parties. This chapter discusses the internal relationship between trust parties in law. The latter two perspectives are addressed in Chapters 4 and 5.

As discussed in Chapter 1, in China, charitable trusts are, in substance, modelled on public welfare trusts but have several significant differences. Drawing on lessons from the failure of public welfare trusts, legislators established a new legal framework for charitable trusts. This new framework shows how legislators expect each actor (i.e., settlors, trustees, and beneficiaries) to act in the creation and ongoing administration of charitable trusts. An examination of this legal framework leads to two main observations. First, the settlor is endowed by law with extensive powers, while the trustee is burdened by law with onerous duties. However, the law does not clearly define what these powers and duties entail and how they could be discharged. This vagueness poses risks to trustees' management of charitable trusts and produces legal uncertainty in some aspects of the relationship between settlors and trustees. Second, the law makes no mention of the role and legal nature of the beneficiaries of charitable trusts. This vagueness has resulted in intense debate among scholars and practitioners on the legal nature of Chinese charitable trusts and the role that beneficiaries can play in the governance setting. This chapter examines these two aspects of governance through an examination of the legislative provisions relating to the parties to charitable trusts. This discussion serves two purposes: first, to identify the extent to which, and the way in which, the new charity law has shaped the governance structure of Chinese charitable trusts and, second, to identify areas where the legal governance framework provides clear guidelines and where it is vague, has gaps, or creates risks for parties in terms of lawful performance of their roles and responsibilities.

II Establishment of the New Legal Governance Framework

As discussed in Chapter 2, the charitable trust model was introduced to overcome the shortcomings of the earlier legal framework for carrying out charitable undertakings. Over the past two decades, legislators have created four legal forms for doing charitable causes: foundations (*jijin hui* 基金会),[1] social associations (*shehui tuanti* 社会团体),[2] privately-operated non-enterprise organizations (*minban feiqiye danwei* or *minfei* 民办非企业单位或者民非),[3] and public welfare trusts (*gongyi xintuo* 公益信托).[4] Different forms have different strengths and weaknesses in the conducting of charitable activities.

The public law model of public welfare trusts was introduced with the enactment of the Chinese Trust Law in 2001. This public law model did not work very well, and the practice in the last twenty years has shown that there is a considerable gap between the advantages that public welfare trusts were supposed to have in developing charitable causes and the limited role they actually play. The failure of public welfare trusts can be linked to the fragmented system of regulation, particularly as it discourages the establishment of a public welfare trust.[5] This is reflected in two respects. First, private actors have difficulty in identifying the administrative authorities (regulators) responsible for the establishment of public welfare trusts. The law requires private actors to submit documents to regulators for registration but makes no mention of who

1 《基金会管理条例》 [Regulations on Administration of Foundations] (People's Republic of China) State Council, 3 August 2004.

2 《社会团体登记管理条例》 [Regulations on Registration Administration of Associations] (People's Republic of China) State Council, 6 February 2016.

3 《民办非企业单位登记管理暂行条例》 [Interim Regulations on the Administration of the Registration of Privately-Operated Non-Enterprise Organizations] (People's Republic of China) State Council, 25 October 1998.

4 《中华人民共和国信托法》 [Trust Law of the People's Republic of China] (People's Republic of China) National People's Congress, 28 April 2001, ch 6.

5 See analysis in Section II of Chapter 4.

these regulators are and how they can be identified. Private actors need to consult various possible government organs to determine to whom a registration application can be submitted.[6] Second, regulators in practice are unwilling to approve the establishment of public welfare trusts. In contrast to the charity-promoting role of public welfare trusts, regulators are more concerned about the risk that may arise from the supervision and management of public welfare trusts.[7]

Over the past decade, academic institutions, law firms, and regulators have hosted numerous conferences and forums to discuss what legislative reforms might be adopted in relation to trusts for the purpose of strengthening their potential to promote the development of charitable causes. In this context, a new model – the Chinese charitable trust – was introduced with the promulgation of the Chinese Charity Law and the Measures for Charitable Trusts in 2016 and 2017, respectively. Legislators created a public–private hybrid model for charitable trusts, which expanded the scope of the civil capacity of legal actors. The checks and balances between settlors and trustees are essential to this new legal governance model. The law grants settlors wide powers, including the powers to appoint trust supervisors and change the management method of charitable assets. This legislative approach enables settlors to not only define the way in which charitable trusts are managed but also be proactive in supervising the performance of trustees' duties. At the same time, trustees are burdened by law with onerous duties, including the duty to act in the best interest of the charitable purposes and the duty to avoid profits. These duties constrain the way in which trustees discharge their roles and motivate them to align the management of trust assets with the charitable purposes defined by the state.

The law sets up the governance framework for charitable trusts but is vague and incomplete in various aspects. As regards the internal relationship between settlors and trustees, the law does not clearly define in what way the two parties should interact. To what extent can a settlor intervene in the disposal of charitable assets? How can the trustee's performance of their duty be assessed? In what way can disputes between settlors and trustees be dealt with in the ongoing management of charitable trusts? The vagueness of the law on these questions not only poses risks to a trustee in its administration of charitable trusts but also produces legal uncertainty in some aspects of the relationship between trust parties.

[6] See analysis in Section I of Chapter 1.

[7] Ibid.

The law is also under-determined in terms of the role and legal status of beneficiaries under a charitable trust. The charity law uses the term 'beneficiary' but does not address the question of what powers or rights a beneficiary may have. This vagueness leads to legal uncertainty regarding in what way and to what extent beneficiaries may play a supervisory role in the governance of charitable trusts. Questions relating to the role of beneficiaries include the following: Can beneficiaries have standing to petition the court for redress in relation to trustees' maladministration of charitable assets? If so, what is the scope of their standing? Is their standing limited to the individualized interest they have in the trust assets? Or can their standing extend to the general administration of charitable trusts, irrespective of how much and what type of interest they have in the trust assets? The law makes no mention of these issues and, currently, there is no judicial interpretation or case law that elaborates how these questions should be answered.

By examining the law relevant to charitable trusts, Sections III and IV explore the ways in which trust parties interact with each other. This examination can help to identify the areas where the legal governance framework is vague and the legal uncertainties that arise from this vagueness. The focus of this chapter is on the internal relationship between trust parties. Chapter 4 addresses the question of how trust parties interact with regulators.

III Tension between Settlors and Trustees

The discussion in Section II indicated that one of the key features of the new legal governance framework is the tension between settlors and trustees. This tension is explored in more detail in this section. The 'tension' can be observed in two matters: the legal title to charitable trust assets and the allocation of powers and duties between settlors and trustees. The law grants settlors the discretion to determine who can retain the legal title to charitable assets. This approach is favourable to protecting a settlor's autonomy in the creation of charitable trusts. After a charitable trust is legally established, settlors are empowered to intervene intensively in the management of charitable trusts, including directing how charitable trusts should be managed and in what way charitable assets can be distributed. Section III-A analyses these two matters for two purposes: first, to investigate how trustees interact with settlors in the internal governance structure of charitable trusts and, second, to identify the legal uncertainties that settlors and trustees may face in the management of charitable trusts.

A *Legal Title to Charitable Trust Assets*

1 Terminology of Entrust

Under Chinese law, settlors are not required to transfer the legal title to trust assets to trustees for the creation of a valid trust. Article 2 of the Measures for Charitable Trusts and article 44 of the Chinese Charity Law use the term 'entrust' to describe the creation of charitable trust relationships. The term 'entrust' is not unique to Chinese charitable trusts. Instead, it is widely used in agency relationships[8] where the transfer of legal title is not necessarily contemplated. The use of the wording 'entrust' raises a years-long debate about what it means in the charitable trust setting. The view of most Chinese academics and commentators is that the meaning of 'entrust' in charitable trusts is akin to that of agency relationships.[9] That is, a relationship of entrustment does not entail the compulsory transfer of legal title to assets from principals to agents. Following this interpretation, the next question that requires examination is 'Does the current law prohibit such a transfer?'. The answer is negative in current law – whether or not the transfer of legal title is made depends entirely on the settlor's own wishes.

2 Legislative Reasons

Failure to give a clear answer as to the vesting of trust assets is not an oversight by Chinese legislators. Rather, it is a deliberate and conscious legal arrangement that can be traced back to the promulgation of the Chinese Trust Law in 2001.[10] Existing literature shows that, in the enactment of the Chinese Trust Law, drafters and experts had carefully

[8] 《中华人民共和国民法典》 [Civil Code of the People's Republic of China] (People's Republic of China) National People's Congress, 28 May 2020, art 163.

[9] On academic works in favour of this argument, see 张淳 [Zhang Chun],《<中华人民共和国信托法>中的创造性规定及其评析》 [The Creative Provisions in the Trust Law of the People's Republic of China and Its Evaluation] (2002) 2 法律科学 *Law Science* 110, 112–13; Lusina Ho, *Trust Law in China* (Sweet & Maxell Asia, 2003) 41; Lusina Ho, Rebecca Lee and Jinping Jin, 'Trust Law in China: A Critical Evaluation of Its Conceptual Foundation' in Lusina Ho and Rebecca Lee (eds.), *Trust Law in Asian Civil Law Jurisdiction: A Comparative Analysis* (Cambridge University Press, 2013) 86; Lusina Ho, 'Trust Laws in China: History, Ambiguity and Beneficiary's Rights' in Lionel Smith (ed.), *Re-Imaging the Trust: Trusts in Civil Law* (Cambridge University Press, 2012) 195–6.

[10] Article 2 of the Chinese Trust Law stipulates that 'trust refers to the act in which the settlor, on the basis of confidence on the trustee, entrusts certain property rights it owns to the trustee and the trustee manages or disposes of the property rights in its own name in accordance with the intentions of the settlor and for the benefit of the beneficiary or for specific purposes'.

examined foreign precedents, commentaries, statutes, and legal practices.[11] Legislators in China fully understood the legal elements of common law trusts and the adjustments and efforts that had been made by their Japanese and South Korean counterparts when transplanting common law trusts into their indigenous civil law systems. It is noteworthy that the adoption of the term 'entrust' was the consequence of 'a last-minute change'[12] made by politicians. All the earlier drafts proposed by drafters and scholars contemplated the transfer of legal title in the creation of a Chinese trust.[13]

There are three main reasons for this legislative arrangement. First, because of the numerus clauses principle in Chinese law,[14] Chinese scholars find it difficult to embrace the concept of 'split ownership of trust property'.[15] Moreover, in practice, trust companies have several problems, such as poor risk management ability and a lack of internal governance rules.[16] In this light, vesting trust assets in the trustee will pose a great risk to the protection of the beneficiary's interest.[17] Second, prior to the introduction of the Chinese Trust Law, the institution of agency was widely used in asset management. The concept of 'trust' is strange to both practitioners and academics in China. They do not have a clear understanding of how trust works and what its constituent elements are. In the eyes of settlors, it is unacceptable to relinquish the legal title to

[11] Frances H. Foster, 'American Trust Law in a Chinese Mirror' (2010) 94 *Minnesota Law Review* 602, 627–31.

[12] Ruiqiao Zhang, 'Trust Law of China and Its Uncertainties: Examination of the Rights and Obligations of Trust and Ownership of Trust Property' (2015) 10 *National Taiwan University Law Review* 45, 69.

[13] 闫荣涛 [Yan Rongtao],《中国信托财产所有权归属分析与建构 》 [Analysis and Reconstruction on the Internal Structure of Trust Ownership in China] (2009) 9 昆明理工大学学报 (社会科学版) *Journal of Kunming University of Science and Technology (Social Sciences)* 60, 62; Ho, 'Trust Laws in China: History, Ambiguity and Beneficiary's Rights' (n 9) 201.

[14] Ho, 'Trust Laws in China: History, Ambiguity and Beneficiary's Rights' (n 9) 207.

[15] Rebecca Lee, 'Convergence and Divergence in the Worlds of the Trust: Duties and Liabilities of Trustees under the Chinese Trust' in Lionel D. Smith (ed.), *The Worlds of the Trust* (Cambridge University Press, 2013) 407.

[16] 《关于<中华人民共和国信托法（草案）>的说明》 [Explanations on the Trust Law of the People's Republic of China (Draft)] (People's Republic of China) Standing Committee of the People's Congress, 24 December 1996;《全国人大法律委员会关于<中华人民共和国信托法(草案)>修改情况的汇报》 [Report of the Law Committee of the National People's Congress on the Revision of Trust Law of the People's Republic of China (Draft)] (People's Republic of China) National People's Congress, 3 July 2000.

[17] Ho, 'Trust Laws in China: History, Ambiguity and Beneficiary's Rights' (n 9) 201.

trust assets solely for the purpose of asset management.[18] The third reason relates to the practice of Chinese trusts. Most of the trusts established in the late 1980s were designed to be collective investment schemes where investors transferred their investment (cash) to the trustee anyway. Thus, legislators considered that it was not urgent to provide a clear answer on the vesting of trust assets.[19]

These three reasons are closely associated with the historical background against which the Chinese Trust Law was enacted. Societal and cultural circumstances have undergone drastic changes in the past fifteen years. Nevertheless, legislative arrangements relating to the vesting of charitable trust assets remain the same. Scholars and practitioners often consult explanatory memoranda when exploring the reason behind specific legislative arrangements. However, the memorandum for the Chinese Charity Law makes no mention of the arrangements relating to the legal title to charitable trust assets. Interviews with scholars and trust lawyers show that there are two reasons behind this 'entrust' approach. First, there have been many scandals involving misuse of charity funds in the past two decades, and therefore the public lacks trust and confidence in charity trustees.[20] In this context, a mandatory requirement of the transfer of legal title to trust assets may discourage the public from using the model of charitable trusts, since settlors can stay away from a legal model that conflicts with their needs.[21] Second, the Chinese Trust Law has the highest legal binding effect on the regulation of trust affairs in China. The Measures for Charitable Trusts, as an administrative regulation, is subordinate to the regulatory framework set out in the Chinese Trust Law. In view of the need for consistency and coherence between superior and subordinate laws, legislators tend to take the same approach on the vesting of trust assets in the charitable trust setting.[22]

B Assignment of Powers and Duties to the Settlor and the Trustee

The idea of entrustment is mirrored in the assignment of powers and duties to settlors and trustees. In the legal governance framework, settlors

[18] Kai Lyu, 'Re-Clarifying China's Trust Law: Characteristics and New Conceptual Basis' (2015) 36 *Loyola of Los Angeles International and Comparative Law Review* 447, 456.

[19] Zhang (n 12) 69.

[20] See analysis in Section II-B of Chapter 2.

[21] See interviews with A1, A7, A8, L2, L8, and T1.

[22] See interviews with A6, A7, L1, and L5.

are able to play a proactive role due to the granting of wide powers to them, such as the powers to define the types of benefits to be created by the charitable trust and the way in which trust parties interact with each other. In contrast, trustees are burdened by law with broad duties, such as the duties to avoid profits, avoid conflicts, and act in the best interest of charitable purposes. Behind this legal governance framework exist numerous ambiguities. The law sets up the internal relationship between settlors and trustees but does not clearly define what the scope of their powers and duties is and how their roles should be performed. This vagueness creates a great deal of uncertainty in the way in which settlors interact with trustees. This section will identify the areas of vagueness and how it affects the way in which settlors and trustees discharge their roles.

1 The Settlor's Wide Powers

Instead of dropping out of the picture, the settlor in Chinese law is granted wide powers,[23] including the powers to change the trust management method, appoint trust supervisors, require the trustee to explain its decisions, be informed on the administration and disposal of trust assets, and check and duplicate the trust accounts. This section discusses the two most important powers that settlors have under a charitable trust: the powers to require the trustee to change the management method and to appoint trust supervisors.

(a) Power to Require the Trustee to Change the Management Method Pursuant to article 20 of the Chinese Trust Law, the settlor has the power to request the trustee to give explanations for its decisions.[24] These explanations allow the settlor to assess whether the

[23] For common law, settlors use the letter of wishes or the mechanism of protector to play a certain role in the management of charitable trusts. See analysis in Section II-B of Chapter 2.

[24] In the United Kingdom and Australia, there is significant conflict within cases about the extent of such disclosures by trustees. The traditional position, however, is that trustees have immunity from the court examining the reasons for their decisions. See *Breakspear* v *Ackland* (2008) 3 WLR 698, [54]–[58]; *Re Londonderry's Settlement* [1965] Ch 918, 928, 936–7; *Re Rabaiott's Settlement* [2000] WTLR 953, 933; *Hartigan Nominees Pty Ltd v Rydge* (1992) 29 NSWLR 405, 436, 442; Mark Pawlowski, 'Confidentiality or Disclosure?' (2008) 96 *Trusts and Estates Law & Tax Journal* 12, 12; Alec Samuels, 'Disclosure of Trust Documents' (1965) 28(2) *Modern Law Review* 220, 222; Tsun Hang Tey, 'Trustee's Duty of Disclosure' (2012) 24 *Singapore Academy of Law Journal* 191, 216; David A. Steele, 'Disclosure of Trust Documents Revisited' (1995) 15 *Estates and Trusts Journal* 218, 226.

trustee's management method is favourable to the realization of the trust's purpose. If the answer is 'no' from the settlor's perspective, it can ask the trustee to modify such method according to article 21 of the Chinese Trust Law. Article 21 of the Chinese Trust Law stipulates that the settlor, due to special causes that were unforeseen when the trust was established, has the power to ask the trustee to change the methods of management of trust assets if the methods are not favourable to the realization of the trust's purposes or do not conform to the interest of the beneficiary. The power to require the trustee to change management methods allows the settlor to perform its supervisory role in the ongoing administration of the affairs of the charitable trust. Nevertheless, the law does not clearly define in what situation a management method is deemed to be unfavourable to the realization of a trust's purposes. Nor does it define the phrase 'special causes that were unforeseen when the trust was established'. Because of these ambiguities, the widest possible discretion that is vested in the settlor may produce a great deal of uncertainty in the trustee's administration of charitable trusts. For example, is there really a gap in current management methods that prevents the charitable trust purpose from being met? How should the risks associated with the change of management methods be appropriately addressed? In the absence of a clear answer to these questions, it is foreseeable that the vagueness of article 21 will easily lead to controversy between settlors and trustees if they disagree on the management of charitable trusts.[25]

The uncertainty in a trustee's autonomous management power is further exacerbated by the fact that settlors are empowered to change trustees in accordance with article 20 of the Measures for Charitable Trusts. This article allows settlors to change trustees if trustees breach their duties or have difficulty in performing their duties. When viewed together with article 21 of the Chinese Trust Law, the wording of article 20 creates several difficulties. For example, what does the phrase 'trustees

In contrast, a later set of cases have suggested that trustees would need to disclose reasons for their decisions to prevent a drawing of adverse inferences from their silence in the face of a case with prima facie evidence. See *Knudsen* v *Kara Kar Holdings Pty Ltd* [2000] NSWSC 715, [112]; *Sharp* v *Maritime Super Pty Ltd* [2012] NSWSC 1350, [176]; *Scott* v *National Trust for Places of Historical Interest or Natural Beauty* (1998) 2 All ER 705, 718–9; *Edge* v *Pensions Ombudsman* [2000] Ch 602, 633.

25 Contractual practice suggests that the parties to charitable trusts tend to use contractual tools to clarify their powers and duties, so as to minimize risks that may arise from the settlor's exercise of power. See analysis in Section III of Chapter 5.

have difficulty in performing their duties' mean? From whose perspective should this phrase be understood – the trustee's or the settlor's? If trustees decline to adopt the management method suggested by settlors, can settlors change trustees on the basis that trustees have breached their duties? The law relevant to charitable trusts does not provide clear answers to these questions. The vagueness of the joint reading of article 20 of the Measures for Charitable Trusts and article 21 of the Chinese Trust Law creates a high level of uncertainty for trustees.

(b) Power to Appoint Trust Supervisors The charity law allows settlors to appoint trust supervisors. By appointing trust supervisors, settlors can keep a close eye on how trustees exercise their powers and on whether trust assets are managed in alignment with the trust's charitable purpose.[26] In contrast to public welfare trusts, a trust supervisor is not mandatory in the charitable trust model[27] – whether a trust supervisor is appointed depends heavily on the settlor's own wishes. At the same time, the law does not provide any detailed criteria for how the powers and obligations of a trust supervisor should be determined.[28] Are supervisors fiduciaries? To whom do supervisors owe their duties? How should supervisors interact with settlors and trustees? The law provides no answers to these questions.

26 中国信托业协会 [China Trustee Association] (ed.),《慈善信托研究》 [Research on the Charitable Trust] (中国金融出版社 [China Financial Publishing House], 2016) 85–6; Stewart E. Sterk, 'Trust Protectors, Agency Costs, and Fiduciary Duty' (2005) 27 *Cardozo Law Review* 2761, 2763; 张淳 [Zhang Chun] (n 9) 119; Foster (n 11) 645.

27 《慈善信托管理办法》 [Administrative Measures for Charitable Trusts] (People's Republic of China) China Banking Regulatory Commission and Ministry of Civil Affairs, 10 July 2017, art 11;《中华人民共和国信托法》 [Trust Law of the People's Republic of China] (People's Republic of China) National People's Congress, 28 April 2001 (n 4) art 64.

28 For common law, trust protectors can be granted various administrative and dispositive powers, such as the powers to appoint and remove the trustee, to consent to the trustee's exercise of power, and to consent to a distribution plan. However, there is no uniform answer as to the nature of the protector's powers, as the purpose of the power and the factual context out of which the power is conferred vary considerably in each trust. See *LGSS* v *Egan* [2002] NSWSC 1171, [113]; *Blenkinsop v Herbert* [2017] WASCA 87, [106]–[110]; Lynton Tucker, Nicholas Le Poidevin, James Brightwell, Thomas Fletcher and Aidan Briggs (eds.), *Lewin on Trusts (Volume I)* (Sweet & Maxwell, 20th ed., 2020) 1266; Jeffrey Evans Stake, 'A Brief Comment on Trust Protectors' (2006) 27 *Cardozo Law Review* 2813, 2814–5; Gregory S. Alexander, 'Trust Protectors: Who Will Watch the Watchmen' (2006) 27 *Cardozo Law Review* 2807, 2809–10; Philip J. Ruce, 'The Trustee and the Trust Protector: A Question of Fiduciary Power – Should a Trust Protector Be Held to a Fiduciary Standard?' (2011) 59 *Drake Law Review* 67, 95; Sterk (n 26) 2775–6.

Interviews with trust lawyers and trustee managers indicate that, in practice, the extent to which supervisors can play a supervisory role varies considerably, depending on the way in which supervisors participate in the management of trust affairs. Two of these ways are summarized here. The first is the establishment of charitable trust committees,[29] on which trust supervisors serve as committee members and have the power to vote on any matters associated with the administration of charitable trusts. With this approach, trust supervisors can play a crucial role, as trust instruments often provide that all decisions relating to the handling of trust affairs shall come into force on the condition that all committee members have reached unanimous consent.[30] Regarding the second approach, the role of trust supervisors is weak and akin to that of a consultant. In this approach, trust supervisors just give advice on how trust assets can be managed and how beneficiaries can be selected. Trust supervisors' suggestions are not legally binding on trustees.[31] Instead, trustees have unfettered discretion in determining how charitable trusts should be managed.

2 The Trustee's Onerous Duties

Under Chinese law, the trustee is burdened with onerous duties, including the duty to act in good faith, the duty to avoid profits, the duty to avoid conflicts, the duty to act in the best interest of the charitable trust's purpose, and the duty to act personally. These duties acknowledge a trustee's powers to make decisions about the management and distribution of charitable assets, but the way in which the powers are exercised can create a risk of deviation from the purpose of the trust or an undermining of the interests of potential beneficiaries. At the same time, the new legal framework for charitable trusts creates several ambiguities in the ways in which trustees are required to perform their duties. It is unclear what the scope of these duties is and how they can be properly discharged. This vagueness makes it difficult to determine whether a trustee's management of charitable trusts is compliant with the requirements of the law. This section discusses the two most important duties that trustees under a charitable trust are burdened with: the duty to avoid profits and the duty to act in the best interest of the charitable trust's purpose.

29 See analysis in Section III-C of Chapter 5.
30 See interviews with T1, L1, L5, and L9.
31 See interviews with L1, L2, and L5.

(a) Duty to Avoid Profits Consensus has been achieved in Chinese academia that article 26[32] of the Chinese Trust Law articulates the no profit rule in China.[33] In the circumstances specified in article 26, there is a risk that a trustee's temptation to acquire personal benefits may 'impede the faithful performance'[34] of its duty as a trustee to duly administer trust assets. The object that this article seeks to achieve is analogous to the purpose in common law jurisdictions under which trustees are precluded 'from being swayed by considerations of personal interest',[35] thereby misusing trust assets for personal gains.[36]

Due to the legal terms used by article 26, the scope of application of the no profit rule is extremely narrow in the context of the Chinese Trust Law. Its application is confined to personal profits that arise from the use of trust assets by a trustee. Gains generated without any connection to the use of trust assets or the personal interests of a trustee do not give rise to the intervention of article 26. This applies to situations such as a trustee receiving commissions or bribes from taking advantage of their trustee position[37] or a trustee utilizing information and opportunities[38] they

32 According to article 26 of the Chinese Trust Law, 'except obtaining remuneration according to the provisions of this Law, the trustee may not seek interests for itself by using the trust property. Where the trustee, in violation of the provisions of the preceding paragraph, seeks interests for itself by using the trust property, the interests gained therefrom shall be integrated into the trust property'.

33 Charles Zhen Qu, 'The Doctrinal Basis of the Trust Principles in China's Trust Law' (2003) 38 *Real Property, Probate and Trust Journal* 345, 369; 陈向聪 [Chen Xiangcong],《信托法律制度研究》 [Research on Trust Law System] (中国检察出版社 [China People's Procuratorate Press], 2007) 206–8; 赵廉慧 [Zhao Lianhui],《信托法解释论》 [Interpretative Theory of Trust Law] (中国法制出版社 [China Legal Publishing House], 2015) 310; 谭振亭 [Tan Zhenting],《信托法》 [Trust Law] (中国政法大学出版社 [China University of Political Science and Law Press], 2010) 124; Ho, Lee and Jin (n 9) 90.

34 *Clay* v *Clay* (2001) 202 CLR 410, [15].

35 *Warman International Ltd* v *Dwyer* (1995) 128 ALR 201, 209.

36 卞耀武 [Bian Yaowu],《中华人民共和国信托法释义》 [Interpretation of the Trust Law of the People's Republic of China] (法律出版社 [Law Press], 2002) 97;周小明 [Zhou Xiaoming],《信托制度: 法理与实务》 [Trust System: Theory and Practice] (中国法制出版社 [China Legal Publishing House], 2012) 277; 高凌云 [Gao Lingyun],《被误读的信托 – 信托法原论》 [A Misreading of Trust: Discussion on the Origin of Trust] (复旦大学出版社 [Fudan University Press], 2010) 114, 116; 赵廉慧 [Zhao Lianhui] (n 33) 310–12, 316; 谭振亭 [Tan Zhenting] (n 33) 124–5; 陈向聪 [Chen Xiangcong] (n 33) 206, 208.

37 The difficulty of applying article 26 here is that the trustee's receipt of commission or bribe is not directly related to the use of trust properties.

38 Although trustees obtain business opportunities in the course of exploring investment possibilities for beneficiaries, article 26 may not be applied where trustees use their own money rather than trust properties to exploit opportunities for themselves. The answer to

have access to by virtue of their position as a trustee; or a trustee using trust assets to offer guarantees for their affiliated party, which seem to be outside the scope of article 26.

The Chinese Company Law also defines the duty to avoid profits, but the scope of the duty to avoid profits in the Chinese Company Law is broader than in the Chinese Trust Law. Article 147 of the Chinese Company Law clearly stipulates that no director, supervisor, or senior manager may take any bribe or illegal gains by abusing his or her powers.[39] At the same time, pursuant to articles 148(3) and 148(5) of the Chinese Company Law, without the consent of the shareholders' meeting or the general meeting, a director or senior manager is prohibited from using company assets to provide a guarantee for others or from using his or her powers to usurp any business opportunities that belong to the company.[40]

whether article 26 applies to this scenario depends on whether 'information and opportunity' can be conceptualized as trust assets. Regarding the relationship between opportunity and property, see 冯果 [Feng Guo],《"禁止篡夺公司机会"规则探究》[Research on the Doctrine of Prohibiting the Usurpation of Corporate Opportunities] (2010) 1 中国法学 *China Legal Science* 96, 98–9; Lusina Ho and Rebecca Lee (eds.), 'Case 3: Protecting Ring-Fenced Assets against Disloyalty of the Asset Manager' in *Trust Law in Asian Civil Law Jurisdiction: A Comparative Analysis* (Cambridge University Press, 2013) 163; *Farah Construction Pty Ltd* v *Say-Dee Pty Ltd* (2007) 236 ALR 209, [119].

39 On account of this article, see 王军 [Wang Jun],《中国公司法》[Corporation Law of China] (高等教育出版社 [Higher Education Press], 2015) 330; 金晓文 [Jin Xiaowen], 《中国公司法原理与适用》[Principles and Application of Chinese Corporation Law] (中国法制出版社 [China Legal Publishing House], 2017) 350; 孔祥俊 [Kong Xiangjun],《公司法要论》 [Key Discussions on Chinese Company Law] (最高人民法院出版社 [Supreme People's Court Press], 1997) 333–5; 甘培忠 [Gan Peizhong],《企业与公司法学》[Enterprise and Company Law] (北京大学出版社 [Peking University Press], 2014) 264.

40 There is an intense debate as to what constitutes the usurpation of corporate opportunities, see 朱锦清 [Zhu Jinqing],《公司法学（下）》 [Company Law (II)] (清华大学出版社 [Tsinghua University Press], 2017) 150–3;《林承恩、李江山、涂雅雅侵占公司机会纠纷案》 [*Lin Chengen and Li Jiangshen* v *Tu Yaya* – Company Opportunity Dispute] [2012], 最高人民法院 [Supreme People's Court], 民四终字第 15 号 [Civil Fourth Division, Appealing Ruling, Case No 15], 6 September 2012;《刘彬与李占军监事损害公司利益纠纷上诉案》 [*Lin Bin* v *Li Zhanjun* – Company Interest Dispute], 北京市第一中级人民法院 [Beijing First Intermediate Court], 民终字第 1099 号 [Civil Division, Appealing Ruling, Case No 1099], 9 March 2010;《冯锦等诉高育新公司利益纠纷案》 [*Feng Jin* v *Gao Yuxin* – Company Interest Dispute], 北京市第一中级人民法院 [Beijing First Intermediate Court], 民终字第 7378 号 [Civil Division, Appealing Ruling, Case No 7378], 31 October 2017; 王军 [Wang Jun] (n 39) 329–30; 金晓文 [Jin Xiaowen] (n 39) 352–3; 孔祥俊 [Kong Xiangjun] (n 39) 335.

Currently, China has built up a relatively comprehensive framework of trust regulations. Subordinated legal instruments provided by the China Banking and Insurance Regulatory Commission (CBIRC)[41] are tasked with defining details about specific requirements or components of the Chinese Trust Law. The Measures for Administration of Trust Companies (MTC)[42] is one example here. Article 34(1) of the MTC relates to the no profit rule in the Chinese Trust Law. This article stipulates, 'The trustee ought not to seek illegitimate interests by taking advantage of their trustee position'. In contrast to article 26 of the Chinese Trust Law, the scope of article 34(1) of the MTC is broader to cover situations in respect of bribery or commissions in the transaction. However, the key phrase 'illegitimate interest' is left unelaborated in the MTC and, currently, no cases have clearly defined its meaning and scope. It is still unclear whether trustees are eligible to enter into transactions where they make use of the 'knowledge possessed by them in virtue of their office'.[43] Furthermore, the MTC is, in nature, an administrative regulation. Regulators thus have wide discretion in interpreting the scope and nature of the phrase 'illegitimate interest'. This discretion allows regulators to easily control a trustee's exercise of power, thereby posing risks to the trustee's management of charitable trusts.[44]

(b) Duty to Act in the Best Interest of the Charitable Purpose In contrast to the express reference to the duty of loyalty in the Chinese Company Law,[45] Chinese trust laws do not adopt the term 'duty of loyalty' in their legal provisions, whether in the Chinese Trust Law or in its subsidiary regulations. Article 25(1) of the Chinese Trust Law only provides that 'the trustee shall abide by the provisions of trust documents and handle trust affairs in the best interest of the beneficiary'.[46] Because of the way this article is couched, numerous scholarly writings have suggested that the basic elements accompanying the duty of loyalty have

[41] This Commission is also one of the regulators of Chinese charitable trusts. On the powers and duties of this Commission, see analysis in Section II-B of Chapter 4.

[42] 《信托公司管理办法》 [Measures for Administration of Trust Companies] (People's Republic of China) China Banking Regulatory Commission, 23 January 2007.

[43] *Regal (Hastings) Ltd* v *Gulliver* (1967) 2 AC 134, 153, 159.

[44] To mitigate risks arising from regulatory scrutiny, trust parties are willing to use contracts to specify the way in which they interact with regulators. See analysis in Section III of Chapter 5.

[45] 《中华人民共和国公司法》 [Company Law of the People's Republic of China] (People's Republic of China) National People's Congress, 26 October 2018, art 147.

[46] 《中华人民共和国信托法》 [Trust Law of the People's Republic of China] (People's Republic of China) National People's Congress, 28 April 2001 (n 4) art 25.

already been recognized by the Chinese Trust Law.[47] In the area of charitable trusts, this duty has been expressed as 'the duty to act in the best interest of the charitable purpose'.[48]

This duty is ambiguous in two respects. First, the wording of the phrase 'in the best interest of the charitable purpose' seems to 'mandate positive actions'[49] to be taken by a trustee, but it is unclear what a trustee ought to do under this heading. One may draw reference from article 25 (2) of the Chinese Trust Law to address this question. However, it is still unclear to what extent and in what way article 25(2) may illuminate the understanding of this phrase. According to article 25(2) of the Chinese Trust Law, 'the trustee shall be careful in performing his duties and fulfil his obligations with honesty, prudence, good faith and efficiency'. Do articles 25(2) and 25(1) run in parallel to each other and thus there is no intersection?[50] Can the duty to handle affairs in the best interest of the purpose be understood as a composite of the duty to act in honesty and the duty to perform tasks with the requisite degree of prudence and care? Or are the terms of honesty, prudence, and care only used as references for assessing whether the performance of a trustee is in the best interest of the purpose? The law does not elaborate on these matters. Because of these ambiguities, the trustee will face numerous problems in the performance of its duties. For example, what factors are relevant to the determination of the performance of 'in the best interest of the charitable

47 See Lusina Ho and Rebecca Lee (eds.), *Trust Law in Asian Civil Law Jurisdiction: A Comparative Analysis* (Cambridge University Press, 2013) 162; Ho, *Trust Law in China* (n 9) 144; Ho, Lee and Jin (n 9) 90; Zhang (n 12) 57; Lyu (n 18) 482; 谭振亭 [Tan Zhenting] (n 33) 123.

48 赵廉慧 [Zhao Lianhui] (n 33) 310.

49 Rosemary Teele Langford, 'High Court of Australia on Fiduciary Theory' in Ken Coghill, Charles Sampford and Tim Smith (eds.), *Fiduciary Duty and the Atmospheric Trust* (Routledge, 2016) 196.

50 The object of article 25(2) is to provide a legal basis for other duties that are imposed on the trustee, such as the duty of care and the duty of honesty. See Zhenting Tan, 'Perfecting the Chinese Law of Trusts: A Critical and Comparative Study of the Australian and the Chinese Law of Trusts' (PhD Thesis, Bond University, 2005) 180; Zhang (n 12) 57; Lyu (n 18) 482; Qu (n 33) 369; 陈向聪 [Chen Xiangcong] (n 33) 202; 赵廉慧 [Zhao Lianhui] (n 33) 329; 谭振亭 [Tan Zhenting] (n 33) 124; 周小明 [Zhou Xiaoming] (n 36) 279. The duty of prudence and diligence in the *Chinese Trust Law* is akin to the duty of care in common law jurisdictions. See Lusina Ho, 'The Reception of Trust in Asia: Emerging Asian Principles of Trust?' [2004] *Singapore Journal of Legal Studies* 287, 290; Antonio Cappiello, 'Using Trusts to Manage Private and Charitable Patrimony: An Overview and Comparison of U.S., EU, and Chinese Law' (2014) 22 *National Italian American Bar Association Law Journal* 13, 17.

purpose'? What acts are mandated and prohibited by the concepts of honesty and prudence in the context of 'in the best interest of the charitable purpose'? What is the connection between acting in the best interest of the charitable purpose and acting in good faith?

The second type of ambiguity relates to the nature of this duty. Most Chinese academics and commentators hold that article 25(1)[51] of the Chinese Trust Law is the clause prescribing the general rule of the duty of loyalty. It is nevertheless worth reconsidering whether this view accords with what the law says. The Chinese Trust Law does not merely say that the trustee ought to handle trust affairs in the best interest of the charitable purpose. Instead, there is a qualifier in front of the description of this duty – that is, the trustee shall abide by the provisions of the trust documents. A textual interpretation of this qualifier suggests that how to protect the best interest of the charitable purpose shall be defined by the trust documents.

The legal duty relating to undertaking to perform a task can arise both outside and within a loyalty relationship. A case in point is where a lessor agrees to lease his or her own property to a lessee. According to contract provisions, the lessor is obliged to deliver the house keys on time and, likewise, the lessee ought to pay the rent on schedule. It is beyond doubt that the terms of a lease are hugely different from those of a trust contract. Nevertheless, the duty of a trustee to act in the best interest of the charitable purpose pursuant to the provisions of the trust is, in nature, the same as the duty of a lessor or a lessee under a lease – namely, a contractual duty to perform tasks that have been mutually agreed on. A trustee is obliged to pursue the best interest of the charitable purpose but merely to the extent necessary to execute the terms in the trust instrument. Applying this train of logic, 'acting in the best interest of the charitable purpose' can be understood as a particular way in which the trustee ought to fulfil its duties under the trust instrument, and the meaning of 'the best interest of the charitable purpose' ought to be ascertained by reference to specific terms of the trust instrument. Based on this understanding, a claim relating to failure to act in the best interest of the charitable purpose is simply a claim for breach of an undertaking to act in a specific manner.[52]

[51] Article 25(1) of the Chinese Trust Law stipulates that the trustee shall abide by the provisions of trust documents and handle trust affairs in the best interest of the beneficiary.

[52] The duty to comply with an undertaking to perform a task is analogous to strict contract duties and not exclusive to the trustee, for anyone who has assumed legally enforceable obligations ought to act in a specific way, whether based on contract or by virtue of a trust. See Ho, *Trust Law in China* (n 9) 144. At the international level, it accords with the common practice where the duty to abide by the provisions of trust instruments is the

C Comparison between Charitable Trusts and Agency Relationships

The above analysis[53] relating to the assignment of powers and duties to the settlor and the trustee suggests that, in the Chinese legal system, there is a close relationship between charitable trusts and agency relationships. On the one hand, both settlors and principals are endowed by law with wide powers to interfere in the disposal of entrusted assets. Settlors and principals are all allowed to be proactive in supervising how entrusted affairs are managed. On the other hand, trustees have autonomous powers to make decisions about the management and distribution of charitable assets, while an agent's discretion in determining how entrusted affairs are managed is heavily constrained. An agent is obliged to follow the principal's instructions strictly. Consistent with this analysis, how and to what extent are charitable trusts similar to, or different from, agency relationships? Published literature has examined the differences and similarities between express private trusts and agency relationships,[54] but has not specifically examined this question. Sections III-C-1 and III-C-2 analyse this question to shed light on how trustees interact with settlors in the legal framework for charitable trusts.

1 Similarities to Agency Relationships

In light of the foregoing analysis, one can identify the similarity between charitable trusts and agency relationships in three aspects. First, both settlors and principals are entitled to reserve the legal title to entrusted assets.[55] Second, both settlors and principals are granted a wide range of

most important of all the rules relating to the duties of trustees. See Arthur Underhill, David J. Hayton, Paul Matthews and Charles Mitchell, *Underhill and Hayton Law Relating to Trusts and Trustees* (LexisNexis Butterworths, 17th ed., 2007) [47.2]; Michael Bryan, Simone Degeling, Scott Donald and Vicki Vann, *A Sourcebook on Equity and Trusts in Australia* (Cambridge University Press, 2016) 369.

53 See Section III-B.

54 Ho, *Trust Law in China* (n 9) 55–6; 赵廉慧 [Zhao Lianhui] (n 33) 62–6; 陈向聪 [Chen Xiangcong] (n 33) 33–6; 高凌云 [Gao Lingyun] (n 36) 32–3; 周小明 [Zhou Xiaoming] (n 36) 96–100.

55 Rebecca Lee, 'Conceptualizing the Chinese Trust' (2009) 58(3) *International & Comparative Law Quarterly* 655, 659;《中华人民共和国慈善法》 [Charity Law of the People's Republic of China] (People's Republic of China) National People's Congress, 16 March 2016, art 44; Lyu (n 18) 471;《慈善信托管理办法》[Administrative Measures for Charitable Trusts] (People's Republic of China) China Banking Regulatory Commission and Ministry of Civil Affairs, 10 July 2017 (n 27) art 2; Qu (n 33) 356; Ho (n 50) 294.

statutory powers to influence the management of entrusted assets.[56] Third, both trustees and agents are subject to onerous duties, including the duty to avoid self-dealing, the duty of care, the duty not to delegate their duties or powers unless authorized, and the duty to obey the directions of the documents (i.e., trust documents or entrusted documents).[57]

There are two reasons for these similarities. The first relates to the background of the enactment of the Chinese Trust Law.[58] Different from the development path of common law trusts, the discussions of 'why the trust system should be transplanted' and 'how a trust system should be established so that the logical coherence of the existing Chinese legal system will not be greatly and adversely affected' were carried out during a period when Chinese agency theories had already been well developed. Accordingly, Chinese lawmakers tended to draw references from agency theories when designing the legal system for Chinese trusts, so that any adverse impact that trust laws may have on the Chinese domestic legal system could be minimized to the largest extent.[59] Furthermore, as

[56] 《中华人民共和国民法典》 [Civil Code of the People's Republic of China] (People's Republic of China) National People's Congress, 28 May 2020 (n 8) arts 168–9;《慈善信托管理办法》[Administrative Measures for Charitable Trusts] (People's Republic of China) China Banking Regulatory Commission and Ministry of Civil Affairs, 10 July 2017 (n 27) arts 11, 20, 33, 38.

[57] 《中华人民共和国民法典》 [Civil Code of the People's Republic of China] (People's Republic of China) National People's Congress, 28 May 2020 (n 8) arts 164, 168–9;《慈善信托管理办法》[Administrative Measures for Charitable Trusts] (People's Republic of China) China Banking Regulatory Commission and Ministry of Civil Affairs, 10 July 2017 (n 27) arts 29, 31.

[58] 《慈善信托管理办法》[Administrative Measures for Charitable Trusts] (People's Republic of China) China Banking Regulatory Commission and Ministry of Civil Affairs, 10 July 2017 (n 27) art 2; 王萍 [Wang Ping],《大陆法代理制度与英美法信托制度之比较》 [Comparison between the Agency System of Mainland Law and Anglo-American Trust Law System] (1998) 3 甘肃政法学院学报 *Journal of Gansu Political Science and Law Institute* 49, 53.

[59] A large number of trust cases from the early 2000s were addressed by recharacterizing trust relationships into a contractual or agency relationship. See《上海岩鑫实业投资有限公司诉华宝信托投资有限责任公司信托合同纠纷案》 [*Shanghai Yanxin Industrial Investment Co Ltd* v *Huabao Trust Investment Co Ltd* – Dispute over Trust Contract], 上海市第一中级人民法院 [Shanghai First Intermediate Court], 沪一中民三（商）初字第 201 号[Civil Division, Initial Ruling, Case No 201], 25 August 2004;《健桥证券股份有限公司与宝鸡钛业股份有限公司委托理财合同纠纷上诉案》 [*Jianqiao Securities Co Ltd* v *Baoji Titanium Industry Co Ltd* – Dispute over Entrusted Financial Management Contract], 最高人民法院 [Supreme People's Court], 民二终字第29号 [Civil Division, Appeal Ruling, Case No 29], 29 April 2005;《北京海淀科技发展有限公司诉深圳市新华锦源投资发展有限公司财产权属纠纷案》 [*Beijing Haidian Technology Development Co Ltd* v *Shenzhen Xinhua Jinyuan Investment Development Co Ltd* – Dispute over the

analysed in Section III-A-2, there is a legal hierarchy between the Chinese Trust Law and the Measures for Charitable Trusts: the latter, as an administrative regulation, is subordinate to the former. For the purpose of maintaining consistency and coherence between superior and subordinate laws, lawmakers tend to follow the approach adopted in the Chinese Trust Law when determining how settlors should interact with trustees in the governance of charitable trusts. The second reason relates to charity practice in China. The analysis in Chapter 2 shows that the media has exposed a series of scandals involving misuse of charity funds over the past two decades.[60] The general public, therefore, lacks trust and confidence in charity trustees' performance of their roles. In this light, allowing settlors to retain legal title to trust assets and granting settlors extensive supervisory powers may play a role in motivating the public to use trusts to develop charitable causes.[61]

2 Differences from Agency Relationships

Agency theories have heavily impacted the construction of the Chinese charitable trust system. Despite this, charitable trusts are, in substance, still distinguishable from agency relationships in three respects. These respects demonstrate the unique characteristics of the structure of charitable trusts and make them in certain scenarios institutionally more advantageous than agency when developing charitable causes. To begin, pursuant to articles 15 and 16 of the Chinese Trust Law, should settlors or trustees become insolvent, charitable trust assets are not subject to the claims of trustees' or settlors' general creditors. In comparison, according to article 71 of the Provisions of the Supreme People's Court on Certain Issues Concerning the Trial of Enterprise Bankruptcy Cases,[62] entrusted assets in an agency relationship will fall into the purview of a principal's liquidation assets upon his insolvency. This means the creditors of a principal are entitled to sue for proper distribution of the entrusted assets in accordance with the *pari passu* principle.

Plaintiff's Property Ownership], 重庆市高级人民法院 [Chongqing High People's Court], 渝高法民初字第14号 [Civil Division, Initial Ruling, Case No 14], 19 March 2007.

60 See analysis in Section II-B of Chapter 2.

61 See interviews with L1, L2, A4, and A5.

62 《最高人民法院关于审理企业破产案件若干问题的规定》 [Provisions of the Supreme People's Court on Certain Issues Concerning the Trial of Enterprise Bankruptcy Cases] (People's Republic of China) Supreme People's Court, 9 January 2002, art 71.

Second, after charitable trusts have been validly established, trustees have the autonomy to determine the management of charitable trusts and the distribution of charitable assets. Allowing trustees to make decisions on their own initiative is an inherent need for trust management.[63] In a formal sense, unless otherwise stipulated in the trust instruments, settlors should leave trustees to make decisions about the management of charitable trusts independently. However, the question of whom trustees' duties are owed to is still subject to debate.[64] Some interviewees in this research posit that trustees' duties are owed to the charitable trust purpose,[65] while others opine that trustees owe their duties to the general public.[66] Despite the lack of a standard answer to this question, scholars and practitioners generally agree[67] that trustees' duties are not owed to settlors. In contrast, it is unquestionable that agents owe strict duties to principals. For agents, answering the question of what steps can be taken to comply with the principals' requirements is crucial to the day-to-day management of entrusted affairs.

Finally, protecting public benefits in the carrying out of charitable purposes is a common thread running through the entire life cycle of a charitable trust. The valid status of charitable trusts would not be adversely affected even in special circumstances, such as when the trustees are dissolved or have lost their statutory qualifications, or when settlors are dead.[68] In comparison, agency relationships are automatically terminated when the agents in question lose their capacity for civil conduct, or the agents or their principals are dead.[69]

63 See interviews with T1, T5, and L5.

64 A trustee shall perform its duties for the best fulfilment of the charitable purpose expressed in the trust documents. See interviews with L3, L8, and A6.

65 See interviews with L1 and L8.

66 See interviews with A1, A2, T1, and T7.

67 See interviews with A1, A3, A6, A7, L1, L2, and L5.

68 《中华人民共和国信托法》 [Trust Law of the People's Republic of China] (People's Republic of China) National People's Congress, 28 April 2001 (n 4) art 52;《慈善信托管理办法》 [Administrative Measures for Charitable Trusts] (People's Republic of China) China Banking Regulatory Commission and Ministry of Civil Affairs, 10 July 2017 (n 27) art 37; 王萍 [Wang Ping] (n 58) 53.

69 Yuanshi Bu (ed.), *Chinese Civil Law* (Hart Publishing, 2013) 18; 朱庆育 [Zhu Qingyu],《民法总论》 [The General Theory of Civil Law] (北京大学出版社 [Peking University Press], 2016) 356–7;《中华人民共和国民法典》 [Civil Code of the People's Republic of China] (People's Republic of China) National People's Congress, 28 May 2020 (n 8) art 173.

IV Uncertain Role of Beneficiaries

Section III discussed the internal relationship between settlors and trustees in law. The analysis showed that, in law, the settlor is granted extensive powers while the trustee is subject to broad duties. The vagueness of the law on what the scopes of these powers and duties are and how the roles of the settlor and the trustee should be performed, however, creates a great deal of uncertainty regarding the administration of charitable trusts. This section will analyse the role of beneficiaries. As already mentioned in Section II, the law makes no mention of the role and legal nature of charitable trust beneficiaries. The silence of the law has resulted in an intense debate among scholars and practitioners on whether the concept of 'beneficiary' truly exists in the context of Chinese charitable trusts. This debate focuses on three inter-related questions. First, are the objects who receive charitable trust benefits 'beneficiaries' or merely 'recipients'? Second, is there any difference between 'beneficiaries' and 'recipients' in terms of standing to sue in respect of trustees' maladministration of charitable trusts? Third, what is the scope of an object's standing? Is their standing limited to the individualized interest they have in the trust assets? Or can their standing extend to the general administration of charitable trusts, irrespective of how much and what kind of interest they have in the trust assets? This section examines these questions to identify in what way and to what extent beneficiaries may play a supervisory role in trustees' performance of their duties.

A Exception to the Requirement of Certainty of Object

Since the introduction of the Chinese Trust Law in 2001, the legal status of purpose trusts has been the subject of much academic and judicial writing. According to article 2 of the Chinese Trust Law, 'the trustee is allowed to administer or dispose of trust property in the interest of a beneficiary or for any intended purposes'. An initial glance at this provision suggests that the Chinese Trust Law permits a purpose trust to be created. However, one reaches a strikingly different conclusion when the law is read and construed as a whole: a trust, pursuant to clause 5 of article 11 of the Chinese Trust Law, is by itself invalid in the absence of identifiable beneficiaries.[70] So far as these two irreconcilable provisions

[70] On account of this aspect, see 江平 [Jiang Ping] and 周小明 [Zhou Xiaoming],《建构大陆的信托法制的若干设想》 [Several Thoughts on the Construction of Trust System in

are concerned, to what extent can trusts for abstract purposes (e.g., purposes for maintenance of one's tomb or for promoting charitable causes) be legally established in China? This question cannot be answered until judicial interpretations or new laws are issued for clarification. In Chinese law, an exception to the uncertainty of the legal status of purpose trusts[71] is the institution of charitable trust, the validity of which has been established by the Chinese Charity Law and the Measures for Charitable Trusts.

Inherent in the valid status of a charitable trust is the notion that it is in the public interest that the validity of charitable trusts should be acknowledged. To prevent trusts from becoming channels for crimes or unregulated flow of funds, article 10 of the Measures for Charitable Trusts takes a negative approach in defining who the beneficiaries could

Mainland China] (1993) 6 政法论坛 *Tribune of Political Science and Law* 5, 8; 江平 [Jiang Ping] and 周小明 [Zhou Xiaoming],《论中国的信托立法》 [Research on the Legislation of Chinese Trust Law] (1994) 6 中国法学 *China Legal Science* 53, 55–6; Ho, Lee and Jin (n 9) 82; Foster (n 11) 627, 629; 赵廉慧 [Zhao Lianhui] (n 33) 96–7; Lee (n 55) 656.

71 For common law, there is an intense debate regarding how the legal status of non-charitable purpose trusts (NCPTs) could be understood. One argument holds that NCPTs are void due to the absence of ascertainable individuals in whose favour the court can decree performance. See *Bowman* v *Secular Society Ltd* [1917] AC 406, 441; *Re Wood* (1949) Ch 498, 501. In contrast, another argument holds that the certainty of object is not a legal necessity, although 'it is reasonable, equitable, and in accordance with the analogies of the law'. See John Chipman Gray, 'Gifts for a Non-Charitable Purpose' (1902) 15(7) *Harvard Law Review* 509, 515. Clauson J expressed the similar view in *Re Thompson* [1934] Ch 342 at 344, 'the object of the gift has been defined with sufficient clearness and is of a nature to which effect can be given'. The essence of this debate lies in the enforceability of NCPTs. See *Re Astor's Settlement Trusts* (1952) 1 All ER 1067, 1071; *Radmanovich v Nedeljkovic* [2001] NSWSC 492, [102], [113]; *Re Denley's Trust Deed* (1969) 1 Ch 373, 377; *Re Hummeltenberg* (1923) All ER Rep 49, 51; Matteo Ho, 'Time to Allow Non-Charitable Purpose Trusts in Hong Kong?' (2014) 44(2) *Hong Kong Law Journal* 519, 522–3; Adam J. Hirsch, 'Trusts for Purposes: Policy, Ambiguity, and Anomaly in the Uniform Laws' (1998) 26 *Florida State University Law Review* 913, 914; Adam J. Hirsch, 'Bequests for Purposes: A Unified Theory' (1999) 56 *Washington and Lee Law Review* 33, 45; Philip Jamieson, 'Trusts for the Maintenance of Particular Animals' (1985) 14(2) *University of Queensland Law Journal* 175, 175. The case law developed over the last century has upheld a limited, though well-recognized, number of NCPTs. See *Bourne* v *Keane* (1919) AC 815; *Pedulla* v *Nasti* (1990) 20 NSWLR 720; *Re Thompson* (1934) Ch 342; *Re Pearce* (1946) SASR 118; *Chesterman* v *Mitchell* (1923) 24 SR (NSW) 108; *Carson* v *Presbyterian Church of Queensland* [1956] St R Qd 466. Nevertheless, the bases on which these exceptional and anomalous trusts are recognized are inconsistent; thus, it is doubtful whether these instances can be followed in light of the recent case law. See David B. Parker and Anthony R. Mellows, *The Modern Law of Trusts* (Sweet and Maxwell, 5th ed., 1983) 177.

be. That is, settlors cannot designate, overtly or covertly, persons or entities who have any interest in the settlors themselves or the trustees as beneficiaries.[72] This approach serves to discourage settlors or trustees from taking advantage of an affiliated relationship to damage the interest of a charitable trust. Article 10 uses the term 'any interest', but it makes no mention of how this term should be defined. For example, what is the legal nature of the 'interest' here: pecuniary or non-pecuniary? Can altruistic or moral interest fall into the purview of the term 'any interest' here? The statute provides no answers to these questions. Nor does there exist case law that deals with this matter. The impreciseness of the term 'any interest' in the law makes it difficult for trustees to select beneficiaries.

B Role of Beneficiaries in the Governance Framework

There are two fundamental questions relevant to the arrangement of a trust. First, what is the analytical nature of this arrangement – that is, trust for purposes or trust for persons? Second, who has the standing to enforce the duties of the trustee? In express private trusts, the two questions are answered in the same way, as the beneficiary is the person to whom the trustee should be accountable. Nevertheless, in common law, when it comes to charitable trusts, the two questions are answered in different ways. As a matter of public policy, an object's entitlement to bring proceedings is granted by legislation or case law,[73] independent of the analytical nature of the trust.[74]

[72] 《慈善信托管理办法》 [Administrative Measures for Charitable Trusts] (People's Republic of China) China Banking Regulatory Commission and Ministry of Civil Affairs, 10 July 2017 (n 27) art 10.

[73] The case law in the United Kingdom and Australia takes the 'special interest' rule to assess whether individuals have standing to file lawsuits against a trustee's maladministration of charitable trusts. See *Re Hampton Fuel Allotment Charity* (1988) 3 WLR 513, 520; *Haslemere Estates Ltd* v *Baker* (1982) 1 WLR 1109, 1122; *Royal Society for the Prevention of Cruelty to Animals* v *Attorney General* (2001) 3 All ER 530, 540; *Metropolitan Petar* v *Mitreski* [2001] NSWSC 976, [6]; *Ngarluma Aboriginal Corp RNTBC* v *Attorney General (WA)* [2014] WASC 245, [46]–[50]; *Laura & Alfred West Cottage Homes Inc* v *Attorney-General (SA)* [2018] SASA 19, [8]–[11]; *Scott* v *National Trust for Places of Historical Interest or Natural Beauty* (n 24) 713–14.

[74] Take Anglo-Australian charitable trusts for example. Several cases, albeit a small number, have in the course of the last century held that there are no beneficiaries in Anglo-Australian charitable trusts. A well-known reference is the judgments of Dixon and Evatt JJ in *Attorney-General for New South Wales* v *Perpetual Trustee Co (Ltd)* (1940) 63 CLR 209, where their honours compared the relationship between charitable trusts and private

It is widely acknowledged that charitable trusts are purpose trusts and, thus, the conceptual distinction between beneficiaries and recipients is not theoretically significant in common law. In contrast, this distinction is particularly meaningful in understanding the nature of Chinese charitable trusts. There is a debate as to how the legal nature of objects can be understood: are the objects who receive benefits from charitable trusts 'beneficiaries' or merely 'recipients'? In law, the term 'beneficiary' is used extensively, suggesting that the objects who receive benefits are beneficiaries in the trust law sense.[75] In contrast, many academic papers or commentaries regard the term 'beneficiary' as speculative and argue that this term can be interpreted as either beneficiary or recipient.[76] This debate focuses on two arguments. The first is the beneficiary argument. This argument is that the concept of 'beneficiary' does not exist as a general proposition – it is only in the phase of

trusts at 222: 'A charitable trust is a trust for a purpose, not for a person . . . to dispose of property for the fulfilment of ends considered beneficiary to the community is an entirely different thing from creating equitable estates and interests and limiting them to beneficiaries'. This statement has been quoted or followed in several subsequent cases. See *Re Cooper Street Property Trust (No 2)* [2017] VSC 291, [29]; *Wright* v *Stevens* [2018] NSWSC 548, [218]; *The Salvation Army (New South Wales) Property Trust* v *Chief Commissioner of State Revenue* [2018] NSWSC 128, [79]; *Bropho* v *City of Perth* [2016] FCA 1098, [60]; *James Cook University* v *Townsville City Council & Anor* [2011] QSC 209, [11]; *Melbourne Jewish Orphan and Children's Aid Society Inc & Anor* v *ANZ Executors and Trustee Company Ltd* [2007] VSC 26, [63]; *Bateman's Bay Local Aboriginal Land Council* v *The Aboriginal Community Benefit Fund Pty Limited* [1998] HCA 49, [28]; *Bropho* v *State of Western Australia* [2007] FCA 519, [345]; *Ngarluma Aboriginal Corp RNTBC v Attorney General (WA)* (n73) [49]; *Metropolitan Petar* v *Mitreski* (n 73) [33]. Hansen J summarized the understanding of 'beneficiary' in a well-known passage in his judgment: 'In such a case there is no person who is a beneficiary. That is for the fundamental reason that a charitable trust is a trust for a purpose and not for a person. A charitable trust does not have a beneficiary'. See *BSH Holding Pty Ltd* v *Commissioner of State Revenue* [2000] VSC 302, [9].

75 See《民政部、中国银行业监督管理委员会关于做好慈善信托备案有关工作的通知》[Notice of Civil Affairs Department and China Banking Regulatory Commission on the Recordation Work for Charitable Trusts] (People's Republic of China) Civil Affairs Department and China Banking Regulatory Commission, 25 August 2016, s 2;《慈善信托管理办法》[Administrative Measures for Charitable Trusts] (People's Republic of China) China Banking Regulatory Commission and Ministry of Civil Affairs, 10 July 2017 (n 27) arts 10–11.

76 谢哲胜 [Xie Zhesheng],《信托法》 [Trust Law] (元照出版公司 [Angle Publishing], 2009) 219; 中国信托业协会 [China Trustee Association] (n 26) 62, 84; 谭振亭 [Tan Zhenting] (n 33) 199–200; 陈向聪 [Chen Xiangcong] (n 33) 278–9; 赵廉慧 [Zhao Lianhui] (n 33) 555.

trust asset distribution that beneficiaries can be identified.[77] Thus, the beneficiary status of an object starts from the date of selection and ends upon receipt of trust assets. During the period where the beneficiary title exists, objects have standing to sue for proper distribution of a certain part of trust assets. The second is the recipient argument – that is, objects who receive trust benefits are considered recipients, rather than beneficiaries as understood in the law of express private trusts.[78] Under this argument, recipients have no role to play at all in the governance structure of charitable trusts, notwithstanding that they may have a particularized interest in trust assets after receiving the notice of distribution from trustees.

1 The Beneficiary Argument

The object with the title of beneficiary is entitled to sue as of right. Several pieces of legislation make provisions on this point. The question about how these different legislative provisions should be read and interpreted together is: pursuant to article 50 of the Chinese Charity Law[79] and article 63 of the Measures for Charitable Trusts,[80] which is applied first. In the absence of relevant provisions in those Measures, the Chinese Charity Law and the Chinese Trust Law are respectively applied in the second and third order. So, one may refer to the Chinese Trust Law to investigate whether the object has standing and, if so, what the scope of the object's standing is, for the Measures for Charitable Trusts and the Chinese Charity Law have no provisions regarding the standing of an object.

The beneficiary's right to sue is stipulated in articles 22 and 49 of the Chinese Trust Law. The two articles, when read and construed as a

[77] 中国信托业协会 [China Trustee Association] (n 26) 62, 84; 谭振亭 [Tan Zhenting] (n 33) 199–200.

[78] 陈向聪 [Chen Xiangcong] (n 33) 278–9; 赵廉慧 [Zhao Lianhui] (n 33) 555; 谢哲胜 [Xie Zhesheng] (n 76) 219.

[79] The wording of article 50 of the Chinese Charity Law is: The establishment of a charitable trust, the management of trust assets, the parties to a trust, the termination and liquidation of a trust, etc., shall be governed by other relevant provisions herein in the absence of relevant provisions in this Chapter, and shall be governed by the Trust Law of the People's Republic of China in the absence of relevant provisions herein.

[80] The wording of article 63 of the Measures for Charitable Trusts is: In the event of any discrepancy between these Measures and relevant prior provisions on charitable trusts, these Measures shall prevail.

whole, prescribe that 'where (a) trustees dispose of trust assets in breach of trust purposes or (b) if losses are caused to the trust assets due to violation of their administrative duties or improper handling of trust affairs, beneficiaries have the right to petition the court to rescind such disposition or ask the trustee to restore trust assets to their former state'.[81] In light of these provisions, a beneficiary's right to sue is confined to a specific focus that solely deals with situations (a) and (b). Therefore, scenarios like trustees receiving commissions or bribes by taking advantage of their position, or trustees using trust assets to offer guarantees for their affiliated parties, are outside the scope of the beneficiary's right to sue as defined in articles 49 and 22 of the Chinese Trust Law.[82] Under the Chinese Trust Law, a beneficiary's right to sue is personal in nature.[83] The scenarios in which a beneficiary is entitled to initiate proceedings have all been prescribed by the Chinese Trust Law. This is in striking contrast to a beneficiary's right to sue in common law jurisdictions, under which the beneficiary's *locus standi* is derived from their proprietary entitlement in respect of the trust assets.[84]

81 Article 22 of the Chinese Trust Law is vague. It is unclear whether the expression 'causing losses to the trust property' is connected to 'disposition in breach of trust purpose'. One argument suggests that the availability of the remedy of rescission is premised on the fulfilment of two conditions: causing losses to the trust property and disposition in breach of trust purposes. See Ho, Lee and Jin (n 9) 95; 赵廉慧 [Zhao Lianhui] (n 33) 476; 卞耀武 [Bian Yaowu] (n 36) 92; 周小明 [Zhou Xiaoming] (n 36) 236. Another argument suggests that breach of the trust purpose alone is sufficient to trigger the remedy of rescission under article 22 of the Chinese Trust Law. See 何宝玉 [He Baoyu],《信托法原理研究》 [Research on the Jurisprudence of Trust Law] (中国政法大学出版社 [China University of Political Science and Law Press], 2005) 183;《吉林省建苑设计集团有限公司与四川信托有限公司信托纠纷案》 [Trust Dispute between Jilin Jianyuan Design Company and Sichuan Trust Company], 四川省成都市中级人民法院 [Chengdu Intermediate People's Court of Sichuan Province], 成民初字第2449号 [Civil Division, Initial Ruling, Case No 2449], 20 October 2016; Ho, *Trust Law in China* (n 9) 149.

82 See also analysis in Section III-B.

83 The beneficiary's right is also personal in nature in Japan, South Korea, and Taiwan. See Ying-Chieh Wu, 'Trusts Reimagined: The Transplantation and Evolution of Trust Law in Northeast Asia' (2020) 68(2) *American Journal of Comparative Law* 441, 459.

84 Objects under a discretionary trust have no proprietary interest in the trust assets, and the majority view is that they have no standing to sue. See *McPhail* v *Doulton* [1971] AC 424, 441; *Kambouris* v *Tahmazis* [2012] VSC 432, [12]; *Lygon Nominees Pty Ltd* v *Commissioner of State Revenue* [2005] VSC 247, [58]; *Walter* v *Registrar of Titles* [2003] VSCA 122, [15]; *Re Cooper Street Property Trust* [2016] VSC 756, [67]; *Richstar Enterprises Pty Ltd* v *Carey (No 6)* (2006) 233 ALR 475, [36]; Lionel Smith, 'Massively Discretionary Trusts' in Richard C. Nolan, Kelvin F. K. Low and Tang Hang Wu (eds.), *Trusts and Modern Wealth Management* (Cambridge University Press, 2018) 135. This majority view has been challenged by Peter Turner and Richard Nolan, see P. G. Turner,

Under the beneficiary argument, the beneficiary title of an object arises from the date of selection by the trustee and ends upon receipt of trust assets. Where the beneficiary status of an object has been ascertained, the scope of its right to sue and the situations in which litigation can be brought against a misbehaving trustee are to be determined by reference to articles 22 and 49 of the Chinese Trust Law. From a literal interpretation of situation (a) under article 22, selected objects with the beneficiary title may be entitled to sue in two circumstances. First, a trustee reneges on the distribution of trust assets to selected objects. Second, the trust benefits distributed are inconsistent with the time of distribution or with the amount or proportion of the trust assets specified in the distribution notice. These two situations lead to the loss of financial trust benefits on the part of the selected objects. Therefore, it is not difficult to interpret the trustee's misbehaviour as falling under 'disposing of trust assets in breach of trust purposes'.

Regarding situation (b) under article 22 – 'losses are caused to trust assets due to trustees' violation of their administrative duties or improper handling of trust affairs' – it is rare for selected objects to rely on this article to safeguard their interests in the proper distribution of trust assets. Unlike beneficiaries under express private trusts, objects under a charitable trust in most cases have limited channels to learn about the management of charitable assets. The information disclosed on the uniform platform Charity in China is sparse and incomplete to provide objects with a clear picture of the handling of trust affairs and the details of the establishment of a charitable trust.[85] While it may be possible for selected objects to know of their entitlement to a certain part of the trust assets from the distribution notice, it is difficult for them to learn about whether a trustee's management has caused losses to trust assets or whether trustees have improperly administered trust affairs. As long as objects' interests in the distribution of trust assets are not prejudiced, it is doubtful whether the objects have the incentive to supervise the trustees' daily management of charitable assets.

'The Entitlements of Objects as Defining Features of Discretionary Trusts' in Richard C. Nolan, Kelvin F. K. Low and Tang Hang Wu (eds.), *Trusts and Modern Wealth Management* (Cambridge University Press, 2018) 247–51; Richard Nolan, 'Invoking the Administrative Jurisdiction: The Enforcement of Modern Trust Structures' in Paul S. Davies and James Penner (eds.), *Equity, Trusts, and Commerce* (Hart, 2017) 160–8.

85 Dejian Li, 'Reform of Charity Governance in China: From Economic and Comparative Perspectives' (PhD Thesis, Faculty of Law, The University of Liverpool, 2017) 225–6.

It can, therefore, be concluded that, under the beneficiary argument, selected objects with the beneficiary title have the standing to sue, and their standing extends to the general administration of charitable trust affairs, as understood under the Chinese Trust Law. However, due to the wording of article 22 of the law, the scenarios under which objects are allowed to institute proceedings are considerably constrained. Also, due to the nature of charitable trust affairs, it is questionable to what extent an object may bring proceedings if a trustee's mismanagement is not relevant to the protection of its own interests in the trust assets.

2 The Recipient Argument

The recipient argument holds that objects that receive trust benefits are recipients, as opposed to beneficiaries as understood in the law of express private trusts. In this view, recipients have no standing to sue, as they are not trust parties and therefore have no right to interfere with trustees' management of charitable trusts.[86] While it appears that a recipient has no standing to sue in the charity law, this does not completely resolve the question. As discussed further in Sections IV-B-2(a) and (b), there is an argument that even without express granting of standing, a recipient may be able to rely on other general provisions in the law that give standing where a person can show harm to a 'direct interest'. As the argument in Sections IV-B-2(a) and (b) show, provisions of the Civil Procedure Law of the People's Republic of China (Civil Procedure Law)[87] and environmental public interest litigations (EPIL) give plaintiffs standing where they can show harm to a direct interest.

This section analyses the interpretation given to 'direct interest' in the two types of cases and considers whether that reasoning may be applied by analogy to the position of a recipient under a charitable trust. While it does not provide a definite answer to the question of the independent standing of a recipient in a charitable trust to sue, the analysis of the two types of cases does provide some indication of the current scope of the 'direct interest' as may be applied to determine the standing of a recipient who cannot otherwise demonstrate a separate right to standing to sue in relation to trustees' administration of charitable assets.

[86] 陈向聪 [Chen Xiangcong] (n 33) 278–9; 赵廉慧 [Zhao Lianhui] (n 33) 555; 谢哲胜 [Xie Zhesheng] (n 76) 219.

[87] 《中华人民共和国民事诉讼法》 [Civil Procedure Law of the People's Republic of China] (People's Republic of China) Standing Committee of the National People's Congress, 24 December 2021, art 122.

Article 122 of the Civil Procedure Law stipulates, 'To bring a lawsuit, the plaintiff must be a citizen, legal person or any other organization that has a direct interest in the case'. The phrase 'direct interest in the case'[88] may provide a basis for granting recipients standing to sue if they can show harm to a direct interest. However, the phrase itself has considerable uncertainty that may create impediments to its application to charitable trusts, since 'direct interest in the case' is not defined in the Civil Procedure Law, and 'the plain and ordinary meaning of the phrase is inexact'.[89] How should the meaning of 'direct interest' be understood in the context of Chinese procedural law? What criterion or criteria should be adopted when assessing whether an interest is direct or not? Does 'direct interest in a case' refer to a direct interest in the subject matter of the lawsuit? In what way and to what extent can a person be regarded as having a direct interest in the case? How direct should an interest be in order to be entitled to protection from Chinese courts? Interest is 'capable of a very wide and general meaning'.[90] Chinese lawmakers did not elaborate on the foregoing questions, and currently no judicial interpretations have been issued for clarification.

(a) Lessons from Private Interest Litigation In the absence of a clear definition of 'direct interest' in law, attention is paid to case law for the interpretation of this phrase. Although case law only plays a marginal role and is not legally binding for subsequent judgments in China, a close inspection of case law, especially cases adjudicated by the Supreme People's Court, can illuminate the factors that Chinese judges have considered in the analysis of standing to sue and shed light on the way to which the phrase 'direct interest in the case' is given effect in judicial practice.

Seventy-two cases adjudicated by the Supreme People's Court were examined for this study. It was found that, despite the lack of clear guidance for the interpretation of 'direct interest in the case', judicial interpretations of 'interest' are mainly focused on a claimant's civil rights

88 This phrase has had twenty-six years of history. It first appeared in article 108 of the Civil Procedure Law (1991) and has been incorporated into article 119 of the Civil Procedure Law (2012), article 119 of the Civil Procedure Law (2017), and article 122 of the Civil Procedure Law (2021).

89 *Re Cooper Street Property Trust* (n 84) [62].

90 *Gartside* v *Inland Revenue Commissioners* [1968] AC 553, 617.

or interests.[91] In the case of *Hu Yunhe* v *Yunnan Xinchao Ronghe Real Estate*, the Supreme People's Court held that the person who has direct interest in the case refers to one whose civil rights or interests are, or may be, adversely affected by the action of the defendant.[92] In cases adjudicated between 2014 and 2020, this interpretation has been extensively quoted and endorsed by courts at both national and provincial levels, and has also been incorporated into the guiding cases[93] issued by the Supreme People's Court.[94] This interpretation can provide insight into two scenarios concerning the standing of recipients under a charitable trust.

In the first scenario, recipients have been notified of the distribution of some of the charity's assets. However, this distribution did not occur within the agreed timeframe for distribution, and it was inconsistent with the amount or form notified by the charity trustees. In this scenario, it can be argued that recipients have been notified by the charity trustees

[91] 《中银投资有限公司与太原市北晨综合开发有限责任公司一般借款合同纠纷二审民事裁定书》 [Civil Order of the Second Instance of the General Loan Contract Dispute between Bank of China Investment Co Ltd and Taiyuan Beichen Comprehensive Development Co Ltd], 最高人民法院 [Supreme People's Court], 民二终字第38号 [Civil Division, Appeal Ruling, Case No 38], 15 June 2014;《杭州市西湖区西湖家园业主委员会与杭州安泰西湖房地产有限公司清算委员会房屋买卖合同纠纷申诉民事裁定书》 [Civil Order of the Appeal of the Housing Sales Contract Dispute between West Lake Home Owners Committee and the Liquidation Committee of Hangzhou Antai West Lake Real Estate Co Ltd], 最高人民法院 [Supreme People's Court], 民提字第100号 [Supreme People's Court, Civil Division, Case No 100], 29 October 2014.

[92] 《胡云河与云南鑫潮融和置业有限公司民间借贷纠纷二审民事裁定书》 [Civil Order of the Second Instance of the Private Lending Dispute between Hu Yunhe and Yunnan Xinchao Ronghe Real Estate Co Ltd], 最高人民法院 [Supreme People's Court], 民一终字第139号 [Civil Division, Appeal Ruling, Case No 139], 16 October 2013.

[93] The courts in China have already recognized the significance of uniformity and consistency in applying legal rules to cases. Regarding the role of guiding cases in judicial interpretations in China, see Shucheng Wang, 'Guiding Cases as a Form of Statutory Interpretation: Expansion of Supreme People's Court's Judicial Lawmaking Authority in China Law' (2018) 48(3) *Hong Kong Law Journal* 1067, 1075–8.

[94] See《吴振庆与哈尔滨现代房地产开发有限公司不当得利纠纷二审民事裁定书》 [Civil Order of the Second Instance of the Unjust Enrichment Dispute between Wu Zhenqing and Harbin Modern Real Estate Development Co Ltd], 最高人民法院 [Supreme People's Court], 最高法民终149号 [Civil Division, Appeal Ruling, Case No 149], 1 March 2017;《河北省直纪元房地产开发有限公司、河北省西山迎宾馆有限公司物权保护纠纷二审民事裁定书》 [Civil Order of the Second Instance of the Property Protection Dispute between Hebei Province Zhijiyuan Real Estate Development Co Ltd and Hebei Province Xi Shanying Hotel Co Ltd], 最高人民法院 [Supreme People's Court], 最高法民终764号 [Civil Division, Appeal Ruling, Case No 764], 16 December 2016.

and therefore already have an individual proprietary interest in the proper distribution of a certain part of charitable assets. Failure to distribute trust assets in compliance with the notice would result in individual losses to these recipients, thereby entitling them to bring proceedings according to the Civil Procedure Law.

In the second scenario, recipients have already received notice from the charity trustees. However, prior to distribution, they discovered the trustees' maladministration and honestly believed that this mismanagement might threaten the proper distribution of trust assets to them. In this scenario, the financial loss to the informed recipients seems imminently likely to occur, rather than merely speculative, and their interest in the proper distribution of trust assets has already materialised upon receiving the notice. Although the statute and the case law are unclear on whether recipients in this scenario have standing, it is arguable that the phrase 'direct interest in the case' can be construed generously to recognise their entitlement to launch litigation. Such an approach can be justified on two policy grounds. First, it serves the purpose of deterring wrongful conduct among charity trustees and protecting public benefit in the carrying out of charitable purposes. Second, it facilitates the invocation of a court's jurisdiction to supervise charitable trusts, so as to protect the public interest in the administration of charitable assets as much as possible.

(b) Lessons from EPIL Based on the analysis in Section IV-B-2(a), the next question to consider is how to define the scope of a recipient's standing. Is their standing limited to the personal interest they have in the trust assets? Or can their standing extend to the general administration of charitable trusts, irrespective of how much and what kind of interest they have in the trust assets? For example, if the recipients discover that the trust assets are poorly managed but such mismanagement would not threaten the distribution of a certain portion of trust assets to them, are they still allowed to bring proceedings in respect of the trustee's improper management of the charitable trust? The key issue behind this question is whether recipients can act as a 'private procurator acting for the public interest',[95] even when their individual interests are not substantially affected by the trustees' mismanagement.

[95] Matthew D. Zinn, 'Policing Environmental Regulatory Enforcement: Cooperation, Capture, and Citizen Suits' (2002) 21 *Stanford Environmental Law Journal* 81, 131. See also James M. Hecker, 'The Citizen's Role in Environmental Enforcement: Private Attorney General, Private Citizen, or Both' (1994) 8(4) *Natural Resources &*

The experience of EPIL may cast light on the questions noted in the previous paragraph. First, EPIL is concerned with public policies that share similar concerns (i.e., protecting public interest) as those of charitable trusts. Second, the criterion for the standing of recipients is expressed in the same terms (i.e., having a direct interest in the subject matter of the litigation) as that of EPIL. The way in which the courts have interpreted its scope and meaning in EPIL can provide some indication that may help determine the standing of recipients under a charitable trust.

(i) The Standing to Sue under EPIL Claims An examination of case law and scholarly writings suggests that three aspects of the institution of EPIL are relevant to our discussion. First, judicial practice has shown that the question of whether individuals are entitled to voice complaints about environmental damage through EPIL is still addressed by interpreting the term 'direct interest'; namely, whether individuals have a direct interest in the outcome of the defendant's acts undermining the environment.[96] The judgment in No 2 of Ten Guiding Cases Regarding Environmental Public Interest Litigations[97] observes that, due to the public nature of the environment, no individual can be said to have a direct interest in the subject matter of an EPIL. In this light, individuals have no entitlement to file EPIL cases due to their failure to satisfy the direct interest test. Second, the institution of EPIL serves to protect the interests of the entire community. In other words, protecting public (not private) interests lies at the heart of EPIL.[98] Individuals whose interests have been severely

Environment 31, 32; Harold Feld, 'Saving the Citizen Suit: The Effect of Lujan v Defenders of Wildlife and the Role of Citizen Suits in Environmental Enforcement' (1994) 19 *Columbia Journal of Environmental Law* 141, 144.

96 Rachel E. Stern, *Environmental Litigation in China: A Study in Political Ambivalence* (Cambridge University Press, 2013) 218; 巩固 [Gong Gu],《大同小异抑或貌合神离? 中美环境公益诉讼比较研究》 [Looking Like Twins: Comparative Research on Environmental Public Interest Litigation between China and United States] (2017) 2 比较法研究 *Journal of Comparative Law* 105, 115, 117.

97 最高人民法院审判委员会 [Judicial Committee of the Supreme People's Court],《最高法发布十起环境公益诉讼典型案例之二: 中国生物多样性保护与绿色发展基金会诉宁夏瑞泰科技股份有限公司环境污染公益诉讼案》 (2016年12月28日) [No 2 of Ten Guiding Cases Regarding Environmental Public Interest Litigations Published by the Supreme People's Court: *China Biodiversity Conservation and Green Development Foundation* v *Ningxia Ruitai Science and Technology Co Ltd*] (28 December 2016).

98 最高人民法院审判委员会 [Judicial Committee of the Supreme People's Court],《最高法发布十起环境公益诉讼典型案例之九: 贵州省六盘水市六枝特区人民检察院诉贵州省镇宁布依族苗族自治县丁旗镇人民政府环境行政公益诉讼案》 (2016年12月28日)

prejudiced due to environmentally damaging acts are allowed to institute litigation under Chinese tort law or property law. Such actions are by nature private litigations, unlike EPIL. Third, the courts are obliged to consider a wide range of policy and social factors when adjudicating EPIL cases. Take government-controlled projects for example. These projects are initiated by local governments, and their execution is supposed to benefit the larger community or society as a whole. Are citizens allowed to institute proceedings to strike them down? The exploration of this question requires consideration of the objectives underlying the projects, the detriments and benefits of the proceedings against the projects, and the substance of the interests that the claimants may have in the execution of these projects. There are also other general policy concerns. For example, would natural persons harass the courts with frivolous and hopeless lawsuits? To what extent may citizen lawsuits contribute to the monitoring of environmental pollution or to an entity's compliance with laws or regulations?[99]

Taking into account the concerns just noted, the current approach that Chinese legislators have adopted for EPIL is to empower qualified social organizations[100] and the people's procuratorate to file lawsuits against activities that pollute the environment, cause ecological damage, or harm the public interest.[101] This approach envisages a balance between the protection of the public interest in EPIL and the prevention of vexatious

[No 9 of Ten Guiding Cases regarding Environmental Public Interest Litigations Published by the Supreme People's Court: *People's Procuratorate of Liuzhi Special District of Liupanshui City, Guizhou Province* v *People's Government of Dingqi Township, Zhenning Buyi and Miao Autonomous County, Guizhou Province* – Environmental Administrative Public Interest Litigation] (28 December 2016).

99 Mark Seidenfeld and Janna Satz Nugent, 'The Friendship of the People: Citizen Participation in Environmental Enforcement' (2005) 73 *George Washington Law Review* 269, 299; 巩固 [Gong Gu],《2015年中国环境民事公益诉讼的实证分析》[An Empirical Analysis of China's Environmental Civil Public Interest Litigation in 2015] (2016) 9 法学 *Law Science* 16, 17–18; Zinn (n 95) 118–19.

100 'Qualified social organizations' here refer to those registered with the civil affairs department of the people's government at or above the level of a city with districts and engaged in public service activities in environmental protection for five consecutive years without any record of violation of laws. See《中华人民共和国环境保护法》[Environmental Protection Law of the People's Republic of China] (People's Republic of China) Standing Committee of the National People's Congress, 24 April 2014, art 58.

101《最高人民法院关于审理环境民事公益诉讼案件适用法律若干问题的解释》[Interpretations of the Supreme People's Court on Several Issues Concerning the Application of Law in the Hearing of Environmental Civil Public Interest Lawsuits] (People's Republic of China) Supreme People's Court, 7 January 2015, art 11.

and meaningless litigation. The granting of standing to qualified social organizations and to the people's procuratorate is a matter of public policy. The social organizations and the procuratorate are selected to represent the interests of the entire community and have been considered as having a direct interest in the outcome of the acts undermining the environment. Allowing them to sue increases the probability of exposing environmentally damaging activities to the courts, thereby enhancing the capacity of the courts to safeguard the public's environmental interests.[102]

At the same time, not all social organizations are eligible to bring EPIL claims: only those that have no record of violation of laws and have engaged in environmental protection activities for five consecutive years are entitled to institute proceedings.[103] The setting up of a protective filter – limiting the standing to qualified social organizations and the people's procuratorate – points to the other end of this balancing act; that is, preventing the courts from being harassed with meaningless lawsuits. In comparison to private individuals, the selected social organizations and the procuratorate have resources in funding and staff to address EPIL.[104] Before initiating an EPIL suit, such organizations will assess whether the activities concerned truly damage the public environment, what the potential social consequences flowing from the launching of such litigation are, and how the courts may look at this litigation in light of the cases they have adjudicated in the past. This holistic assessment minimizes the risk of wasting judicial resources on merely speculative cases and assists the courts in focusing their attention on addressing environmentally damaging activities that have already occurred or are imminently likely to occur.

(ii) Implications for the Chinese Charitable Trust Given the foregoing analysis, what insights can be derived from EPIL when analysing a recipient's standing to sue under the Chinese charitable trust legislation? Charitable trusts and EPIL share similar policy concerns in terms of

102 王丽萍 [Wang Liping],《突破环境公益诉讼启动的瓶颈: 适格原告扩张与激励机制构建》 [Breaking the Bottleneck of Initiating Environmental Public Interest Litigation: Expansion of Standing and Construction of Incentive Mechanisms] (2017) 3 法学论坛 *Legal Forum* 89, 93.

103 《中华人民共和国环境保护法》 [Environmental Protection Law of the People's Republic of China] (People's Republic of China) Standing Committee of the National People's Congress, 24 April 2014 (n 100) art 58.

104 王丽萍 [Wang Liping] (n 102) 93.

protecting the public interest, and the criterion for the standing of recipients under charitable trusts is expressed in the same terms as that for EPIL. These similarities provide the basis for drawing insights from the EPIL when analysing the standing of recipients under a charitable trust. At the same time, differences do exist between EPIL and charitable trusts that may limit the extent to which the experience of EPIL can be referenced.

Two major differences are summarized here. First, in EPIL claims, environmental injuries are frequently probabilistic; for instance, the increased possibility of getting a serious disease owing to continuous exposure to toxic materials in the air.[105] It is, therefore, difficult to exactly define the number of practical or potential victims under the EPIL. In comparison, in a charitable trust where the charitable purpose and the selection criteria are specified, it is not hard for a trustee to ascertain the list of potential recipients for the purpose of distributing charitable assets. Second, charitable trust claims are, by nature, jurisdictionally distinct from those brought under the EPIL. In contrast to the public law-leaning tendency of EPIL, the charitable trust is a public law–private law hybrid[106] where private law norms are essential to its establishment and ongoing administration. The checks and balances between trust parties are vital to the supervision of a trustee's performance of their duties. In contrast, the EPIL stands entirely within the public law sphere, and the initiation of EPIL proceedings is heavily reliant on public organs and selected social organizations.

Given the similarities and differences mentioned in the previous paragraph, the experience of the EPIL suggests that, in analysing the standing of a recipient, a distinction can be made between a recipient's claim in respect of their own interest in the trust assets and a claim in respect of the trustee's general administration of charitable trusts. The denial of a citizen's standing in EPIL does not necessarily exclude the possibility of granting standing to recipients under a charitable trust. Where a recipient can show harm to their direct interest in the distribution of charitable assets, article 122 of the Civil Procedure Law can be referenced to determine the recipient's standing to sue. Where a recipient brings proceedings for the purpose of holding the trustee accountable to its management of charitable trust, rather than for the purpose of claiming its own interest in the trust assets, the experience of EPIL

[105] Feld (n 95) 163.

[106] See analysis in Section III of Chapter 2.

suggests that a lenient approach may be taken in the determination of standing to sue. The policy concerns underlying the creation and regulation of charitable trusts are relevant to the analysis of a recipient's entitlement to sue. Because of the public interest in the enforcement of charitable trusts, courts may tend towards a lenient approach in their interpretation of 'direct interest in the case'. This approach may increase the possibility of exposing charity trustees' misconduct to the courts and facilitate the protection of the public interest in the distribution of charitable assets as much as possible. Yet, from the foregoing analysis, two further questions arise. How generous could the interpretation of the principles governing standing to sue be in light of the policy aspects of Chinese charitable trusts? How should a balance be struck between the promotion of charitable causes and the avoidance of vexatious litigation in the charitable trust context? The experience of the EPIL is not particularly helpful in resolving these questions.

V Conclusion

This chapter has analysed the internal relationship between trust parties in the legal governance framework for charitable trusts. This analysis raised two key observations. The first relates to the tension between settlors and trustees in the legal governance framework. The settlor is granted extensive powers by law, while the trustee is burdened by law with onerous duties. This legislative approach allows settlors to not only define the ways in which charitable trusts are administered but also be proactive in supervising the performance of trustees' duties or responsibilities. This approach is consistent with the private law norms in the legal structure of charitable trusts.

The legislative regime governing charitable trusts is also incomplete and vague in various respects. This chapter has explored the areas where the legal governance is vague and the legal uncertainties that arise therefrom. It showed that the vagueness of the law may pose two types of risks to a trustee's management of charitable trusts. First, settlors are empowered to intervene intensively in the administration of charitable trust affairs. The impreciseness of the scope of settlors' powers and how they should be exercised can lead to disputes between settlors and trustees with respect to the management of charitable trusts. Second, trustees are obliged to perform their duties in alignment with the trust's charitable purposes. However, the law does not elaborate the scope of trustees' duties and how trustees should interact with settlors. This ambiguity makes it difficult for trustees to assess whether their management is compliant with the requirements of the law and regulatory measures. Furthermore, the lack of clear criteria for assessing a trustee's performance makes it easy for the public to criticise their management of charitable trusts. The two types of risks together motivate settlors and trustees to take actions to clarify their powers and duties and to define the ways in which they should interact. These private actions will be discussed in more detail in Chapter 5.

The second key observation raised by the analysis in this chapter relates to the role of beneficiaries in the governance framework of charitable trusts. The charity law adopts the term 'beneficiary' but makes no mention of what powers or rights a beneficiary may have in the governance setting. Academics and practitioners have proposed two arguments about the nature of charitable trust beneficiaries: the beneficiary argument and the recipient argument. This chapter has examined how beneficiaries may play a supervisory role under each argument. The beneficiary argument indicates that the object with the title of beneficiary is entitled to sue where trustees cause losses to trust assets due to the violation of their duties or improper handling of trust affairs. However, due to the language of the Chinese Trust Law, the scenarios under which objects are allowed to institute proceedings are considerably constrained. Moreover, because of the nature of charitable trust affairs, it is questionable to what extent an object may institute proceedings if a trustee's mismanagement is not relevant to the protection of the particular beneficiary's interests in the trust assets.

In contrast, the recipient argument suggests that recipients have no standing to sue, as they are not trust parties and thus have no right to interfere with a trustee's management of charitable trusts. It appears that a recipient has no standing to sue in the charity law, but this does not entirely resolve the question. Under the recipient argument, this chapter has examined the Civil Procedure Law and EPIL and considered whether the reasoning of 'direct interest' in these two cases may be applied by analogy to the position of recipients under a charitable trust. This examination showed that a recipient may be able to sue if they can show harm to a direct interest. For example, if recipients have already received notice from charity trustees, it can be argued that their proprietary interest in the proper distribution of a certain part of charitable assets has materialized. Therefore, recipients may be entitled to bring proceedings if the distribution of trust assets does not comply with the notice. On the other hand, it is still unclear whether recipients have standing to sue where they have no substantial interest in the outcome of a trustee's mismanagement. Through examining the similarities and differences between charitable trusts and EPIL, it was found that a lenient approach can be taken where a recipient brings proceedings for the purpose of holding the trustee accountable to its management of charitable trust, rather than for the purpose of claiming its own interest in the trust assets. However, how lenient could the approach be in light of the policy aspects of Chinese charitable trusts? In what way ought a sensible balance be struck between the promotion of charitable undertakings and the prevention of frivolous lawsuits in the charitable trust setting? These questions remain unanswered under the recipient argument.

4

Administrative Regulation

I Introduction

Chapter 2 engaged in an analysis of the public law–private law nature of Chinese charitable trusts and argued that this hybrid nature permeates and informs the design of the governance framework for such trusts. Chapter 3 analysed legal provisions in relation to the relationship between trust parties and argued that the vagueness of the law has created multifaceted layers of uncertainty regarding the scope of settlors' powers and how they should be exercised, the scope of trustees' duties, the relationship between settlors and trustees, and the legal nature and role of the beneficiaries under charitable trusts. Chapter 4 now turns to an analysis of the practice of the regulatory oversight of charitable trusts. The key questions examined in this chapter involve the powers granted to regulators and how they are exercised in practice. In Chinese law, it is unclear how regulatory powers should be exercised over charitable trusts and what obligations regulators have when performing their supervisory roles. Interviews with actors who have experience with charitable trusts suggest that, in practice, regulators tend to take a proactive role in the creation and ongoing administration of these trusts. In this chapter, I further explore how the vagueness in the law has motivated regulators to adopt strategies to implement the law in ways that minimize risks to themselves.

Meanwhile, as government organs, regulators are required to follow the directives of the central government in China. Legislators introduced the charitable trust model to further and develop charitable undertakings defined by the state. The social and policy environment in which charitable trusts are established and operate is significant in determining how regulators engage with the law. This chapter examines both the legislative framework and regulatory practice. It considers the degree to which regulators are responsive to extra-legal concerns in the exercise of their powers. Three of these concerns are examined: the regional development agenda, the tension between regulatory capacity and regulatory objectives, and regulators' perceptions of risk. According to the findings, extra-legal concerns supplement, and sometimes prevail over, legal rules in guiding the supervisory work of regulators.

Drawing on the interview data collected, this chapter analyses the regulation of Chinese charitable trusts by exploring three questions. First, what are the statutory powers assigned to regulators? Second, how have these powers been exercised by regulators? Third, what measures are undertaken by regulators? The legislators who introduced the charitable trust model were influenced by public welfare trusts. Therefore, comparisons with public welfare trusts will be conducted where appropriate in order to delineate the unique characteristics of the regulatory framework for charitable trusts. Based on the examination of the above three questions, the chapter then discusses the administrative style of charitable trust regulation. The strategies adopted by regulators to guide the performance of their responsibilities are examined, with the purpose of identifying the factors shaping the regulatory framework and the way in which these factors take effect under the administration and supervision of charitable trusts.

II The Structure of the Regulatory Framework

As analysed in Chapter 2, prior to the promulgation of the Chinese Charity Law in 2016, there was another institution performing the same function as charitable trusts, namely public welfare trusts. In contrast to charitable trusts, the responsibility for the regulation of public welfare trusts was shared by civil affairs departments, bureaus of public security, and a wide range of government organs or agencies at provincial, municipal, and county levels. This fragmented system governing public welfare trusts[1] contributed to rising compliance costs on the part of trust parties and dissuaded people from establishing public welfare trusts. At the same time, it also gave rise to the recommendation for the establishment of an independent regulator for charitable trusts.[2]

[1] See analysis in Section II-A of Chapter 2.

[2] 吕鑫 [Lyu Xin],《从公益信托到慈善信托：跨国移植及其本土建构》[From Public Welfare Trusts to Charitable Trusts: Transnational Transplantation and Local Construction] (2019) 10 社会科学战线 *Social Science Front* 199, 203–4.

This thinking materialized in the enactment of article 6 of the Chinese Charity Law[3] and article 6 of the Measures for Charitable Trusts.[4] Under these two articles, banking regulatory authorities (BRAs) and civil affairs departments (CADs) were empowered to regulate the creation and day-to-day administration of charitable trusts. The law endows these two regulators with extensive powers, such as the powers to assess charitable trusts and revoke the registration licenses of trustees. These powers enable the regulators to intervene extensively in the creation and ongoing administration of charitable trusts. However, similar to the vagueness of the law regarding the internal relationship between settlors and trustees, it is also vague on the role of regulators and the relationship between regulators and trust parties. The law does not clearly define what these regulatory powers entail and how they should be exercised; neither does it provide a clear definition of the liability of regulators for the unlawful performance of their powers and responsibilities. This vagueness creates scope for regulators to consider extra-legal factors when determining how to engage with the law.

Sections II-A, II-B, and II-C discuss the structure of the regulatory framework for charitable trusts. This discussion is spread over three parts. The first relates to the relationship between the two regulators in the contexts of law and practice. The second relates to the legal powers that these regulators can exercise in the creation and ongoing administration of charitable trusts and how these powers are exercised in practice. The third part relates to the educative measures that the two regulators have taken to encourage the development of charitable trusts and exercise their supervisory powers in China.

A The Relationship between CADs and BRAs

1 The Domain of Law

Article 6 of the Measures for Charitable Trusts stipulates that CADs and BRAs are responsible for regulating the creation and administration of charitable trusts. However, the law and explanatory memoranda do not provide a clear definition of the relationship between the two regulators.

[3] 《中华人民共和国慈善法》 [Charity Law of the People's Republic of China] (People's Republic of China) National People's Congress, 16 March 2016.

[4] 《慈善信托管理办法》 [Administrative Measures for Charitable Trusts] (People's Republic of China) China Banking Regulatory Commission and Ministry of Civil Affairs, 10 July 2017.

A possible clue regarding their relationship, however, may be drawn from article 48 of the Measures for Charitable Trusts: CADs and BRAs 'shall establish a regular regulatory cooperation mechanism to strengthen an interim and ex post regulation, and effectively improve the effectiveness of regulatory operations'. The wording of article 48 indicates that there is, or should be, a cooperative relationship between the two regulators; however, the key unanswered question is what this cooperation mechanism looks like in law and practice.

Articles 47, 49, and 51 of the Measures for Charitable Trusts may provide insights into this cooperative mechanism. Two observations can be drawn here. First, the law prescribes collaboration between BRAs and CADs in supervising the administration of charitable trusts – BRAs are 'responsible for the supervision of charitable trust businesses of trust companies and the custody of funds in charitable trust accounts by commercial banks';[5] CADs 'at and above the county level are responsible for the recording of charitable trusts and their related supervision and administration'.[6] A good illustration of this cooperation mechanism is the exercise of the power to revoke registration licenses. The current law states that, where trustees commit violations in administering trust affairs, depending on the identity and nature of the trustee in question, BRAs are empowered to revoke the registration licenses of the trust companies[7] concerned and that CADs are empowered to revoke the registration licenses of charitable organizations.[8]

The second observation relates to the considerable overlap between CADs and BRAs in the exercise of statutory powers. According to the law, both CADs and BRAs are empowered to inspect trustees in the performance of their duties;[9] entrust third-party agencies to assess the management of charitable trusts[10] and conduct supervisory conversations (*jianguan tanhua* 监管谈话) with the principal persons in charge of

[5] Ibid., art 47.

[6] Ibid.

[7] 《信托公司管理办法》 [Measures for Administration of Trust Companies] (People's Republic of China) China Banking Regulatory Commission, 23 January 2007, art 59.

[8] 《中华人民共和国慈善法》 [Charity Law of the People's Republic of China] (People's Republic of China) National People's Congress, 16 March 2016 (n 3) art 98.

[9] 《慈善信托管理办法》[Administrative Measures for Charitable Trusts] (People's Republic of China) China Banking Regulatory Commission and Ministry of Civil Affairs, 10 July 2017 (n 4) art 49.

[10] Ibid., art 50.

charitable trusts.[11] However, the law is silent on how the two regulators should cooperate with each other in exercising these overlapping powers. Should they communicate and reach a consensus before issuing regulatory decisions? Should they exercise powers separately without communicating? These questions remain persistent and need to be clarified in future judicial interpretation or legislation.

2 The Practice Domain

What the law says is not necessarily consistent with practice, for 'all jurisdictions have some gap between aspirational rules and their practical enforcement'.[12] The relationship between the two regulators is illustrative of this point. The law stipulates that CADs should cooperate with BRAs in the regulation of charitable trusts.[13] Based on this understanding, the next question focuses on the manner in which this cooperation mechanism operates in practice. Answering this question will help re-examine the legislative arrangements for the assignment of powers to the two regulators. An examination of interview data suggests two findings relating to this question. First, there are no streamlined means of data exchange between the two regulators. Without clear data-sharing processes between CADs and BRAs, it is highly likely that the current regulatory framework will impose 'reporting red tape'[14] on recorded charitable trusts. Among the actors interviewed, three trustee managers[15] expressed that they had been asked to submit similar or duplicate reports to different regulators.

Second, it is questionable whether BRAs are appropriate regulators for charitable trusts. As opposed to the flourishing development of charitable trusts in common law,[16] nearly 80 per cent of the trusts created in China

[11] Ibid., art 51.

[12] Tarunabh Khaitan, *A Theory of Discrimination Law* (Oxford University Press, 2015) 13.

[13] 《慈善信托管理办法》[Administrative Measures for Charitable Trusts] (People's Republic of China) China Banking Regulatory Commission and Ministry of Civil Affairs, 10 July 2017 (n 4) art 48.

[14] Australian Charities and Not-for-profits Commission, *Strengthening for Purpose: Australian Charities and Not-for-Profits Commission Legislative Review* (2018) 106.

[15] See interviews with T1, T5, and T7.

[16] Kathryn Chan, *The Public–Private Nature of Charity Law* (Hart, 2016) 22; Alison Dunn, 'As Cold as Charity: Poverty, Equity and the Charitable Trust' (2000) 20 *Legal Studies* 222, 223; Allan D. Vestal, 'Critical Evaluation of the Charitable Trust as a Giving Device' (1957) 1957(3) *Washington University Law Review* 195, 195–6; John H. Langbein, 'The Secret Life of the Trust: The Trust as an Instrument of Commerce' (1997) 107 *Yale Law Journal* 165, 188.

are commercial in nature.[17] The Chinese Trust Law and its subordinated legal instruments are all centred on the regulation of commercial businesses operated by trust companies. Regulatory practice over the last two decades has enabled BRAs to gain extensive experience in supervising commercial trust businesses. These commercial trust businesses focus on providing private benefits to individuals (e.g., settlors and trust companies) whose objectives are fundamentally different from those of charitable trust businesses. A series of notices (*tongzhi* 通知) or opinions (*yijian* 意见) have been issued by BRAs to assist trust companies in controlling or preventing risks (e.g., liquidity risk, credit risk, or market risk) arising from the operation of commercial trust businesses.[18] However, the extent to which BRAs are capable of supervising the administration of charitable trusts remains unclear.

Regulatory practice shows that, compared to the BRAs, CADs currently play a dominant role in the supervision of charitable trusts[19] and face greater policy pressure in the regulation of charitable trusts.[20] Although the law does not elaborate on how the two regulators should cooperate with each other in the exercise of their powers, CADs have tended to take measures to specify what the law says about their roles and how their powers can be exercised in practice. CADs are also willing to issue letters or notices to inspect whether charitable trusts are administered in

[17] 中国人民大学信托与基金研究所 [Institute of Trust and Fund of Renmin University of China],《中国信托业发展报告（2018）》[The Development Report of Chinese Trust Business (2018)] (中国经济出版社 [China Economic Publishing House], 2018) 113–15; Lusina Ho, 'Business Trusts in China: A Reality Check' (2020) 88(3) *University of Cincinnati Law Review* 767, 768; Lingyun Gao, 'The Development of Private Trusts in Mainland China: Legal Obstacles and Solutions' (2014) 20(4) *Trusts & Trustees* 350, 350–1.

[18] 《中国银监会办公厅关于进一步加强信托公司风险监管工作的意见》 [Opinions of the General Office of the China Banking Regulatory Commission on Further Strengthening the Work of Supervising the Risks of Trust Companies] China Banking Regulatory Commission, 18 March 2016, s 2;《中国银行业监督管理委员会办公厅关于信托公司房地产信托业务风险提示的通知》[Notice of the General Office of the China Banking Regulatory Commission on Risk Reminders for the Real Estate Trust Business of Trust Companies] (People's Republic of China) General Office of the China Banking Regulatory Commission, 12 November 2010;《中国银监会办公厅关于进一步明确信托公司风险监管责任的通知》[Notice by the General Office of the China Insurance Regulatory Commission of Further Clarifying the Risk Supervision Responsibilities of Trust Companies] China Banking Regulatory Commission, 25 June 2013.

[19] See interviews with R1, R2, and R3.

[20] See analysis in Section III-B.

alignment with the state's public welfare policy.[21] In contrast, BRAs have not played a proactive role in supervising trustees in the performance of their roles. Contrary to CADs, BRAs do not suffer under intense policy and administrative pressures in the regulation of charitable trusts, which is outside the focus of their supervisory work. Thus, BRAs do not have strong incentives to specify what procedures they should follow in order to exercise their powers and how they should interact with charity trustees in the day-to-day management of charitable trusts. Where risks in relation to the administration of charitable trusts arise, BRAs may consult relevant CADs to determine what measures should be taken and what administrative punishments (if any) could be imposed on trustees.[22]

B The Content and Scope of Regulatory Powers

With the existence of numerous policies regarding the intensive supervision of charitable activities,[23] CADs and BRAs, as specialized regulators of Chinese charitable trusts, are endowed by law with wide regulatory and supervisory powers to approve the establishment of charitable trusts and supervise their ongoing administration. In the creation phase, CADs are empowered to determine whether or not a charitable trust can be recorded. Where a charitable trust is legally established, the two regulators have the powers to ask trustees to submit annual reports, revoke the registration licenses of trustees, assess the operation of charitable trusts, and conduct supervisory conversations. This legislative arrangement allows regulators to maintain a high degree of control over the creation and ongoing administration of charitable trusts. Sections II-B-1 and II-B-2 discuss the content and scope of these regulatory powers and the ways in which the two regulators exercise these powers in practice.

21 See interviews with R1, R2, L1, and L2.

22 See interviews with L1, L2, L3, L5, L9, T5, and A6.

23 《国务院关于促进慈善事业健康发展的指导意见》 [Guiding Opinions of the State Council on Promoting Healthy Development of Charitable Causes] (People's Republic of China) State Council, 24 November 2014, ch 4;《民政部关于贯彻落实<国务院关于促进慈善事业健康发展的指导意见>的通知》[Notice of the Ministry of Civil Affairs on Implementing the 'Guiding Opinions of the State Council on Promoting the Healthy Development of Charitable Causes'] (People's Republic of China) Ministry of Civil Affairs of People's Republic of China, 15 December 2014, chs 2–3;《中国慈善事业发展指导纲要（2011–2015年）》[Guidelines for the Development of China's Charitable Causes (2011–2015)] (People's Republic of China) Ministry of Civil Affairs, 15 July 2011, ch 3.

1 The Creation of Charitable Trusts

Pursuant to article 15 of the Measures for Charitable Trusts, CADs at or above the county level have the power to determine whether or not a charitable trust can be recorded (bei'an 备案). Prior to the enactment of the Chinese Charity Law, a public welfare trust came into existence only when the settlors or trustees obtained approval from public welfare administration authorities.[24] This approval requirement endowed relevant authorities with a high level of discretion to reject applications in cases where, according to their judgement, the purpose of a trust was considered inconsistent with the public welfare purposes prescribed by law. Second, the Chinese Trust Law provides no criteria for the identification of relevant administration authorities for the establishment of public welfare trusts. Responsibilities for the registration of public welfare trusts may be shared by CADs, bureaus of public security, and a wide range of government organs or agencies, depending on the purpose of the trust, the identity of relevant trust parties, and the activities that the trust intends to carry out.[25] The parties to public welfare trusts thus need to consult various government organs to determine the recipient of a registration application. Due to these two reasons, no more than twenty public welfare trusts have been successfully established over the last two decades.[26] In view of the experience of public welfare trusts, the charity law stipulates that CADs and BRAs are specialized regulators, with recording (*bei'an* 备案) enacted as the measure for the creation of charitable trusts.[27]

The law makes no mention of the legal nature of recording or the distinction between recording and registration (*dengji* 登记). The interviewees had a range of views on these two issues. Seven of them[28] reported that the examination conducted by regulators regarding the creation of a charitable trust should be formal rather than substantive, with the majority

[24] 《中华人民共和国信托法》 [Trust Law of the People's Republic of China] (People's Republic of China) National People's Congress, 28 April 2001, art 62.

[25] See also analysis in Section II of Chapter 3.

[26] For details on these established public welfare trusts, see 赵廉慧 [Zhao Lianhui], 《信托法解释论》 [Interpretative Theory of Trust Law] (中国法制出版社 [China Legal Publishing House], 2015) 526–9.

[27] 《慈善信托管理办法》[Administrative Measures for Charitable Trusts] (People's Republic of China) China Banking Regulatory Commission and Ministry of Civil Affairs, 10 July 2017 (n 4) ch 3; 《中华人民共和国慈善法》 [Charity Law of the People's Republic of China] (People's Republic of China) National People's Congress, 16 March 2016 (n 3) art 45.

[28] See interviews with L8, L9, A1, A2, A3, A6, and A7.

of them[29] holding that, in practice, the examination is substantive as opposed to formal. There have been cases in which applications for recording were declined by the CADs in Beijing and Shanghai, although the documents submitted were in full compliance with the requirements specified by law and, thus, ought to have been recorded. Four of the ten lawyers with recording experience stressed that, in practice, the CADs in Beijing, Shanghai, Shenzhen, and Guangzhou have a high degree of discretion in the recording of charitable trusts. For example, three lawyers[30] said that the regulatory officials in Beijing have refused to record open-ended charitable trusts (the term ‘open-ended’ means that the trust properties can be increased and that the criteria for selecting beneficiaries can be changed during the ongoing operation of a charitable trust) and, more importantly, there has been no legal recourse against the refusal of such applications. In contrast, the CADs in Guangzhou and Shanghai are more positive about recording open-ended charitable trusts. In fact, the recording information on the Charity in China platform shows that more than ten open-ended charitable trusts have successfully been recorded in these two cities.

The three regulatory officials interviewed held that the recording of charitable trusts was in fact a substantive, not formal, examination.[31] The interviewees provided two reasons for this. First, since the law does not clearly define the legal nature of recording or provide guidance on the relationship between recording and registration, regulators have the discretion to determine the type of examination. Second, charitable trusts are still in their infancy and, therefore, regulators elect to exercise substantive examination of the trust documents to determine possible risks[32] in relation to the creation of charitable trusts. Pre-communication practice in Shanghai, Beijing, and Guangzhou provides evidence of this thinking. Before submitting documents to CADs for recording, trustees often first communicate with relevant officials on certain issues, including the nature and scope of the charitable purpose, the criteria for selecting beneficiaries, the scale and type of trust assets, and the identity of each trust party. In this process, the regulatory officials concerned often provide advice to the trust parties regarding ambiguous terms in

29 See interviews with R1, R2, R3, T1, T2, T3, T6, T7, L1, L2, and L5.

30 See interviews with L1, L2, and L3.

31 See interviews with R1, R2, and R3.

32 See analysis in Section III.

the trust documents and how they should be modified.[33] From the perspective of trustees, submitting recording applications is futile and a waste of time for both parties, unless the terms of the trust documents already meet all the regulators' requirements.[34]

2 The Ongoing Administration of Charitable Trusts

In the ongoing administration of charitable trusts, both CADs and BRAs are empowered to assess the operation of charitable trusts, conduct supervisory conversations, and require information disclosure. The law grants these two regulators wide supervisory powers but does not clearly define what these powers entail and how they should be exercised.

(a) Power to Assess Charitable Trusts The law stipulates that CADs and BRAs can entrust third-party agencies[35] to assess (*pinggu* 评估) whether charitable trust affairs are managed in alignment with regulatory measures and whether charitable trust assets are used in compliance with charitable purposes.[36] Assessment is not unique to charitable trusts. The Ministry of Civil Affairs of the People's Republic of China issued the Administrative Measures for the Assessment of Social Organizations (hereinafter the Measures for Assessment)[37] on 20 December 2010, with the objective of regulating the assessment of social associations, foundations, and privately-operated non-enterprise entities registered at CADs at all levels of the government.[38] In response to this national law, subnational CADs issued local guidance and administrative measures concerning the assessment of social organizations in their own jurisdictions.[39]

33 See analysis in Section III of Chapter 5.

34 See interviews with L1, L2, L5, L8, T1, T3, T5, T6, and T7.

35 The agencies here mainly refer to accounting firms and legal firms. See interviews with R2, A1, A2, and A6.

36 《慈善信托管理办法》[Administrative Measures for Charitable Trusts] (People's Republic of China) China Banking Regulatory Commission and Ministry of Civil Affairs, 10 July 2017 (n 4) art 50.

37 《社会组织评估管理办法》 [Administrative Measures for the Assessment of Social Organizations] (People's Republic of China) Ministry of Civil Affairs, 20 December 2010.

38 Ibid., arts 1–3.

39 See 《天津市社会组织评估管理办法》 [Administrative Measures for the Assessment and Management of Social Organizations in Tianjin] (People's Republic of China) Tianjin Civil Affairs Bureau, 28 May 2012; 《深圳市社会组织评估管理办法（试行）》 [Administrative Measures for the Assessment and Management of Social Organizations in Shenzhen (Trial)] (People's Republic of China) Shenzhen Civil Affairs Bureau, 21 September 2011; 《广州市社会组织评估管理办法》 [Administrative Measures for the Assessment and Management of Social Organizations in Guangzhou] (People's Republic of China)

Pursuant to articles 9 and 10 of the Measures for Assessment, assessment committees for social organizations were set up by CADs at each level and are responsible for developing assessment plans, forming assessment expert teams, organizing assessments, and announcing assessment results.[40]

Two questions emerge from looking at the assessment of charitable trusts: (1) what is the working system or mechanism for assessing charitable trusts?; and (2) what is the identity of the third-party assessment agency? As no government documents or laws have been issued for reference, these questions remain unanswerable. Over the last three years, CADs at both the central and local levels have carried out numerous collaborative research projects on the assessment of charitable trusts with independent research institutes or Chinese universities. The main topics of these research projects include the following: the specification of assessment indices for charitable trusts,[41] the criteria for appointing assessment agencies, the powers of these agencies, and the way in which they receive remuneration.[42] Prior to the clarification of these issues, CADs in Beijing, Shanghai, Guangzhou, and Hangzhou were disinclined to conduct assessment work over the operation of charitable trusts,[43] as evidenced by the complete absence of assessment work conducted in any of these four cities since the enactment of the Chinese Charity Law in 2016.

Guangzhou Civil Affairs Bureau, 2 December 2013;《潮州市全市性社会组织评估实施办法》[Implementation Measures for the Assessment of Social Organizations in Chaozhou] (People's Republic of China) Chaozhou Civil Affairs Bureau, 8 July 2011;《惠州市民政局关于社会组织评估管理的实施办法》[Implementation Measures of Huizhou Civil Affairs Bureau on the Assessment and Management of Social Organizations] (People's Republic of China) Huizhou Civil Affairs Bureau, 12 October 2011;《无锡市社会组织评估管理办法》[Measures for the Assessment and Management of Social Organizations in Wuxi] (People's Republic of China) Wuxi Civil Affairs Bureau, 28 April 2013.

40 《社会组织评估管理办法》[Administrative Measures for the Assessment of Social Organizations] (People's Republic of China) Ministry of Civil Affairs, 20 December 2010 (n 37) art 11.

41 Based on extensive solicitation of public opinions, the Ministry of Civil Affairs formulated assessment indicators for national industry associations, foundations, and privately-operated non-enterprise entities in 2011. See《民政部关于印发各类社会组织评估指标的通知》[Notice of the Ministry of Civil Affairs on Printing and Distributing the Assessment Indicators of Various Social Organizations] (People's Republic of China) Ministry of Civil Affairs, 23 August 2011.

42 See interviews with L1, L2, L8, L9, T1, and A8.

43 See interviews with R1, R2, R3, A1, A4, A7, and A8.

(b) Power to Conduct Supervisory Conversations Where trustees are suspected of violating the law, the two regulators can initiate separate supervisory conversations with the persons in charge of the trustee companies, compelling them to explain their management decisions.[44] This also includes the power to conduct on-site inspections of the domiciles of trustees and the places where charitable trust affairs are carried out,[45] as well as inspect and duplicate materials relevant to the administration of charitable trusts.[46] In practice, there are two situations that may motivate regulators to conduct supervisory conversations: (1) when regulators receive complaints or accusations from public report complaint hotlines in relation to maladministration by charity trustees or (2) when regulators themselves identify non-compliance risks when carrying out on-site inspections. The interview data[47] suggest that the supervisory conversation is, in essence, a form of administrative investigation (*xingzheng diaocha* 行政调查) carried out by government organs. It is part of the ongoing administrative decision-making process and includes both educative and disciplinary elements. It is educative in the sense that regulators seek to advise trustees on how their minor violations of the law can be rectified and what steps can be taken to comply with the requirement of regulatory measures through the supervisory conversation.[48] It is also disciplinary in the sense that regulators

44 《信托公司管理办法》 [Measures for Administration of Trust Companies] (People's Republic of China) China Banking Regulatory Commission, 23 January 2007 (n 7) art 53; 《慈善信托管理办法》[Administrative Measures for Charitable Trusts] (People's Republic of China) China Banking Regulatory Commission and Ministry of Civil Affairs, 10 July 2017 (n 4) art 51.

45 《中华人民共和国慈善法》 [Charity Law of the People's Republic of China] (People's Republic of China) National People's Congress, 16 March 2016 (n 3) art 93; 《信托公司管理办法》 [Measures for Administration of Trust Companies] (People's Republic of China) China Banking Regulatory Commission, 23 January 2007 (n 7) art 47. Because of the short inspection time and the small number of supervisors involved in on-site inspections, it is difficult for regulators to judge the authenticity of the documents submitted by trustees. See interviews with L1, L2, and T5.

46 《中华人民共和国慈善法》 [Charity Law of the People's Republic of China] (People's Republic of China) National People's Congress, 16 March 2016 (n 3) art 93.

47 See interviews with R2, A1, A3, A6, A7, A8, T1, L1, and L8.

48 孟强龙 [Meng Qianglong], 《行政约谈法治化研究》 [Study on Legalization of Administrative Interviews] (2015) 6 行政法学研究 *Administrative Law Review* 99, 105–6; 王虎 [Wang Hu], 《风险社会中的行政约谈制度: 因应、反思与完善》 [The System of Administrative Interviews in Risk Society: Response, Reflection, and Improvement] (2018) 1 法商研究 *Study of Law and Business* 22, 26; 邓禾 [Deng He], 鲁颖然 [Lu Yingran] and 孙凌佼 [Sun Lingjiao], 《环境行政约谈的实践考察及制度完善》 [The Practice and Perfection of Environmental Administrative Interview System]

have wide discretion in the process of conducting supervisory conversations and, thus, may issue administrative punishments to trustees where their management of charitable trusts severely contravenes the laws or regulations. In such a scenario, the conduct of a supervisory conversation will lead to change or an elimination of the rights or obligations of the actor being interviewed.[49]

Supervisory conversations have been used extensively by environmental and food safety regulators over the last ten years. Where private parties engage in minor infringements of the law, the regulators concerned will employ means such as conversations, guidance, and warnings to advise these parties that they should rectify their wrongdoing in a timely manner so as to prevent serious legal liabilities resulting from the perpetuation of the illegal acts concerned.[50] However, several problems feature alongside the broad application of supervisory conversations. Much of the criticism from academics focuses on the ambiguity surrounding the legal nature of these supervisory conversations, their scope of application, and the procedures for conducting them.[51] Because of these ambiguities, regulators have a high degree of discretion in exercising their power to conduct supervisory conversations. Furthermore, because of this broad discretion, regulators have sizeable incentives to carry out supervisory conversations when investigating violations.[52]

As the Chinese Charity Law was only enacted in 2016, to date, the CADs and BRAs in Beijing, Shanghai and Guangzhou have yet to conduct any supervisory conversations with charity trustees.[53] Nevertheless, it is foreseeable that future supervisory conversations for charitable trusts will face the same ambiguities mentioned in the previous paragraph. On 25 October 2015, the Beijing Civil Affairs Bureau promulgated the

(2018) 4 重庆大学学报 (社会科学版) *Journal of Chongqing University (Social Sciences)* 156, 158–9.

49 朱新力 [Zhu Xinli] and 李芹 [Li Qin],《行政约谈的功能定位与制度建构》[The Functional Orientation and Institutional Design of Administrative Interviews] (2018) 4 国家行政学院学报 *Journal of Chinese Academy of Governance* 91, 93–4; 孟强龙 [Meng Qianglong] (n 48) 105.

50 See interviews with A3, A7, L1, and L2.

51 王利 [Wang Li],《我国环保行政执法约谈制度探析》[Analysis of Chinese Interview System of Administrative Enforcement in Environmental Protection] (2014) 5 河南大学学报 (社会科学版) *Journal of Henan University (Social Sciences)* 62, 64–6; 邓禾 [Deng He], 鲁颖然 [Lu Yingran], and 孙凌佼 [Sun Lingjiao] (n 48) 160–2; 王虎 [Wang Hu] (n 48) 26–7; 朱新力 [Zhu Xinli] and 李芹 [Li Qin] (n 49) 92.

52 See interviews with L2, A3, and A5.

53 See interviews with R1, R2, A1, A3, A4, and A7.

Measures of Administrative Interviews for Social Organizations in Beijing.[54] Later, on 16 March 2016, the Provisions on the Interview Works in the Administrative Law Enforcement by Social Organization Registration and Administration Organs (for Trial Implementation)[55] was issued by the Ministry of Civil Affairs at the central government level. These two government documents stipulate the procedure for conducting supervisory conversations with persons in charge of social organizations.[56] These documents may provide insights regarding the conduct of supervisory conversations in the area of charitable trusts. In the eyes of the parties to charitable trusts, clarification of the procedure and content of supervisory conversations by regulators of charitable trusts is of tremendous practical significance. This matters not only for assessing the potential liabilities of those in charge of charitable trusts but also for the availability of remedial relief in response to administrative punishments that may arise from supervisory conversations.

(c) **Power to Require Information Disclosure** CADs and BRAs are empowered to require charity trustees to disclose relevant information to the public. Regulatory practice over the last three years shows that the two regulators exercise this power strictly.[57] There are two reasons for this. First, the misuse of charity funds over the last two decades has led to a significant reduction in public trust in the charity sector.[58] To increase public trust and confidence in how charitable trusts are created and operated, regulators monitor the ongoing administration of these trusts, and information disclosure is a good way for them to learn about the

54 《北京市社会组织行政约谈办法》[Measures of Administrative Interviews for Social Organizations in Beijing] (People's Republic of China) Beijing Civil Affairs Bureau, 25 October 2015.

55 《社会组织登记管理机关行政执法约谈工作规定（试行）》 [Provisions on the Interview Works in the Administrative Law Enforcement by Social Organization Registration and Administration Organs: For Trail Implementation] (People's Republic of China) Ministry of Civil Affairs, 16 March 2016.

56 《北京市社会组织行政约谈办法》 [Measures of Administrative Interviews for Social Organizations in Beijing] (People's Republic of China) Beijing Civil Affairs Bureau, 25 October 2015 (n 54) arts 2–18;《社会组织登记管理机关行政执法约谈工作规定（试行）》[Provisions on the Interview Works in the Administrative Law Enforcement by Social Organization Registration and Administration Organs: For Trail Implementation] (People's Republic of China) Ministry of Civil Affairs, 16 March 2016 (n 55) arts 2–15.

57 See interviews with R1, R2, R3, L1, A4, A5, T1, and T5.

58 See analysis in Section II-B of Chapter 2.

management of charitable trust affairs.[59] Second, since the promulgation of the Chinese Charity Law three years ago, governments at all levels have continued to increase their policy support for the development of charitable trusts. To ensure that these policy privileges are not abused by trust parties, CADs issue letters or notices to verify whether the information required by law has been disclosed in a timely and adequate manner.[60]

Article 56 of the Measures for Charitable Trusts stipulates that trustees are obliged to disclose four types of information: (a) details of the establishment of charitable trusts; (b) reports on asset conditions and the handling of trust affairs; (c) reasons for the change and termination of charitable trusts; and (d) other information disclosure requirements from CADs for processing the recording of charitable trusts. Failure to make public the handling of charitable trust affairs and the financial conditions of charitable trust assets may raise legal liabilities on the part of trustees.[61] Interviews with trust lawyers[62] and trustee managers[63] suggest that the fourth type of information mainly relates to the assessment and administrative punishment of specific charitable trusts. The interviewed CAD officials[64] held that disclosure of disciplinary action is essential to maintaining public trust and confidence, for the general public needs to be assured that CADs and BRAs are effective regulators and perform their jobs well. Nevertheless, given that a charitable trust's reputation is critical to its ability to carry out its work, the three officials also stated that considerable caution was required in terms of issuing punishments with respect to potential or actual offences.

The law stipulates that charity trustees should disclose to the public the four types of information listed in the previous paragraph, but it does not clarify what each type of information entails. The vagueness of the law creates a number of ambiguities that impede the proper operation of this

59 See interviews with R1, R3, A4, and T5.

60 See interviews with R1, R2, R3, A5, T1, and T5.

61 The legal liabilities include warnings, making corrections by the prescribed deadline, or a fine of between RMB 20,000 and RMB 200,000. See《中华人民共和国慈善法》[Charity Law of the People's Republic of China] (People's Republic of China) National People's Congress, 16 March 2016 (n 3) art 105;《慈善信托管理办法》[Administrative Measures for Charitable Trusts] (People's Republic of China) China Banking Regulatory Commission and Ministry of Civil Affairs, 10 July 2017 (n 4) art 59.

62 See interviews with L1 and L2.

63 See interviews with T1 and T5.

64 See interviews with R1, R2, and R3.

information disclosure system in China. For example, should the level of transparency required of a charitable trust be differentiated by the scale and type of its assets or the nature of its charitable purpose? To what extent should the information regarding trust asset conditions be disclosed? At a macro level, some of the unanswered questions include: What factors should be considered when determining the extent and scope of information disclosure? How should the tension between private parties' right to privacy and the public interest in information disclosure regarding charity activities be dealt with? In what way could the public's trust and confidence be protected, maintained, and enhanced in the process of carrying out charitable trust purposes? In the absence of clarification, it is difficult to determine whether there is sufficient transparency to inform regulators and the public more broadly that trust assets are being used for appropriate purposes.

C *The Regulatory Approach of Public Education*

In the last five years, CADs and BRAs have undertaken numerous educative and consultative measures to promote public awareness about charitable trusts. Regulators aim to use these measures to educate private actors and encourage them to use charitable trusts to promote the public welfare goals defined by the state. Pursuant to the Guiding Opinions of the State Council on Promoting Healthy Development of Charitable Causes (Opinions on Development of Charitable Causes), regulators are given the clear administrative task of educating and supporting charity participants on best practices for carrying out charitable activities.[65] Similarly, at the local level, according to the Key Work Points of Civil Affairs Bureaus, CADs in several areas[66] are required to organize training or educational programmes in relation to the recording of charitable trusts, the management of charitable trust affairs, and the disposition of charitable assets. Consistent with such policy rhetoric, CADs have taken a wide range of educative and consultative

[65] 《国务院关于促进慈善事业健康发展的指导意见》 [Guiding Opinions of the State Council on Promoting Healthy Development of Charitable Causes] (People's Republic of China) State Council, 24 November 2014 (n 23) chs 4–5.

[66] See, e.g.,《2020年上海慈善事业促进工作要点》[Key Work Points of Shanghai Charity Promotion Work in 2019] (People's Republic of China) Shanghai Civil Affairs Bureau, 20 March 2020, s 1;《杭州市民政系统2017年工作总结和2018年工作要点》[Work Summary of Hangzhou Civil Affair System in 2017 and Key Work Points in 2018] (People's Republic of China) Hangzhou Civil Affairs Bureau, 13 February 2018, s 2.

programmes to help the public understand what charitable trusts are and how they can be used to further the development of charitable undertakings in China.

More specifically, CADs at the central government level have initiated various research projects and training programmes around charitable trusts, some of which are conducted in cooperation with local trust associations and academic institutions. At the same time, in the last three years, local-level CADs have held a variety of forums and conferences for leading trustees, including trust companies and charitable organizations, to share best practices around the administration of trust affairs. Regulatory agencies at the forefront of the charitable trust sector have increasingly focused on creating partnerships with private charitable actors when framing or setting up their regulatory goals. For example, the Notice of the Shanghai Bureau of Civil Affairs on the Implementation of the Chinese Charity Law and the Implementation Plan for Promoting the Development of Charitable Causes in the Haidian District of Beijing stress that 'the public plays a positive role in the implementation of charity-related policies'.[67] The strategy around charitable trusts in Zhejiang and Jiangsu envisions a collaborative mechanism in which the government enacts charity-promoting policies, and the public oversees how these policies are implemented in practice.[68] In addition, CADs in the eastern coastal areas, such as Guangzhou and Zhejiang, have issued charity progress reports for their jurisdictions or awarded and praised leaders with outstanding charitable trust performance.[69] In such a

[67] 《上海市民政局关于贯彻落实<中华人民共和国慈善法>的通知》 [Notice of the Shanghai Bureau of Civil Affairs on the Implementation of the Charity Law of the People's Republic of China] (People's Republic of China) Shanghai Bureau of Civil Affairs, 26 August 2016, pt 1;《北京市海淀区关于促进慈善事业发展的实施方案》 [Implementation Plan for Promoting the Development of Charitable Causes in Haidian District of Beijing] (People's Republic of China) Haidian District Government of Beijing, 14 March 2017, s 7.

[68] 《浙江省实施<中华人民共和国慈善法>办法》 [Measures for the Implementation of the Chinese Charity Law in Zhejiang Province] (People's Republic of China) Standing Committee of Zhejiang Provincial People's Congress, 30 November 2018, arts 5–6, 35;《江苏省慈善信托备案管理暂行实施办法》 [Interim Measures for the Administration of Recording of Charitable Trusts in Jiangsu Province] (People's Republic of China) Jiangsu Provincial Civil Affairs Department and Jiangsu Office of the China Banking Regulatory Commission, 23 October 2017, arts 51, 57–8.

[69] Individuals and enterprises that have made outstanding contributions to the development of charity in China are entitled to participate in the selection of the China Charity Awards (*zhonghua cishan jiang* 中华慈善奖). See《"中华慈善奖"评选表彰办法》 [Method for the Selection and Commendation of 'China Charity Award'] (People's Republic of China)

favourable environment, an increasing number of actors outside the CAD and BRA framework have sought to improve the understanding and administration of charitable trusts. Such efforts include establishing free-standing research and training institutes, advisory services associated with Chinese universities,[70] and, sometimes, individual legal and accountancy firms. One illustrative instance is the research cooperation between the national CAD and the China Philanthropy Development Institute of Shanghai Jiao Tong University (CPD). In this collaborative programme, the CPD was asked to design and update the criteria for the assessment of the performance of charity trustees in their administration of charitable affairs and devise potential measures that may cultivate capable and responsible assessment agencies in the near future.[71] Overall, the collaborative and research-based approach taken on by CADs reflects the latest changes in the regulatory environment of the charitable trust sector.

The wide application of educative measures shows that charity sector regulators have transitioned from control to cooperation in terms of regulatory philosophy. Nevertheless, drawing on experiences from environment and labour law enforcement, this transition raises an important concern: is it too easy for trust parties to negotiate compliance with regulators? The six interviewees[72] who answered this question expressed a common experience: unlike environment and labour law regulation,[73] charitable trust regulators are powerful and are unlikely to be easily

Ministry of Civil Affairs, 3 June 2014, art 2;《民政部关于表彰第十届"中华慈善奖"获得者的决定》[Decision of the Ministry of Civil Affairs on Commending the Winners of the 10th China Charity Award] (People's Republic of China) Ministry of Civil Affairs, 10 September 2018. At the local level, the CADs in Jiangsu and Zhejiang Provinces have also set up the Jiangsu Charity Award and Zhejiang Charity Award, respectively. See《2019年江苏省民政工作要点》[Key Points of Civil Affairs Work in Jiangsu Province in 2019] (People's Republic of China) Jiangsu Civil Affairs Department, 19 February 2019, s 8;《浙江省实施<中华人民共和国慈善法>办法》[Measures for the Implementation of the Chinese Charity Law in Zhejiang Province] (People's Republic of China) Standing Committee of Zhejiang Provincial People's Congress, 30 November 2018 (n 68) art 25.

70 For example, Peking University, Shanghai Jiao Tong University, Beijing Normal University, and Zhejiang University of Technology have each established public welfare research centres.

71《上海交通大学中国公益发展研究院<中国社会组织评估发展报告(2018)>蓝皮书发布》[The Blue Book of 'China Social Organization Evaluation and Development Report (2018)' Released by China Philanthropy Development Institute of Shanghai Jiaotong University] (29 December 2018) <https://Dzb.Sjtu.Edu.Cn/Data/View/3309>.

72 See interviews with R1, R2, T1, T5, T6, and T7.

73 For scholarly writings on the enforcement gap in environment and labour law regulations, see Carlos Wing-Hung Lo, Gerald E. Fryxell, Benjamin van Rooij, Wei Wang and

influenced by trustees. This conclusion was founded by considering two factors. First, CADs and BRAs are conferred with broad powers under the law.[74] This allows them to play a proactive role in addressing non-compliance issues. Second, as explained in Chapter 1, regulators have witnessed a large number of scandals in the last two decades involving misuse of charity funds. Therefore, it is not difficult for them to identify potential risks arising from the administration of charitable trusts. Moreover, regulatory officials themselves are fully aware that any regulatory failure or scandal would result in irrevocable reputational damage and serious administrative punishments for them. As such, regulators have a greater incentive to exercise their powers in a strict manner when dealing with violations of the law and tend to disclose their disciplinary decisions so as to demonstrate to the public that they are performing their jobs properly.

III Regulatory Style in Practice

Section II examined the regulatory framework for charitable trusts by showing that CADs and BRAs are endowed by law with extensive powers and broad discretion as to how to exercise them. These powers allow regulators extensive interference in the creation and day-to-day management of charitable trusts. However, the law is vague and does not clarify how these powers should be exercised. This vagueness motivates regulators to take strategies to protect their interests from being adversely affected in the implementation of the law. Meanwhile, in view of the Chinese administrative system, regulators have long been subject to policy and administrative pressures and, thus, tend to be responsive to extra-legal concerns when discharging their supervisory roles. These concerns significantly influence the decision-making of regulatory officials. Sections III-A and III-B analyse these strategies and extra-legal factors in order to demonstrate how CADs and BRAs perform their responsibilities in practice.

Pansy Honying Li, 'Explaining the Enforcement Gap in China: Local Government Support and Internal Agency Obstacles as Predictors of Enforcement Actions in Guangzhou' (2012) 111 *Journal of Environmental Management* 227, 234–5; Virginia E. Harper Ho, 'From Contracts to Compliance: An Early Look at Implementation under China's New Labor Legislation' (2009) 23 *Columbia Journal of Asian Law* 35, 101–2; Benjamin van Rooij, Rachel E. Stern and Kathinka Fürst, 'The Authoritarian Logic of Regulatory Pluralism: Understanding China's New Environmental Actors' (2016) 10(1) *Regulation & Governance* 1, 4–6.

[74] See analysis in Section II-B.

A The Existence of Administrative Considerations

The analysis in Section II showed that regulators do in fact carry out a substantive examination of the documents submitted by trust parties. There are two reasons for this regulatory practice. First, the law does not elaborate on the legal nature of recording or the difference between recording and registration. CADs and BRAs, therefore, have the discretion to determine what type of examination to conduct. Second, to identify risks relating to the creation of charitable trusts and ensure that these trusts are used to advance the state's public welfare goals, CADs and BRAs seek to exercise substantive examinations of the trust documents in the recording phase.[75] Interviews with trust managers and lawyers with charitable trust experience show that whether a charitable trust can be successfully recorded in practice depends heavily on two considerations.[76] The first relates to the purpose of the charitable trust – the more politically or socially sensitive the purpose of a charitable trust, the more difficult its review and approval process. The second concerns the identity of the trust parties – allowing influential government organs to participate in the creation of charitable trusts facilitates trust approval. These considerations are consistent with the fact that regulators in China have long been subject to direct and intense administrative and policy influences. Extra-legal factors supplement legal rules and play an important role in the decision-making of regulatory officials.

B The Application of Administrative Factors

Administrative and policy considerations run through the regulatory practice of charitable trusts from Western to Eastern China. The interview data show that regulators mainly consider three types of administrative factors when performing their legal roles: the regional development agenda, the tension between regulatory capacity and regulatory objectives, and regulators' perceptions of risk. These administrative factors affect the way in which regulators engage with the law. Furthermore, the application of these administrative factors has led to regional differences: a supportive regulatory environment in the east and a conservative one in the west. Sections III-B-1, III-B-2, and III-B-3 closely analyse the three factors in terms of how they interact with each other in the regulatory practice of

[75] Ibid.

[76] See interviews with T1, T3, T7, L1, L2, L7, L8, and L9.

charitable trusts and the ways in which they each contribute to the emergence of regional differences in regulation.

1 Regional Development Agenda

In the Chinese administrative system, the central government establishes the overall policy objectives that guide administrative work in all parts of China. Various levels of local governments are required to translate these policy objectives into more specific, concrete, and measurable performance targets and put great emphasis on achieving these targets.[77] The central policies in this 'translation' process are interpreted and applied in varying degrees – promoted heavily in some regions while followed loosely in others.[78] The application of the central policies relating to charitable trusts is a typical example as these policies find enthusiastic adoption in eastern coastal areas but far less spirited engagement in western undeveloped areas.

Let us first consider the situation in western undeveloped areas. As analysed in Chapter 1, there are a substantial number of central government policies relating to the development of charitable trusts. In most cases, however, these policies are vague, poorly defined, abstract, and difficult to measure in an objective and fair way. Detailed guides are lacking in relation to the evaluation standards regarding policy accomplishments, the weight awarded to each criterion, the procedures for carrying out appraisal work, and the mechanisms for punishment or reward. Since it is difficult to objectively measure the work around charity development, local government officials in western undeveloped areas may be inclined to apply the limited resources they have to achieving objectives that are more practical in nature as well as more easily quantified and assessed.[79] In such areas, policy priority is mainly given to alleviating poverty or helping the needy.[80] This approach is in

[77] Jie Gao, 'Governing by Goals and Numbers: A Case Study in the Use of Performance Measurement to Build State Capacity in China' (2009) 29(1) *Public Administration and Development* 21, 22; Hon S. Chan and Jie Gao, 'Performance Measurement in Chinese Local Governments' (2008) 41 *Chinese Law & Government* 4, 5.

[78] Kwai Hang Ng and Xin He, *Embedded Courts: Judicial Decision-Making in China* (Cambridge University Press, 2017) 124.

[79] See interviews with A3, A6, and A7.

[80] The national performance evaluation system (the *kaohe* 考核 mechanism for government officials) guides the work priorities of civil servants at both the central and local levels. See Maria Edin, 'State Capacity and Local Agent Control in China: CCP Cadre Management from a Township Perspective' (2003) 173 *China Quarterly* 35, 39; Alex L. Wang, 'The Search for Sustainable Legitimacy: Environmental Law and Bureaucracy in China' (2013)

line with the central government's policy in the region,[81] namely that poverty is the most prominent problem in China's economic and social development, and western undeveloped areas continue to have large numbers of destitute people who live below the poverty line. Improving the living conditions of the poor is, pursuant to the 13th Five-Year Plan for Poverty Alleviation,[82] a clear task assigned to the governments of Western China. Under this logic, it is hardly surprising that local governments in western undeveloped areas tend to focus their limited resources on poverty alleviation. When it comes to charitable trusts, the vagueness of the law on recording creates scope for regulators to consider development agendas in determining what types of charitable trusts can and cannot be established. Consequently, in western provinces such as Gansu and Qinghai, almost 95 per cent of the recorded charitable trusts are related to poverty alleviation. This recording practice is consistent with the needs of local governments and the complex policy challenges they face.[83]

In contrast to western undeveloped areas, the economic conditions in eastern coastal areas are relatively stable. Due to the rapid rate of economic development, eastern-area CADs face greater policy pressures in the development of charitable trusts than their western counterparts.[84] This national policy pressure sets the prevailing agenda for regulators in Eastern China. In response to this pressure, the CADs in the eastern

37 *Harvard Environmental Law Review* 365, 382–3; Carl F. Minzner, 'Riots and Cover-Ups: Counterproductive Control of Local Agents in China' (2014) 31 *University of Pennsylvania Journal of International Law* 53, 57–8; van Rooij, Stern and Fürst (n 73) 4; Chan and Gao (n 77) 5; Gao (n 77) 29.

81 《中共中央、国务院关于打赢脱贫攻坚战的决定》 [Decision of the Central Committee of the Communist Party of China and the State Council on Winning the Battle against Poverty] (People's Republic of China) Central Committee of the Communist Party of China and the State Council, 29 November 2015, chs 1–2;《全国人民代表大会关于国民经济和社会发展第十三个五年规划纲要的决议》[Resolution of the National People's Congress on the Outline of the Thirteenth Five-Year Plan for National Economic and Social Development] (People's Republic of China) National People's Congress, 16 March 2016, chs 56–8;《民政部关于推进深度贫困地区民政领域脱贫攻坚工作的意见》[Opinions of the Ministry of Civil Affairs on Promoting Poverty Alleviation in the Field of Civil Affairs in Deep Poverty Stricken Areas] (People's Republic of China) Ministry of Civil Affairs, 7 April 2018, ch 1;《中国农村扶贫开发纲要（2011–2020年）》[Outline of Poverty Alleviation and Development in China Rural Areas (2011–2020)] (People's Republic of China) Central Committee of the Communist Party of China and State Council, 27 May 2011, chs 2–3.

82 《"十三五"脱贫攻坚规划》 ['13th Five-Year Plan' for Poverty Alleviation] (People's Republic of China) State Council, 23 November 2016.

83 See interviews with L1, L2, T1, and T7.

84 See interviews with A3, A6, A7, T1, and L9.

regions such as Beijing, Shanghai, and Guangzhou have sought to remedy the vagueness in the law by developing clear guidelines and criteria for the implementation of legislated governance goals. A representative example of efforts by coastal regulators is the flurry of administrative measures or guides being enacted at both municipal and provincial levels.[85] One common theme can be discerned from investigating these local laws, namely encouraging the general public and the media to supervise the operations of charitable trusts and expose the violations of parties to charitable trusts.[86] Besides the enactment of laws,[87] other regulatory

[85] From 2016 to 2019, the Beijing Administrative Measures for Charitable Trusts (Beijing Measures for CT), the Regulations on the Management of Charitable Trusts in Guangdong Province (Guangdong Regulation of CT), the Interim Measures for the Administration of the Recording of Charitable Trusts in Jiangsu Province (Jiangsu Measures of CT), and the Measures for the Implementation of the Chinese Charity Law in Zhejiang Province (Zhejiang Measures for Charity Law) were, respectively, enacted. See 《北京慈善信托管理办法》 [Beijing Administrative Measures for Charitable Trusts] (People's Republic of China) Beijing Bureau of Civil Affairs, 21 September 2016, art 1; 《关于慈善信托管理工作的实施细则》 [Regulations on the Management of Charitable Trusts] (People's Republic of China) Guangdong Provincial Civil Affairs Department and Guangdong Office of the China Banking Insurance Regulatory Commission, 21 February 2019, art 1; 《浙江省实施<中华人民共和国慈善法>办法》 [Interim Measures for the Administration of Recording of Charitable Trusts in Jiangsu Province] (People's Republic of China) Jiangsu Provincial Civil Affairs Department and Jiangsu Office of the China Banking Regulatory Commission, 23 October 2017 (n 68) art 1; 《浙江省实施<中华人民共和国慈善法>办法》 [Measures for the Implementation of the Chinese Charity Law in Zhejiang Province] (People's Republic of China) Standing Committee of Zhejiang Provincial People's Congress, 30 November 2018 (n 68) art 1.

[86] 《江苏省慈善信托备案管理暂行实施办法》 [Interim Measures for the Administration of Recording of Charitable Trusts in Jiangsu Province] (People's Republic of China) Jiangsu Provincial Civil Affairs Department and Jiangsu Office of the China Banking Regulatory Commission, 23 October 2017 (n 68) art 58; 《北京慈善信托管理办法》 [Beijing Administrative Measures for Charitable Trusts] (People's Republic of China) Beijing Bureau of Civil Affairs, 21 September 2016 (n 85) art 37; 《关于慈善信托管理工作的实施细则》 [Regulations on the Management of Charitable Trusts] (People's Republic of China) Guangdong Provincial Civil Affairs Department and Guangdong Office of the China Banking Insurance Regulatory Commission, 21 February 2019 (n 85) art 63.

[87] The concept of charitable trust has become a regular focus of policy roundtables and conferences, many involving provincial and local regulatory authority leaders. Social organizations and the public are encouraged to actively participate in the drafting and deliberation of charity-related laws. Legislative hearings and the solicitation of public opinions by publicizing legislative drafts are two essential institutions. Several legislative hearings were carried out in the process of the enactment of the Measures for CT in Beijing, the Measures of CT in Jiangsu, and the Measures for Charity Law in Zhejiang. See interviews with R2, L1, A1, A4, and A7.

innovations[88] designed to facilitate charitable trusts include incorporating the objective of developing charitable trusts as part of the performance appraisal system (the *kaohe* 考核 mechanism in the Chinese bureaucratic system) of local officials;[89] awarding and praising leaders with outstanding charitable trust performance[90] and holding forums or educational programmes around the development of charitable trusts.[91] With such a supportive environment created by eastern coastal regulators, the development of charitable trusts has recorded enormous growth in the last five years: for all the charitable trusts recorded to date, almost 65 per cent have been established in eastern developed areas, covering a wide range of charitable purposes, including science, culture, education, and health.

2 Tension between Regulatory Capacity and Regulatory Objectives

The second factor that affects regulatory practice in relation to charitable trusts is the tension between regulatory capacity and regulatory objectives.

88 The decentralization policy in respect of legislative powers was implemented in China in the late 1970s. See Sarah Biddulph, Sean Cooney and Ying Zhu, 'Rule of Law with Chinese Characteristics: The Role of Campaigns in Lawmaking' (2012) 34(4) *Law & Policy* 373, 394; Young Nam Cho, 'The Politics of Lawmaking in Chinese Local People's Congresses' (2006) 187 *China Quarterly* 592, 594–5; SEN LIN, 'A New Pattern of Decentralization in China: The Increase of Provincial Powers in Economic Legislation' (1992) 7(3) *China Information* 27, 28; Ho (n 73) 50; Gao (n 77) 23. With the implementation of this decentralization policy, many municipal and provincial CADs play a leading role in the innovation of regulatory practice in their respective jurisdictions. See interviews with A1, A3, and A6.

89 Regional regulators following this initiative include the Jiangsu Provincial Civil Affairs Department and the Guangdong Provincial Civil Affairs Department. See《江苏省慈善信托备案管理暂行实施办法》[Interim Measures for the Administration of Recording of Charitable Trusts in Jiangsu Province] (People's Republic of China) Jiangsu Provincial Civil Affairs Department and Jiangsu Office of the China Banking Regulatory Commission, 23 October 2017 (n 68) art 52;《关于慈善信托管理工作的实施细则》[Regulations on the Management of Charitable Trusts] (People's Republic of China) Guangdong Provincial Civil Affairs Department and Guangdong Office of the China Banking Insurance Regulatory Commission, 21 February 2019 (n 85) art 55.

90 See analysis in Section II-C.

91 A number of regulatory authorities, including the Shandong and Guangdong provincial CADs and the Shanghai municipal CAD, have held various forums and educational programmes in which professionals such as charity lawyers and trust academics, representatives of trustee companies and charitable organizations, government officials and members of local legislative committees have been invited to discuss the role that the charitable trust should play in developing local charitable causes and the measures that can be taken to effectively regulate the charitable trust. See interviews with A4, A5, A7, L1, and L9.

For the effective implementation of legal rules, regulators must ensure the availability of a certain level of budget and staff resources.[92] CADs and BRAs do seek to carry out substantive examinations of trust documents, and regulatory officials in coastal areas have a more open and positive attitude towards the creation of charitable trusts than those in western undeveloped areas. An examination of the interview data shows that one of the key reasons for this disparity lies in the allocation of budgets and personnel (in terms of incentive, quantity, and quality) in the CAD of each area.

In the eastern coastal regions, municipal-level CADs have, on average, three or four full-time staff in charge of the regulation of charitable trusts – for example, three in Beijing, four in Guangzhou, and three in Shanghai.[93] Although almost 75 per cent of charitable trusts were established in these developed areas, each area receives no more than fifty charitable trust applications annually. Regulatory practice suggests that, at present, the CADs in Shanghai, Beijing, and Guangzhou have adequate staff and budget resources to maintain consistent communication and interaction with the trustees being regulated.[94] Examining no more than fifty annual charitable trust reports per year is not very difficult in practice.[95] As regards charitable trusts related to the material interests of the local government, which are too politically or socially sensitive for CADs to cope with, regulatory officials conduct consultations with local government leaders. Where non-compliance arises in the operation of charitable trusts, the regulators in Eastern China can flexibly adjust their enforcement measures to best ensure compliance – for some regulated trustees, a punitive response to the violation is necessary; for others, a persuasive and educational approach may be preferred.[96] Because the regulatory resources in Eastern China can handle the number of charitable trusts requiring inspection, the regulators in these areas have

[92] Lesley K. Mcallister, 'Dimensions of Enforcement Style: Factoring in Regulatory Autonomy and Capacity' (2010) 32(1) *Law & Policy* 61, 65; Benjamin van Rooij, 'Implementation of Chinese Environmental Law: Regular Enforcement and Political Campaigns' (2006) 37(1) *Development and Change* 57, 64; Benjamin van Rooij, Gerald E. Fryxell, Carlos Wing-Hung Lo and Wei Wang, 'From Support to Pressure: The Dynamics of Social and Governmental Influences on Environmental Law Enforcement in Guangzhou City, China' (2013) 7(3) *Regulation & Governance* 321, 324.

[93] See interviews with R2, R3, and A8.

[94] See interviews with A1, A2, A4, A5, R1, and R2.

[95] See interviews with R1, R2, A4, and A5.

[96] Mcallister (n 92) 66.

incentives to make a concerted effort to create a favourable environment for carrying out legislated governance goals.

In comparison, the regulators in western undeveloped areas do not have enough employees[97] to thoroughly and consistently carry out legal enforcement work, especially in Gansu, Inner Mongolia, and Qinghai, where a limited number of regulatory officials have to cover a large geographical area. Whether regulatory officials in Western China have the capacity to detect violations of regulatory law should be further tested. In addition to the shortage of staff, a number of the lawyers[98] and scholars[99] interviewed also complained that regulatory officials in the western areas may not have been properly trained and that they lack adequate knowledge of charitable trusts.[100] The levels of official expertise vary considerably across regions – certain applications for recording are being declined only because regulatory officials deem that the internal governance arrangements for these charitable trusts are too innovative.[101] Due to this resource constraint, regulators in Western China do not actively raise awareness about charitable trusts. Rather, they adopt a conservative attitude regarding trust applications that are not associated with poverty alleviation.

3 Regulators' Perceptions of Risk

The final factor under consideration here involves regulators' risk perceptions associated with the supervision of charitable trusts. As discussed in Section III-B-2, regulators in western undeveloped areas, which are funded by local governments, often suffer from resource constraints that render them unable to carry out proactive and consistent enforcement

97 The CADs in Qinghai and Gansu have two full-time staff members responsible for the regulation of charitable trusts. See interview with A5.

98 See interviews with L1, L2, L3, and L4.

99 See interviews with A3 and A4.

100 In contrast, government documents indicate that the recruitment and training of regulatory officials in Eastern China have become more professionalized in recent years. See《2020年上海慈善事业促进工作要点》[Key Work Points of Shanghai Charity Promotion Work in 2019] (People's Republic of China) Shanghai Civil Affairs Bureau, 20 March 2020 (n 66) s 6;《杭州市民政系统2017年工作总结和2018年工作要点》[Work Summary of Hangzhou Civil Affair System in 2017 and Key Work Points in 2018] (People's Republic of China) Hangzhou Civil Affairs Bureau, 13 February 2018 (n 66) s 1;《2019年江苏省民政工作要点》[Key Points of Civil Affairs Work in Jiangsu Province in 2019] (People's Republic of China) Jiangsu Civil Affairs Department, 19 February 2019 (n 69) s 10.

101 See interviews with L1 and L2.

work; therefore, their inspections are generally prompted by public complaints.[102] Due to a shortage in funding and staffing, these regulators tend to avoid making decisions on matters that may expose them to administrative punishment.[103] At the same time, charitable trusts are a newly emerging institution, and so there are numerous uncertainties in regulation that have yet to be tested. Regulatory officials may also lack sufficient knowledge regarding the regulation of charitable trusts. For these two reasons, regulatory officials in western undeveloped areas tend to decline the recording of charitable trusts as public critiques of their work may lead to local CADs suffering irrecoverable reputational damage and serious administrative punishments. Over the last twenty years, a large number of scandals around the misuse of charity funds have been exposed by the general public; therefore, regulatory officials are clearly aware of the potential reputational risks arising from the day-to-day supervision of charitable trusts. This thinking has been further reinforced by the unspoken rules of Chinese bureaucracy: media exposure of regulatory scandals or failures brings about rapid governmental intervention to redress wrongs,[104] and an official may be demoted or, in extreme situations, dismissed from their position once a public incident has caught the attention of higher-level authorities.[105] For these reasons, CADs in western regions take a conservative attitude towards the recording of charitable trusts.[106]

When reviewing recording documents, CADs from eastern developed areas also consider the same legal and reputational risks as those in western areas. However, eastern-area CADs take a supportive and open approach that is considerably different from that of their western counterparts. There are two key reasons for this regional difference. The first relates to the fact that regulators in eastern areas have adequate resources to carry out inspections thoroughly and consistently.[107] Given the increasing policy pressure in Eastern China, CADs with a high degree of regulatory capacity are willing to invest resources in promoting the development of charitable trusts. The second reason concerns the

[102] See interviews with R2, A1, A4, A5, T7, L1, and L2.

[103] Mcallister (n 92) 66.

[104] Sean Cooney, 'Making Chinese Labor Law Work: The Prospects for Regulatory Innovation in the People's Republic of China' (2007) 30 *Fordham International Law Journal* 1050, 1095.

[105] Chan and Gao (n 77) 8; Ng and He (n 78) 130.

[106] See interviews with A1, A4, A5, A8, L1, L2, T1, and T7.

[107] See analysis in Section III-B-2.

reciprocal relationship between the level of public participation and the performance of regulators. As analysed in Section III-B-1, regulators in coastal areas have taken a series of measures to encourage the public to actively participate in the development of charitable trusts. The growing level of public participation is instrumental in motivating regulators to play a proactive role in developing and overseeing charitable trusts within their own jurisdictions. Some of the government officials[108] and scholars[109] interviewed reported that, in areas where the public is deeply interested in charity, the regulators concerned are more motivated to promote the development of charitable trusts. The reason is not difficult to understand: the higher the level of public participation, the higher the public's expectation that regulators will properly execute their roles and duties. In this regard, the increasing degree of public participation in charitable trusts may create external pressure, thereby encouraging regulators to proactively perform their supervisory and educational roles.

IV Conclusion

This chapter discussed two aspects of the practice of regulatory oversight of charitable trusts. The first was an analysis of the legal allocation of powers and responsibilities to regulators and the relationship between them. The second considered the administrative and policy pressures on regulators, combined with vagueness in the law, to influence the ways in which they perform their responsibilities.

Drawing on the experience of public welfare trusts, the law tasks CADs and BRAs to regulate the creation and ongoing administration of charitable trusts. This chapter first examined this new regulatory framework and discovered that the law does not provide a clear definition of the relationship between the two regulators. The law stipulates that CADs and BRAs should cooperate with each other in the performance of their powers and responsibilities. However, the law makes no mention of what this cooperation mechanism should look like. Regulatory practice suggests that CADs play a more proactive role in the regulation of charitable trusts compared to BRAs. CADs face greater policy pressure in the supervision of charitable trusts and, thus, have greater incentives to take measures to inspect the management of charitable trusts. BRAs, in contrast, do not suffer under intense policy pressures in the regulation

[108] See interviews with R1, R2, and R3.

[109] See interviews with A1, A3, A4, A5, and A6.

of charitable trusts and, thus, lack a strong inclination to maintain consistent interaction with the trustees being regulated. In practice, there is no clear cooperation mechanism between the two regulators. They tend to exercise their regulatory powers independent of each other. If risks related to the management of charitable trusts occur, BRAs may consult relevant CADs to determine the measures to be taken and whether administrative penalties should be imposed on the trustees.

This chapter then analysed the assignment of powers to each regulator. The analysis showed that CADs and BRAs are granted extensive powers and broad discretion on how to exercise them. However, the law does not clarify what these powers entail in substance and how they should be exercised. The law puts into effect recording as the measure for the creation of charitable trusts. However, the vagueness of the law on the meaning of recording creates scope for CADs to conduct substantive examinations of the trust documents and advise trust parties on how these documents should be amended. In the ongoing administration of charitable trusts, both regulators are independently empowered to assess the operation of charitable trusts, conduct supervisory conversations, and require information disclosure. However, the law makes no mention of the mechanism for assessing charitable trusts, the procedure for conducting supervisory conversations, and the level of transparency required of charitable trusts. This vagueness motivates regulators to devise strategies to protect their own institutional interests from being adversely affected in the implementation of the law. For example, both regulators are disinclined to conduct assessment work; they have greater incentives to initiate supervisory conversations when investigating violations; and they seek to advise trust parties on what types of information should be disclosed.

Finally, based on an analysis of the law, this chapter examined regulatory practices in light of China's particular political, social, and economic conditions. In the Chinese administrative system, regulators are strongly responsive to extra-legal factors when implementing the law. Meanwhile, the vagueness of the law also creates scope for regulators to consider extra-legal factors when discharging their supervisory roles. In terms of regulatory practices, CADs and BRAs were shown to mainly consider three administrative factors in the performance of their responsibilities: the regional development agenda, the tension between regulatory capacity and regulatory objectives, and regulators' perceptions of risk. The three extra-legal factors are inter-related and have a significant effect on the decision-making of regulatory officials.

The regional development agenda differs between eastern developed areas and western undeveloped areas. The central government's policy priority in Western China is poverty alleviation and, therefore, local regulators tend to focus their limited resources on alleviating poverty or helping the needy. It is difficult to establish trusts in areas whose purposes have no connection to poverty alleviation. In contrast, eastern-area CADs face greater policy pressure in the development of charitable trusts. In response to this pressure, CADs in Eastern China create a supportive regulatory environment and encourage the public to establish charitable trusts with diverse purposes.

The second factor is the tension between regulatory capacity and regulatory objectives. The regulatory resources in Eastern China can handle the number of charitable trusts requiring inspection. Thus, the regulators in these areas are willing to intervene intensively in the creation and ongoing administration of charitable trusts. In comparison, regulators in western undeveloped areas do not have sufficient budgets and personnel to carry out supervisory work and, therefore, are unwilling to take measures to promote public awareness of charitable trusts.

The final factor involves regulators' perceptions of risk. Regulators in both areas are cognisant of the potential legal and reputational risks arising from the day-to-day supervision of charitable trusts. Together with the shortage of regulatory resources, the perception of risk motivates regulators in Western China to adopt a conservative attitude towards the recording of charitable trusts. In comparison, because of the high degree of regulatory capacity and policy pressure, the perception of risk alone does not dissuade eastern-area regulators from playing a proactive role in the supervision of charitable trusts.

5

Contractual Regulation

I Introduction

The analysis in Chapter 3 showed that the law is under-determined and does not provide a clear definition of how settlors should interact with trustees in the governance of charitable trusts. This vagueness creates a great deal of uncertainty in relation to trustees' management of charitable trusts. In Chapter 4, the analysis showed that the law is also vague on the relationship between CADs and BRAs and in terms of the scope and content of the powers that each of the two regulators exercises. Chapter 4 explored the correlation between the vagueness of the law and the consideration of extra-legal factors by regulators when performing their legal roles. It showed that, based on China's particular environment, regulators have great incentives to intensively intervene in the creation and ongoing administration of charitable trusts.

This chapter turns towards analysing the use of contractual tools by trust parties. Due to the vagueness of the law and administrative practice, trust parties tend to use contracts to clarify their powers and duties as well as define the ways in which they should interact. It is widely acknowledged by contract theorists that contracts are widely used as tools to guide the performance of relevant parties and allocate powers and risks between them. However, in the Chinese charitable trust setting, the way in which contracts are used is distinct. There are two reasons for this.

The first relates to the trust parties' risk perceptions. Due to the vagueness of the law, trust parties have difficulty knowing how their performance will be assessed and whether their management is compliant with the requirements of the law. This chapter explores three types of risk that might be perceived by trust parties: the risk of the vagueness of the law, the risk of public scrutiny, and the risk of regulatory scrutiny. It examines the ways in which the perception of these risks influences the distribution of the powers and duties of the trust parties in the contract.

The second reason relates to the regulatory practice of charitable trusts. As discussed in Chapter 4, the law sets up the regulatory framework for charitable trusts, but it is incomplete and vague on how regulators should exercise their powers. To mitigate risks in respect of the use of charitable assets, I examined the ways in which regulators might be willing to intensively intervene in the creation and ongoing administration of charitable trusts. They tend to advise trust parties regarding what clauses should be incorporated in trust documents, when clauses in the trust documents are ambiguous, and how they might be modified. This regulatory strategy is consistent with the administrative style of the regulation of charitable trusts, which was discussed in Chapter 4.

Based on the twenty-eight charitable trust contracts examined in this research, this chapter offers an in-depth analysis of contractual practice. This analysis serves two purposes: one is to better understand the main uses of the contract and the reasons behind them, and the other is to identify the extent to which the function and scope of the legal governance framework for charitable trusts are shaped by the contractual arrangement between the trust parties.

II Perceptions of Risk by Trust Parties

This section introduces three types of risk that might be perceived by the parties to charitable trusts: the risk of the vagueness of the law, the risk of public scrutiny, and the risk of regulatory scrutiny. These three types of risk may also involve different levels of reputational, legal, or management risk. For example, failure to comply with regulatory measures may give rise to reputational and legal risks for trust parties. Likewise, when a trustee's misconduct is made known to the relevant regulators, reputational and legal risks to the charitable trust will ensue. When disagreement occurs between trust parties, management risks will arise as disputes over the disposal of trust assets or the selection of beneficiaries may not be effectively resolved.

Driven by the imperative of risk allocation, trust parties tend to use contractual tools in a variety of ways. For example, settlors and trustees tend to use contract clauses to clarify the powers and duties they have and the interaction between them. In comparison, regulators are inclined to use their regulatory powers to influence contractual planning between trust parties so as to mitigate potential risks in the discharge of their legal roles. This section presents an overview of the three types of risk perceived by trust parties. Section III discusses specific risks and how trust parties use contracts to address them.

A The Risk of the Vagueness of the Law

The first risk stems from the vagueness of the law. As analysed in Chapter 3, the law sets up the internal relationship between settlors and trustees but is vague and incomplete in relation to how they should interact and in what ways their legal roles should be performed. This vagueness enables settlors to easily interfere in the management of charitable trusts and creates a great deal of uncertainty in relation to trustees and the performance of their duties. An illustrative example is article 28 of the Chinese Trust Law, according to which settlors are empowered to check or duplicate trust accounts and request that trustees provide explanations of their management decisions.[1] Exercising this power enables settlors to assess whether trustees manage trust affairs in compliance with charitable trust purposes and whether trustees breach administrative duties or improperly handle trust affairs. If the answer is negative in the settlors' view, pursuant to article 22 of the Chinese Trust Law, they can apply to the court to annul the disposition and ask trustees to restore trust assets to their former state or proceed with compensation.[2] The vagueness regarding the ways in which articles 22 and 28

[1] For an account of settlors' powers, see 卞耀武 [Bian Yaowu],《中华人民共和国信托法释义》[Interpretation of the Trust Law of the People's Republic of China] (法律出版社 [Law Press], 2002) 88–91; 周小明 [Zhou Xiaoming],《信托制度: 法理与实务》 [Trust System: Theory and Practice] (中国法制出版社 [China Legal Publishing House], 2012) 229–30; 陈向聪 [Chen Xiangcong],《信托法律制度研究》 [Research on Trust Law System] (中国检察出版社 [China People's Procuratorate Press], 2007) 172–3; 高凌云 [Gao Lingyun],《被误读的信托 – 信托法原论》 [A Misreading of Trust: Discussion on the Origin of Trust] (复旦大学出版社 [Fudan University Press], 2010) 267; Zhenting Tan, 'The Chinese Law of Trusts: A Compromise between Two Legal Systems' (2001) 13 (1) *Bond Law Review* 224, 228; Rebecca Lee, 'Conceptualizing the Chinese Trust' (2009) 58 (3) *International & Comparative Law Quarterly* 655, 661; Lusina Ho, 'The Reception of Trust in Asia: Emerging Asian Principles of Trust?' [2004] *Singapore Journal of Legal Studies* 287, 297; Ruiqiao Zhang, 'Trust Law of China and Its Uncertainties: Examination of the Rights and Obligations of Trust and Ownership of Trust Property' (2015) 10 *National Taiwan University Law Review* 45, 57.

[2] 《中华人民共和国信托法》 [Trust Law of the People's Republic of China] (People's Republic of China) National People's Congress, 28 April 2001, art 22; Kai Lyu, 'Re-Clarifying China's Trust Law: Characteristics and New Conceptual Basis' (2015) 36 *Loyola of Los Angeles International and Comparative Law Review* 447, 460; 赵廉慧 [Zhao Lianhui],《信托法解释论》 [Interpretative Theory of Trust Law] (中国法制出版社 [China Legal Publishing House], 2015) 476–8; Tan (n 1) 236; Zhang (n 1) 64; 高凌

work together raises three questions. First, in what situations can management be considered inconsistent with a charitable trust purpose? Second, in what way can the handling of trust affairs be thought to be 'improper'? Third, to what extent may a trustee's performance be recognized as deviating from its administrative duties? In the absence of detailed contract terms clarifying how these three questions should be dealt with, the interview data suggest that disputes likely arise between settlors and trustees in relation to the management of charitable trusts.[3]

Seven trustee managers with charitable trust practice were interviewed and asked the following question: under what circumstances will there be disputes between trust parties? They all responded that disputes arise when trust parties have different understandings of their duties and powers.[4] When such disputes are settled through litigation, the information about the litigation quickly becomes public knowledge, and the trustees against whom the legal judgments are entered suffer severe reputational damage. This concern is increasingly apparent when government organs act in the capacity of settlors and trust purposes are related to administrative tasks that local governments are obliged to undertake. In the eyes of both settlors and trustees, an entity's reputation is highly important in business relationships. Based on this understanding, settlors and trustees have strong incentives to specify what each party's powers entail and how the performance of each party's duties is assessed so as to mitigate potential risks arising from the management of charitable trusts.

B The Risk of Public Scrutiny

The second type of risk derives from public supervision. Public scrutiny can be understood in two dimensions. The first concerns the factors that motivate the public to play a supervisory role. Aside from charity-promoting policies,[5] another factor lies in the fact that the public lacks trust and confidence in the management of charities. The last two decades have seen a number of scandals involving the misuse of charity

云 [Gao Lingyun] (n 1) 267; 卞耀武 [Bian Yaowu] (n 1) 91–3; 周小明 [Zhou Xiaoming] (n 1) 234–6.

3 An examination of the charitable trust contracts suggests that trust parties prefer to use contractual instruments to minimize the potential risks arising from the exercise of settlors' powers. For a detailed account of this aspect, see Section III-A.

4 See interviews with T1, T2, T3, T4, T5, T6, and T7.

5 See analysis in Section II-C of Chapter 4.

funds. In the area of charitable trusts, it is hardly surprising that the public also lacks confidence in the performance of trustees' duties.[6] When a charitable trust is created for politically or socially sensitive purposes, the public, echoing a distrustful sentiment, may wish to check whether the charitable trust concerned benefits the community as a whole or merely benefits a particular section of the public and whether its assets are distributed in alignment with charitable purposes. However, as analysed in Section II-A, the law is vague on the internal relationship between settlors and trustees. This vagueness has created a high level of uncertainty in relation to trustees' management of charitable trusts. The lack of clear criteria for assessing a trustee's performance makes it easy for the public to criticize trustees' management of charitable trusts. This concern has imposed pressure on trust parties and incentivized them to distribute such risk through contracts.[7]

The second dimension relates to the potential role of stakeholders in supervising the management of charitable trusts. The last three years have witnessed rising levels of stakeholder participation in the development of charitable trusts.[8] The establishment of public supervision channels (i.e., a hotline and complaint mailbox) at provincial, municipal, and county levels allows stakeholders to voice complaints or report violations.[9] This regulatory practice is consistent with the policy that a tough and stringent environment should be created for regulating charitable trusts. Reporting does not require those reporting to disclose their identity information (e.g., name, domicile, and means of communication) and is, therefore, effective in challenging violations, since reporters are able to act without regard to political or institutional pressures.[10]

[6] See analysis in Section II-A of Chapter 2.

[7] See interviews with L1, L2, T1, and T5.

[8] Chinese governments encourage social organizations and the public to actively participate in the drafting and deliberation of charity-related laws. See interviews with R2, A1, A3, A5, A7, L1, L8, and L9.

[9] The Chinese Charity Law and the Measures for Charitable Trusts both prescribe that any individuals uncovering violations of the laws and regulations of charitable trusts may lodge complaints or tip-offs to CADs, BRAs, or other regulatory departments. See《中华人民共和国慈善法》 [Charity Law of the People's Republic of China] (People's Republic of China) National People's Congress, 16 March 2016, art 97;《慈善信托管理办法》 [Administrative Measures for Charitable Trusts] (People's Republic of China) China Banking Regulatory Commission and Ministry of Civil Affairs, 10 July 2017, art 54.

[10] On scholarly writings discussing the active role of private enforcers or citizen supervisors in challenging violations, see Barton H. Thompson, 'The Continuing Innovations of Citizen Enforcement' (2000) 2000 *University of Illinois Law Review* 185, 187; Karl S. Coplan, 'Citizen Litigants Citizen Regulators: Four Cases Where Citizen Suits Drove

In the last four years, regulators in Shanghai, Guangzhou, Hangzhou, and Shenzhen received no fewer than fifteen public calls or emails per day covering a wide range of topics, such as clues about on-site inspections of trustees' domiciles, recommendations for expanding the extent and scope of disclosures, and delays by trustees in issuing annual reports.[11] The growing level of stakeholder participation has affected the way in which trust parties perform their legal roles. In an environment where regulators are proactive in raising awareness about charitable trusts and stakeholders are willing to play a supervisory role, trust parties have greater incentives to devise strategies to deal with the vagueness of the law, such as using contractual tools to clarify their powers and duties and defining the interaction between them.

C The Risk of Regulatory Scrutiny

The third type of risk comes from trust parties' violations of regulatory measures. This risk is related to the second type of risk mentioned in Section II-B as public scrutiny may expose infringements of the law by trust parties and, thus, attract regulatory scrutiny. Prior to the enactment of the Chinese Charity Law in 2016, there were no uniform laws at the national level governing foundations,[12] social associations,[13] or privately-operated non-enterprise organizations,[14] the three major organizational forms for conducting charitable causes. Key elements for regulating charitable organizations are contained in myriad notices (*tongzhi* 通知),[15]

Development of Clean Water Law' (2014) 25 *Colorado Natural Resources, Energy & Environmental Law Review* 61, 119; Jody Freeman, 'The Private Role in the Public Governance' (2000) 75 *New York University Law Review* 543, 662–3.

11 See interviews with R1, R2, R3, A3, A5, and A8.

12 《基金会管理条例》 [Regulations on Administration of Foundations] (People's Republic of China) State Council, 3 August 2004.

13 《社会团体登记管理条例》 [Regulations on Registration Administration of Associations] (People's Republic of China) State Council, 6 February 2016.

14 《民办非企业单位登记管理暂行条例》 [Interim Regulations on the Administration of the Registration of Privately-Operated Non-Enterprise Organizations] (People's Republic of China) State Council, 25 October 1998.

15 《民政部关于贯彻落实<国务院关于促进慈善事业健康发展的指导意见>的通知》 [Notice of the Ministry of Civil Affairs on Implementing the 'Guiding Opinions of the State Council on Promoting the Healthy Development of Charitable Causes'] (People's Republic of China) Ministry of Civil Affairs of People's Republic of China, 15 December 2014, ch 2.

opinions (*yijian* 意见),[16] and subnational laws of varying consistency and authority.[17] Under this fragmented legal system, there are two problems regarding the regulatory framework for charitable organizations. First, there is a gap between enforcement rhetoric and local realities in the regulatory practice of charities. At the local level, governments are reluctant to spend funds on developing charitable causes.[18] Regulators, as part of local governments, tend to decline applications for the registration of charities.[19] Second, regulators of charitable organizations are not

16 See, e.g.,《国务院关于促进慈善事业健康发展的指导意见》[Guiding Opinions of the State Council on Promoting Healthy Development of Charitable Causes] (People's Republic of China) State Council, 24 November 2014, ch 3;《中国慈善事业发展指导纲要（2011–2015年）》[Guidelines for the Development of China's Charitable Causes (2011–2015)] (People's Republic of China) Ministry of Civil Affairs, 15 July 2011, ch 3;《民政部、国资委关于支持中央企业积极投身公益慈善事业的意见》[Opinions of the Ministry of Civil Affairs and the State-Owned Assets Supervision and Administration Commission on Supporting the Central Enterprises to Actively Participate in Charitable Causes] (People's Republic of China) Ministry of Civil Affairs and State-Owned Assets Supervision and Administration Commission, 19 May 2015, ch 3;《民政部关于加强和创新慈善超市建设的意见》[Opinions of the Ministry of Civil Affairs on Strengthening and Innovating the Construction of Charity Supermarkets] (People's Republic of China) Ministry of Civil Affairs, 31 December 2013, ch 2.

17 See, e.g.,《北京市促进慈善事业若干规定》[Several Regulations for Developing Charity in Beijing] (People's Republic of China) Beijing Municipal People's Government, 1 January 2014;《江苏省慈善事业促进条例》[Regulations of Charity Promotion in Jiangsu Province] (People's Republic of China) Standing Committee of the People's Congress of Jiangsu Province, 1 May 2010;《甘肃省慈善捐助管理办法》[Measures for the Management of Charitable Donations in Gansu Province] (People's Republic of China) The People's Government in Gansu Province, 1 May 2006;《长沙市慈善事业促进条例》[Regulations of Charity Promotion in Changsha City] (People's Republic of China) Standing Committee of the People's Congress of Changsha City, 1 September 2012;《宁波市慈善事业促进条例》[Regulations of Charity Promotion in Ningbo City] (People's Republic of China) Standing Committee of the People's Congress of Ningbo City, 1 October 2011;《宁夏回族自治区慈善事业促进条例》[Regulations of Charity Promotion in Ningxia Hui Autonomous Region] (People's Republic of China) Standing Committee of the People's Congress of Ningxia Hui Autonomous Region, 1 November 2011;《宝鸡市慈善爱心基金管理暂行办法》[Interim Measures for the Administration of Charity Love Fund in Baoji City] (People's Republic of China) The People's Government of Baoji City, 10 January 2008.

18 Virginia E. Harper Ho, 'From Contracts to Compliance: An Early Look at Implementation under China's New Labor Legislation' (2009) 23 *Columbia Journal of Asian Law* 35, 50; Benjamin van Rooij, 'Implementation of Chinese Environmental Law: Regular Enforcement and Political Campaigns' (2006) 37(1) *Development and Change* 57, 59; Benjamin van Rooij, Gerald E. Fryxell, Carlos Wing-Hung Lo and Wei Wang, 'From Support to Pressure: The Dynamics of Social and Governmental Influences on Environmental Law Enforcement in Guangzhou City, China' (2013) 7(3) *Regulation & Governance* 321, 324.

19 See interviews with L8, L9, A1, A6, and A7.

powerful. There is a lack of clear procedures to promote good or punish poor inspection work.[20] Those in charge of charitable organizations are willing to negotiate compliance with regulators, and the deterrent effect of administrative measures has been heavily moderated in practice.

By drawing on experiences from regulatory practice in respect of charitable organizations, the Chinese Charity Law has established a new regulatory framework for the charitable trust model: by law, CADs and BRAs are granted broad supervisory powers and wide discretion on how to exercise them. In practice, as analysed in Chapter 4, the vagueness of the law and the political objectives underlying charitable trusts create scope for regulators to consider extra-legal factors when performing their responsibilities. Administrative and policy pressures have a substantial impact on the implementation of the law.[21] As a result, regulators in both eastern developed areas and western undeveloped areas tend to exercise their legal powers in a strict manner when dealing with violations of the

[20] 谢琼 [Xie Qiong], 《立体监管：我国慈善事业发展的理性选择》[Stereoscopic Supervision: Rational Choice for the Development of Charitable Causes in China] (2015) 4 国家行政学院学报 *Journal of Chinese Academy of Governance* 73, 74. See also interviews with A1, A3, A4, A6, A7, and T1.

[21] Karla W. Simon, 'Regulation of Civil Society in China: Necessary Changes after the Olympic Games and the Sichuan Earthquake' (2008) 32 *Fordham International Law Journal* 943, 972, 986; Sarah Biddulph, 'The Production of Legal Norms: A Case Study of Administrative Detention in China' (2003) 20 *UCLA Pacific Basin Law Journal* 217, 277; van Rooij (n 19) 66; Ho (n 19) 98. It is common for Chinese governments to use short-term political pressures to achieve the implementation of laws. One illustrative example is the conduct of political campaigns in China. For a detailed account of anti-crime campaigns, see Sarah Biddulph, *Legal Reform and Administrative Detention Powers in China* (Cambridge University Press, 2007) 123–38; Murray Scot Tanner, 'State Coercion and the Balance of Awe: The 1983–1986 "Stern Blows" Anti-Crime Campaign' (2000) 44 *China Journal* 93, 107–8; Susan Trevaskes, 'Yanda 2001: Form and Strategy in a Chinese Anti-Crime Campaign' (2003) 36(3) *Australian & New Zealand Journal of Criminology* 272, 272–84. On account of anti-corruption campaigns, see Benjamin van Rooij, 'China's War on Graft: Politico-Legal Campaigns against Corruption in China and Their Similarities to the Legal Reactions to Crisis in the US' (2005) 14(2) *Pacific Rim Law & Political Journal* 289, 309. For an analysis of environmental pollution campaigns, see Carlos Wing-Hung Lo, Gerald E. Fryxell, Benjamin van Rooij, Wei Wang and Pansy Honying Li, 'Explaining the Enforcement Gap in China: Local Government Support and Internal Agency Obstacles as Predictors of Enforcement Actions in Guangzhou' (2012) 111 *Journal of Environmental Management* 227, 228; van Rooij (n 19) 66; van Rooij et al. (n 19) 325. On account of wage arrears campaigns, see Sarah Biddulph, Sean Cooney and Ying Zhu, 'Rule of Law with Chinese Characteristics: The Role of Campaigns in Lawmaking' (2012) 34(4) *Law & Policy* 373, 382–90; Sean Cooney, 'Making Chinese Labor Law Work: The Prospects for Regulatory Innovation in the People's Republic of China' (2007) 30 *Fordham International Law Journal* 1050, 1094–5.

law. Among the actors interviewed, seven[22] had experience dealing with regulators. They stressed that regulatory officials were proactive in issuing letters or notices to inspect whether the disposal of trust assets was compliant with charitable purposes and whether information on trust management had been properly disclosed. The interview data show that, in practice, regulatory officials have greater incentives to interfere intensively with the creation and ongoing administration of charitable trusts. In order to simplify their supervisory work, regulators tend to require trust parties to incorporate or amend certain contract clauses in the recording phase. At the same time, for the purpose of mitigating risks from regulatory scrutiny, trust parties also tend to consult regulators when contract clauses are ambiguous and for guidance on how they might be modified.

III Contractual Arrangements for Risk Allocation

Section II analysed the types of risk perceived by trust parties. This section will now discuss the way in which trust parties use contracts to allocate these risks. This discussion is based on an analysis of the twenty-eight charitable trust contracts collected as part of this study. At present, charitable trust contracts are not available on the uniform Charity in China platform and, therefore, are inaccessible to the general public. Given this limitation, I was able to collect twenty-eight contracts for this research: eleven were collected through interviews at the five fieldwork sites (i.e., Beijing, Shanghai, Guangzhou, Hangzhou, and Shenzhen), and another seventeen were collected from trust lawyers and trustee managers who had personal relationships with me prior to the commencement of the interview sessions. These contracts cover charitable trusts established in both eastern developed areas and western undeveloped areas in China and involve a wide range of charitable trust purposes, such as the promotion of education, environmental protection, and poverty alleviation.

To minimize reliance on contracts that were of a unique and case-sensitive nature, I liaised with the relevant interviewees to verify how widely these contracts were being used and the extent to which they represented contractual practice. Through these efforts, I confirmed that, of the twenty-eight contracts, twenty-five were standard contracts and

[22] See interviews with L1, L5, L9, T1, T3, T5, and T7.

widely used in charitable trust practice, and the other three (two recorded in Xi'an and one recorded in Qinghai) were unique, with separately planned clauses based on the special requirements of the trust parties. An examination of these contracts suggests that charity trustees prefer standardized precedent documents and negotiate contract terms on the basis of these precedent documents.

I examine these twenty-eight contracts here in order to explore two specific questions: first, how trust parties use contracts for guidance in performing their legal roles and, second, how the contractual arrangement between trust parties shapes the function and scope of the legal governance framework for charitable trusts.

A The Use of Contract

The Chinese law stipulates that the establishment of charitable trusts shall be conducted in written form, which includes trust contracts, wills, or other written documents prescribed by laws and administrative regulations.[23] The law itself indicates that trust parties have the freedom to determine the type of written form used to create charitable trusts. Nevertheless, the interviews with the trustee managers and regulatory officials suggest that the contract form is more generally used in practice. The three officials[24] interviewed provided two reasons for this practice: (1) charitable trusts are still in their infancy, and the use of trust contracts can help clarify the powers and duties between the trust parties; and (2) by advising trust parties on how to modify contract terms, regulators can direct the management of charitable trusts and the use of charitable assets in light of the state's public welfare policy. These two reasons show that regulators have played an active role in the establishment of charitable trusts, one that is consistent with the administrative style of regulating such trusts.[25]

Compared to commercial trust contracts, the contract terms of charitable trusts have unique characteristics. The parties to charitable trusts often spend large amounts of time negotiating how perceived risks could

[23] 《慈善信托管理办法》 [Administrative Measures for Charitable Trusts] (People's Republic of China) China Banking Regulatory Commission and Ministry of Civil Affairs, 10 July 2017 (n 10) art 13; 《中华人民共和国信托法》 [Trust Law of the People's Republic of China] (People's Republic of China) National People's Congress, 28 April 2001 (n 2) art 8; 卞耀武 [Bian Yaowu] (n 1) art 59.

[24] See interviews with R1, R2, and R3.

[25] See analysis in Section III of Chapter 4.

be allocated and how their powers and duties could be discharged. In creating contractual relationships, the relevant parties may plan for specific issues.[26] From the perspective of trust parties, the degree to which the relevant issues are planned for depends heavily on the types of risks that may arise in each given case, the extent to which this risk could be minimized through contractual planning and how the relative powers between the trust parties are distributed. For example, when settlors wish to play a proactive role in the management of trust affairs, trustees may wish to specify both the manner in which and the extent to which settlors exercise their legal powers through the contract. However, the extent to which a trustee's desire can be given effect depends on the extent of its perceptions of the risks associated with a settlor's intervention and how powerful the trustee is in trying to impose constraints on the settlor. Similarly, when trustees wish to minimize the reputational risk flowing from the disposition of charitable trust assets, they may elect to use collective decision-making mechanisms to share and dilute potential responsibilities. However, the extent to which the trustee's desire takes effect depends on its perception of the complexity of the management of charitable trusts and the extent to which a settlor is willing to participate in the decision-making process. In these two examples, although the focus of the planned contract clauses is different, the logic behind them is the same – the use of contractual tools to distribute risks between trust parties. To conduct an in-depth analysis of the ways in which contractual planning responds to trust parties' perceptions of risk, Section III-B, III-C and III-D. will examine the factors of relevance to contractual planning and the way in which each factor affects trust parties' decision-making.

B Planning for the Risk of the Vagueness of the Law

Contract theorists acknowledge that contracts are widely used as tools to allocate risks between relevant parties.[27] In light of the ambiguities in the

[26] Stewart Macaulay, 'Non-Contractual Relations in Business: A Preliminary Study' (1963) 28(1) *American Sociological Review* 55, 56.

[27] See Jeannie Marie Paterson, Andrew Robertson and Arlen Duke, *Contract: Cases and Materials* (Thomson Reuters, 2016) 540; Stephen A. Smith, *Contract Theory* (Oxford University Press, 2004) 308; Stewart Macaulay, 'An Empirical View of Contract Law' (1985) 1985 *Wisconsin Law Review* 465, 475; Alan Schwartz and Robert E. Scott, 'Contract Theory and the Limits of Contract Law' (2003) 113(3) *Yale Law Journal* 541, 555; Macaulay (n 27) 63.

legislative framework, trust parties tend to use contractual tools to clarify how they should interact in the ongoing management of charitable trust affairs, how the performance of their duties can be assessed, and how disputes between them can be resolved. As analysed in Chapter 3, under the legislative framework for charitable trusts, the role of the trustee is more akin to that of an agent of the settlor than that of a trustee in common law jurisdictions. Settlors have extensive statutory powers and, therefore, are able to play a proactive role in the administration of charitable trusts.[28] The gateway through which settlors intervene in the management of charitable trusts is largely relaxed, in that very few restrictions are imposed on the exercise of their powers, and there is uncertainty regarding how the performance of trustees' duties should be assessed. Recognizing this, for the purpose of mitigating disputes associated with the administration of trust affairs, trustees may wish to specify both the scenario in which and the extent to which settlors can intervene, and settlors may wish to clarify how trustees' duties work and what each duty entails. Following from this logic, trust parties often design contract clauses to guide how they interact in the day-to-day governance of charitable trusts.

1 On the Part of the Settlor

Where a consensus has been reached that settlors will play a role in the ongoing management of charitable trusts, the ensuing discussion involves the extent and ways in which the settlors will play their roles. In the data collection, all the trustee managers interviewed were asked the following: Under what circumstances are you willing to use contractual tools to limit the exercise of settlors' powers? Five managers answered this question,[29] declaring that their motivation to create contractual constraints was primarily related to the vagueness of article 21 of the Chinese Trust Law. Pursuant to this article, where special reasons are not anticipated at the time the trusts are created, settlors are entitled to ask trustees to modify management methods where the methods in question are not favourable to the attainment of charitable purposes. The current law does not provide clarity around situations in which a management method can be said to be unfavourable to the realization of trust purposes, neither does it specify special reasons in the context of article 21. This vagueness creates a great deal of uncertainty regarding trustees'

[28] See analysis in Section III-B of Chapter 3.
[29] See interviews with T1, T2, T3, T5, and T6.

administration of trust affairs. For example, to what extent does the current management method impede the execution of charitable trust purposes? What are the appropriate ways in which risks associated with the modification of management methods should be addressed? How would regulators look at the modification of management methods? If there are no contractual clauses defining the way in which article 21 works, these questions will likely lead to controversy between the trust parties. Consistent with this analysis, among the twenty-eight charitable trust contracts collected, twenty-two had incorporated a similar provision[30] limiting the potential application of article 21; that is, because some situations are unexpected at the time trusts are created, any suggestions on changing management methods must be submitted to regulatory agencies for approval. It is not difficult to understand the reason behind this provision: a layer of protection could be attached to trust parties if regulatory agencies are involved in the decision-making process.[31]

Nevertheless, contractual practice also raises a new question: how should the legal effect of these contractual constraints be understood? Although these constraints are imposed on the basis of the mutual assent of trust parties, the legal validity of such constraints remains unclear. The interviewees had different views on this issue. Some proposed that these contractual constraints should be legally valid, provided that their imposition did not involve fraud, duress, or undue influence on the part of the trustee; others were of the view that the settlors' powers in article 21 of the Chinese Trust Law were granted by statute, the exercise of which could not be burdened with contractual constraints.[32] The legality of these constraints remains unclear, and this issue remains unanswerable until judicial interpretations or new laws are issued for clarification.

2 On the Part of the Trustee

The charitable trust, a business with low commercial profits but high reputational risks, is not welcomed by trustees in practice. An analysis of the interview data presented two explanations for managers' reluctance

[30] Whether contractual constraints can be imposed depends on the balancing of various factors, including the relative bargaining power between trust parties and whether the constraints imposed are consistent with the interest of each party. See interviews with A1, A6, and R1.

[31] See interviews with T1, T3, T5, L1, L2, and L9.

[32] See interviews with A6, A7, and R1.

regarding handling charitable trust affairs. The first is the lack of specific indicators to assess the performance of managers who are responsible for charitable trusts.[33] The second is the high risk associated with the administration of charitable trusts. Nevertheless, the interview data show that trust companies may be willing to engage in the charitable trust business if the potential benefits are thought to outweigh the costs and risks. In the eyes of trustees, the benefits of conducting charitable trust business mainly include two factors. The first is the benefit that trust companies can receive in respect of industry ratings. The China Trustee Association evaluates and grades the performance of trust companies annually. Although the grade issued by this association is not official, it has been considered a de facto authority for the ranking of trust companies in China. Undertaking charitable trust businesses can help trust companies score well under the social responsibility column.[34] The second benefit relates to the positive effect that trust companies can achieve for image building.[35] Engaging in charitable trust businesses can bring certain promotional benefits to trust companies, for example, demonstrating that they are fulfilling their social responsibilities and have good social ethos. In consideration of such benefits, and the possibility of allocating potential risks through the use of contractual tools, trust companies have engaged in much charitable trust businesses. The information disclosed on the Charity in China platform shows that of the 582 charitable trusts recorded over the last five years, trust companies have accepted the office of trust for 531 of them.

Once trust companies have participated in the charitable trust business, the next question that trustees consider focuses on the possible

[33] Most trust companies do not have specific indicators to assess the performance of managers responsible for charitable trust affairs. These companies use indicators for commercial trusts (i.e., the rate of return on investment) to assess the performance of charitable trusts. However, pursuant to article 30 of the Measures for Charitable Trusts, charitable trust properties can only be invested in low-risk assets such as bank deposits, government bond, central bank bills, and money market funds. In contrast, the investment areas for commercial trust assets are wide, including infrastructure industry, the security market, the real estate industry, and commercial enterprises. According to the assessment indicators for commercial trusts, no matter how diligent managers are, it is extremely difficult to achieve good performance when handling charitable trust affairs. See interviews with L1, L8, T1, T2, T3, and T5.

[34] See《信托公司行业评级指引（试行）》 [Guidelines for Industry Rating of Trust Companies (Trial)] (People's Republic of China) China Trustee Association, 14 September 2017, arts 7, 11. See also interviews with T1, T3, T7, L1, and L8.

[35] See interviews with T1, T5, L1, L5, L9, and A1.

measures that can be taken to prevent their reputation from being damaged in the process of managing charitable trust affairs. The law does not delineate the scope and content of the managerial or distributive powers held by trustees. Rather, it stipulates that trustees shall practice due diligence and perform their duties with integrity and prudence when disposing of trust assets.[36] Given the vagueness in the definition of trustees' duties and powers, the twenty-eight charitable trust contracts show that trustees often employ three types of contractual planning for managing trust affairs: (1) specifying the way in which the investment power is exercised; (2) clarifying the way in which the statutory duties are performed; and (3) establishing charitable trust committees for collective decision-making.

(a) The Investment Power Most trustees are willing to develop detailed and complete contractual terms for managing trust affairs. Pursuant to article 30 of the Measures for Charitable Trusts, charitable trust assets must be invested in low-risk assets such as bank deposits or government bonds. However, settlors and trust companies can agree to exceptions[37] to the

[36] 《中华人民共和国信托法》 [Trust Law of the People's Republic of China] (People's Republic of China) National People's Congress, 28 April 2001 (n 2) art 25;《慈善信托管理办法》 [Administrative Measures for Charitable Trusts] (People's Republic of China) China Banking Regulatory Commission and Ministry of Civil Affairs, 10 July 2017 (n 10) art 24.

[37] The Interim Measures for the Management of Value-Added and Investment Activities of Charitable Organization (hereinafter Measures for Charitable Organizations) was issued on 30 October 2018. There is a conflict between the Measures for Charitable Organizations and the Measures for Charitable Trusts. The Measures for Charitable Trusts stipulates that charitable trust assets shall be used for low-risk assets, but an exception can be made where agreements are concluded between trust companies and settlors. See《慈善信托管理办法》[Administrative Measures for Charitable Trusts] (People's Republic of China) China Banking Regulatory Commission and Ministry of Civil Affairs, 10 July 2017 (n 10) art 30. Given this, when charitable organizations assume the office of trustee, they cannot invest high-risk assets by making special agreements with settlors. In contrast, the Measures for Charitable Organizations releases this limitation, stating that charitable organizations can invest in asset management products issued by financial institutions. See《慈善组织保值增值投资活动管理暂行办法》 [Interim Measures for the Administration of the Investment Activities for Value Preservation and Appreciation of Charitable Organizations] (People's Republic of China) Ministry of Civil Affairs, 30 October 2018, art 4. One question arises as to which Measures should be followed when charitable organizations invest charitable trust assets. If we follow the principle 'new law superior to old law', the Measures for Charitable Organization should be applied first, thereby expanding the investment power of charitable organizations. However, if we follow the principle 'special law superior to general law', the Measures for Charitable Trusts should be applied first, with charitable organizations acting as trustees.

investment of trust assets.[38] Five of the seven trustee managers interviewed said that they were reluctant to retain broad investment power when managing charitable trust assets,[39] whereas the remaining two expressed that it made no difference whether or not flexible investment power was reserved, for all investment decisions must be approved by the settlor.[40] Distinct from commercial trusts where managers are entrusted to invest in pursuit of profitable gains, stability and low risk are of crucial concern when investing charitable trust assets. Thus, trustees of charitable trusts tend to devise detailed plans on how trust assets could be invested and define the procedure for making investment decisions in the contract. Among the twenty-eight charitable trust contracts, twenty-three contained a similar clause narrowing the investment scope to limited types of assets, such as bank deposits, central bank bills, and financial bonds. As to the other five contracts in which the trustees were authorized to make flexible investment decisions, the decision-making procedure was set forth clearly in the contract. Finally, even more significantly, all twenty-eight trust contracts were written with a clear investment disclaimer marked in bold. Under the disclaimer was a series of warnings outlining the potential risks (e.g., market risks and policy risks) from investing charitable trust assets.

(b) The Statutory Duty Trustees of charitable trusts must comply not only with the Chinese Charity Law but also with the regulations applicable to trust companies[41] or charitable

In this light, the investment power of charitable organizations is strictly limited. See 金锦萍 [Jin Jinping],《慈善信托的规制之道 – 兼评<慈善信托管理办法>》 [Regulation of Charitable Trusts: Comment on 'Administrative Measures for Charitable Trusts'] (2017) 16 中国社会组织 *China Social Organization* 23, 26.

[38] In contrast to the investment of charitable trust properties, the trustees of public welfare trusts have no freedom to make investments, and trust parties cannot use contractual agreements to waive this investment restriction. See《中国银监会办公厅关于鼓励信托公司开展公益信托业务支持灾后重建工作的通知》 [Notice of the General Office of China Banking Regulatory Commission on the Encouragement of Charitable Trust Business of Trust Companies to Support Post-Earthquake Reconstruction] (People's Republic of China) General Office of China Banking Regulatory Commission, 6 February 2008, s 6(3).

[39] See interviews with T1, T2, T3, T5, and T6.

[40] See interviews with T4 and T7.

[41] For regulations that apply to trust companies, see, e.g.,《信托公司管理办法》 [Measures for Administration of Trust Companies] (People's Republic of China) China Banking Regulatory Commission, 23 January 2007;《信托公司集合资金信托计划管理办法》 [Administrative Measures for Collective Investment Trust Schemes of Trust Companies] (People's Republic of China) China Banking Regulatory Commission,

organizations.[42] However, these legal instruments all lack clear guidance regarding the definition of trustees' duties and how the performance of these duties should be assessed. Meanwhile, because of intense administrative and policy influences, regulators are inclined to exercise their powers in a strict sense when dealing with non-compliance with regulatory measures or violations of the law.[43] Given these two concerns, when designing contractual terms, trustees tend to be concerned less about how to acquire more powers vis-à-vis the other party but more about what clauses can be used to guide the discharge of their legal roles.

In twenty-five of the contracts, two duties were shown to be carefully planned: the duties to segregate and disclose. The duty to segregate is stipulated in article 27 of the Measures for Charitable Trusts: the assets of a charitable trust must be separated from those of the trustee. Two issues do not receive further elaboration in this article. First, to what extent and in what way can the duty to segregate be performed? Second, how may the trustee manage and compile separate accounts for the assets of different charitable trusts? In practice, trustees have taken a variety of approaches to address these two questions, especially in terms of specifying the way in which this duty works through a contract. This approach has been evidenced by contractual practice. A common clause dealing with the duty to segregate was incorporated into all the twenty-eight contracts collected: 'The trustee is responsible for setting up a special bank account for each charitable trust it handles, and signing a contract with professional custodians (commercial bank) to safeguard charitable trust assets and review the net asset value of the assets; different

4 February 2009;《信托公司净资本管理办法》 [Measures for the Administration of Net Capital of Trust Companies] (People's Republic of China) China Banking Regulatory Commission, 24 August 2010;《信托投资公司信息披露管理暂行办法》 [Interim Measures for the Administration of Information Disclosure by Trust Companies] (People's Republic of China) China Banking Regulatory Commission, 18 January 2015.

42 For regulations that apply to charitable organizations, see, e.g.,《基金会管理条例》 [Regulations on Administration of Foundations] (People's Republic of China) State Council, 3 August 2004 (n 13);《社会团体登记管理条例》 [Regulations on Registration Administration of Associations] (People's Republic of China) State Council, 6 February 2016 (n 14);《民办非企业单位登记管理暂行条例》 [Interim Regulations on the Administration of the Registration of Privately-Operated Non-Enterprise Organizations] (People's Republic of China) State Council, 25 October 1998 (n 15);《慈善组织保值增值投资活动管理暂行办法》 [Interim Measures for the Administration of the Investment Activities for Value Preservation and Appreciation of Charitable Organizations] (People's Republic of China) Ministry of Civil Affairs, 30 October 2018 (n 38).

43 See analysis in Section II-C of Chapter 4.

charitable trusts shall be independent of each other in terms of account setup, bookkeeping record and fund allocation'.[44]

Clarification of disclosure duties through the contract serves the same purpose of facilitating the management of trust affairs. Two observations can be offered here. To begin with, the current law on information disclosure is overly vague and incomplete. The law stipulates that trustees are obliged to disclose charity-related information in an adequate and timely manner. However, little guidance is provided on how this duty could be performed.[45] In the eyes of trustees, two questions remain pertinent: (1) to what extent should the information regarding trust asset conditions be disclosed, and (2) should the level of transparency required of a charitable trust be differentiated by the scale and type of its assets or the nature of its charitable purposes?[46] In the eyes of the regulators, the crucial concern is whether there is sufficient transparency to inform regulators and stakeholders that trust assets are being used for appropriate purposes. In order to simplify the supervisory work and mitigate the risks associated with the supervision of charitable trusts, regulators often require trust parties to specify how the information disclosure in the contract works and what information is involved. The regulatory officials in Guangzhou and Beijing even said that the degree of specificity of the information disclosure clause was essential to determining whether or not a charitable trust would be recorded.[47] Among the trustee managers

[44] See also interviews with L1, L2, L5, L9, T1, T3, T5, and T7. Compared to the Measures for Charitable Trusts, the Administrative Measures for Collective Investment Trust Schemes of Trust Companies prescribes that, after the establishment of a trust scheme, the trust company shall deposit assets under the trust scheme into a special bank account; meanwhile, during the term of a trust scheme, the trust company shall select a commercial bank with stable operations as the custodian. See《信托公司集合资金信托计划管理办法》 [Administrative Measures for Collective Investment Trust Schemes of Trust Companies] (People's Republic of China) China Banking Regulatory Commission, 4 February 2009 (n 42) arts 18–19. Although the Measures for Collective Investment Trusts Schemes does not apply to charitable trusts, trust companies often draw reference from the experience of collective investment trusts when engaging in charitable trust business.

[45] 《慈善信托管理办法》[Administrative Measures for Charitable Trusts] (People's Republic of China) China Banking Regulatory Commission and Ministry of Civil Affairs, 10 July 2017 (n 10) arts 14, 56;《中华人民共和国慈善法》 [Charity Law of the People's Republic of China] (People's Republic of China) National People's Congress, 16 March 2016 (n 10) art 71.

[46] See also analysis in Section II-C of Chapter 4.

[47] See interviews with R1 and R2.

and trust lawyers interviewed, four[48] had experience of modifying contract clauses pursuant to regulators' suggestions. They stated that, on one hand, the regulators' interference with their contractual planning was outside the scope of their expectation; on the other hand, the regulators' suggestions on how the information disclosure clause should be modified were insightful, for they could discern the regulators' concerns and use this experience to continually update and modify standard contractual terms for future use.

(c) **The Charitable Trust Committee** The charitable trust committee mechanism is widely used in practice to guide the management of charitable trust affairs. The charitable trust committee generally comprises the trustee, settlor, and trust supervisor (if any). In this committee, the members agree in advance that any decision relating to the selection of beneficiaries or the distribution of trust assets can only come into force when unanimous consent is achieved between the members.[49] The committee, a mechanism unique to Chinese charitable trusts, is rarely used in commercial trusts. What is the rationale behind the establishment of this committee? Why do trustees wish to involve settlors and trust supervisors in the decision-making process? Through interviews with trust lawyers and trustee managers, I identified two reasons. First, trustees must abide by the duties of care, skill, and prudence when managing and distributing charitable trust assets. However, the current law is silent on definitions of these duties. In the eyes of trustees, it may become easier to meet the requirements of 'due care', 'skill', and 'prudence' if the charitable trust committee is involved in the decision-making process.[50] Second, compared to the asset scale of the individual collective investment trust (amounting to RMB 0.135 billion or USD20.63 million on average),[51] the asset scale of the individual charitable trust is not large,

48 See interviews with L1, L2, L3, and T5.

49 In charitable trusts where local governments act in the capacity of settlors, the relevant governments tend to use the mechanism of the charitable trust committee and be proactive in supervising the management of trust affairs. Meanwhile, because these governments have resources and experience in selecting beneficiaries, they are willing to advise trustees on how to choose beneficiaries and distribute trust assets. See interviews with L1 and T1.

50 Interviewees in favour of this opinion include A1, A6, A4, L1, L3, and T7.

51 中国人民大学信托与基金研究所 [Institute of Trust and Fund of Renmin University of China],《中国信托业发展报告（2016）》 [The Development Report of Chinese Trust Business (2016)] (中国经济出版社 [China Economic Publishing House], 2018) 127.

ranging approximately from RMB 10,000 to RMB 10 million (from USD 1,396.65 to USD 1.39 million).[52] Charitable trusts are not the core business of trust companies. However, trustees are exposed to different levels of legal and reputational risk when managing charitable trusts. In view of these two reasons, most of the trustees interviewed were inclined to use the committee mechanism to administer trust affairs – by allowing settlors and trust supervisors to participate in the decision-making process, the responsibilities associated with the management of charitable trusts can be shared and diluted.

However, it is worth noting that, among the twenty-eight contracts, the three contracts from Western China made no mention of how charitable trust affairs should be managed and how the responsibilities and duties of each party should be performed. On its surface, this phenomenon suggests that there may be a regional variation in terms of contractual planning. Nevertheless, interviews with the trust lawyers and trustee managers[53] in charge of the creation and management of the three trusts suggest that this phenomenon is not contrary to the argument developed in this chapter that there is substantial contractual planning for risk allocation. According to the interview data, the charitable purposes of the three trusts were all related to poverty alleviation. They all lasted less than six months; the distribution was one-off; and the trustees had no discretion as to how trust assets should be distributed or how beneficiaries should be selected. The parties to these three trusts had previously reached a consensus concerning all managerial and distribution affairs. Thus, they were of the view that the perceived risks mentioned earlier were less likely to materialize and that the need for substantial planning of the contract terms for risk allocation was neither imperative nor urgent.

C *Planning for the Risk of Public Scrutiny*

As analysed in Chapter 3, under the law, settlors are empowered to play a proactive role in the day-to-day governance of Chinese charitable trusts. The granting of wide powers to settlors is consistent with the objective of securing the autonomy of settlors and serves to encourage the public to

[52] This data is accessible through the uniform information platform 'Charity in China'.
[53] See interviews with L1, L2, and T1.

take advantage of trusts to develop charitable causes.[54] In practice, there is no uniform answer as to the extent to which and the way in which settlors intervene in the management of charitable trusts. Among the actors interviewed, some expressed the view that settlors should play a dominant role in the administration of charitable trusts.[55] In contrast, others suggested that it was not proper to simply say that settlors play a proactive or conservative role. The extent to which a settlor intervenes in each trust varies considerably. This depends on the balancing or weighing of multiple factors, including the settlors' wishes and identity, the scale of trust assets, the nature of the charitable purpose, and the duration of the charitable trust.[56] The weight allocated to each of these factors varies, and two factors are especially important in settlors' decision-making process: the scale of the trust assets and the nature of the charitable purposes. The larger the scale of trust assets, or the more politically or socially sensitive the charitable trust purpose, the greater the likelihood that the settlor will play an active role. A common pattern can be discerned from this observation: the degree of likelihood to which settlors will bear legal or reputational risk determines how willing they are to perform supervisory roles.

1 The Nature of the Charitable Purpose

The first factor affecting a settlor's decision-making is the nature of the charitable purpose. This does not mean that the charitable purposes themselves are closely related to settlors' interests and that, therefore, settlors are inclined to keep a close eye on carrying them out. Instead, what motivates settlors to play a proactive role is the degree of likelihood that they will bear legal or reputational risks when the purposes to be carried out are politically or socially sensitive. Three illustrative examples are the Charitable Trust of Targeted Poverty Alleviation (*jingzhun fupin* 精准扶贫) – Zhejin Wulanchabu City Chahar Right Back Banner (the Back Banner Charitable Trust);[57] the China Credit Trust – the

[54] Hui Jing, 'The Legal Nature of the Chinese Charitable Trust' in Matthew Harding and Ying Khai Liew (eds.), *Asia-Pacific Trusts Law: Theory and Practice in Context* (Hart, 2021) 271, 280. See also the analysis in Section III-B of Chapter 3.

[55] See interviews with L2, L8, and A2.

[56] See interviews with A1, A3, A4, A6, R2, L1, L3, T1, and T7.

[57] Relevant information on the Charity in China platform includes: (a) this trust was recorded by the Hangzhou Bureau of Civil Affairs on 14 December 2018; (b) the settlor was the Poverty Alleviation and Development Office of Charhar Right Back Banner; (c) the trustee was the Zheshang Jinhui Trust Company; (d) the trust supervisor was the

2018 Annual Charitable Trust of Poverty Alleviation (the Credit Charitable Trust)[58] and the SDIC Taikang Trust – the 2018 Gansu Lintao Industry Charitable Trust of Poverty Alleviation (the SDIC Charitable Trust).[59] In these three trusts, local poverty alleviation and development offices (government agencies) serve in the capacity of settlors.[60] Interviews with trustees and trust lawyers responsible for creating and managing the three trusts suggest two reasons why government agencies wish to play a proactive role.[61] First, the task of alleviating poverty is a crucial policy objective of both the central and local governments.[62] Media exposure of scandals will bring about rapid governmental

JINGTIAN & GONGCHENG Law Firm; and (e) the charitable purpose was to alleviate poverty and help the poor and engage in other charitable activities that are compliant with the Chinese Charity Law, the Chinese Trust Law, and the Measures for Charitable Trusts.

58 Relevant information on the Charity in China platform includes: (a) this trust was recorded by the Beijing Bureau of Civil Affairs on 9 July 2018; (b) the settlor was the Poverty Alleviation and Development Office of Lintao County; (c) the trustee was the China Credit Trust Company; (d) the trust supervisor was the Beijing ZHONGSHENG Law Firm; and (e) the charitable purpose was to alleviate poverty and help the poor, support the development of characteristic industries in poverty-stricken areas of Gansu Province, and provide educational and cultural assistance for local people who are destitute.

59 Relevant information on the Charity in China platform includes: (a) this trust was recorded by the Beijing Bureau of Civil Affairs on 26 March 2018; (b) the settlor was the Poverty Alleviation and Development Office of Lintao County; (c) the trustee was the SDIC Taikang Trust Company; (d) the trust supervisor was the Beijing ZHONGSHENG Law Firm; and (e) the charitable purpose was to alleviate poverty and help the poor, and to provide educational and living assistance for local poor people by supporting the development of characteristic industries in poverty-stricken areas of Gansu.

60 Three aspects require attention here. First, the trust assets of the three trusts come from private donors rather than government funds. Second, in all three trusts, private actors donate assets to government agencies and reach agreement with these agencies that the donated assets shall be used exclusively for charitable purposes. Third, government agencies adopt the form of charitable trusts for the reason that trust companies have expertise in investing and managing trust assets. See interviews with T1 and L2.

61 See interviews with T1 and L2.

62 For policy documents on poverty alleviation, see, e.g.,《中共中央、国务院关于打赢脱贫攻坚战的决定》 [Decision of the Central Committee of the Communist Party of China and the State Council on Winning the Battle against Poverty] (People's Republic of China) Central Committee of the Communist Party of China and the State Council, 29 November 2015, chs 1–2;《全国人民代表大会关于国民经济和社会发展第十三个五年规划纲要的决议》 [Resolution of the National People's Congress on the Outline of the Thirteenth Five-Year Plan for National Economic and Social Development] (People's Republic of China) National People's Congress, 16 March 2016, chs 56–8;《民政部关于推进深度贫困地区民政领域脱贫攻坚工作的意见》 [Opinions of the Ministry of Civil Affairs on Promoting Poverty Alleviation in the Field of Civil Affairs in Deep

intervention to redress wrongdoing,[63] and an official may be demoted or, in extreme situations, dismissed from their position once a public incident has caught the attention of higher-level authorities.[64] Second, the task of alleviating poverty is closely related to the public interest. Accordingly, the public is willing to pay close attention to the administration of charitable trusts that are relevant to poverty alleviation. As we all know, any public speculation about the use of charitable assets may result in irrevocable reputational damage to the governments concerned. Given this reputational risk, government agencies are willing to play a proactive role in the ongoing management of trust affairs, and all trust parties involved tend to have a strong desire to execute detailed plans of how these agencies may perform their roles.

2 The Scale of Trust Assets

The second factor affecting settlors' decision-making is the scale of trust assets. Where the scale of trust assets is large in the eyes of settlors, it is highly likely that these settlors will play a proactive role in the management of trust affairs. Two explanations are available here. The first relates to the settlors' wishes. As benevolent property owners, settlors place a certain amount of their assets in charitable trusts and, therefore, their desire to see how the money is going to be used is understandable. Furthermore, the courts are also willing to uphold such wishes in consideration of the notion that owners are provided with maximal freedom in disposing of their assets.[65] The second explanation derives from the settlors' risk perceptions. Over the last two decades, settlors in China

Poverty Stricken Areas] (People's Republic of China) Ministry of Civil Affairs, 7 April 2018, ch 1; 《中国农村扶贫开发纲要（2011–2020年）》 [Outline of Poverty Alleviation and Development in China Rural Areas (2011–2020)] (People's Republic of China) Central Committee of the Communist Party of China and State Council, 27 May 2011, chs 2–3; 《"十三五"脱贫攻坚规划》 ['13th Five-Year Plan' for Poverty Alleviation] (People's Republic of China) State Council, 23 November 2016.

63 Cooney (n 22) 1095.

64 Hon S. Chan and Jie Gao, 'Performance Measurement in Chinese Local Governments' (2008) 41 *Chinese Law & Government* 4, 8; Kwai Hang Ng and Xin He, *Embedded Courts: Judicial Decision-Making in China* (Cambridge University Press, 2017) 130. See also the analysis in Section III-B of Chapter 4.

65 Simon Gardner, *An Introduction to The Law of Trusts* (Oxford University Press, 3rd ed., 2011) 296; John D. Morley and Robert H. Sitkoff, 'Making Directed Trusts Work: The Uniform Directed Trust Act' (2019) 44(1) *ACTEC Law Journal* 3, 8; Robert H. Sitkoff, 'Trusts and Estates: Implementing Freedom of Disposition' (2014) 58 *Saint Louis University Law Journal* 643, 651; John H. Langbein, 'Mandatory Rules in the Law of Trusts' (2004) 98(3) *Northwestern University Law Review* 1105, 1121.

have witnessed enormous levels of instability and failure in the charity sector. They are aware of the risk of misappropriation arising from the day-to-day operation of charitable trusts. Interviews with trust lawyers suggest that the reputation of a charitable trust is critical to its ability to carry on its purpose. Scandals exposed by media to the public at large may signal that settlors are largely responsible for the misuse of charitable assets, even though the misuse itself is not related to the conduct of settlors.[66] Given these reputational and legal risks, settlors are willing to keep a close eye on trustees and the performance of their duties.

D *Planning for the Risk of Regulatory Scrutiny*

Following a consideration of the contractual plans relating to the risks of public scrutiny and the vagueness of the law, this section will examine how contractual tools are used to allocate risks of regulatory scrutiny. As noted in Section II, the Chinese Charity Law applies a new, significant regulatory framework to charitable trusts. The parties to charitable trusts are fully aware of the policy objectives that this new framework is designed to achieve and the possible negative consequences of violating them. As a result, the parties involved in the charitable trust business often use contracts to guide how they discharge their legal duties so that their behaviours or activities could be in alignment with the public welfare policy of the regulatory authority. A close examination of the twenty-eight contracts shows that, for the purpose of allocating the risk of regulatory scrutiny, trust parties often use contractual tools to plan three aspects: the dispute resolution clauses, the termination of charitable trusts, and the defective performance of trust parties.

1 The Dispute Resolution Clause

Pursuant to article 23 of the Measures for Charitable Trusts, charitable trust assets and the proceeds thereof must be used for charitable purposes.[67] Failure to comply with this 'all charitable use' requirement will

[66] See interviews with L1, L2, and L3.

[67] See《慈善信托管理办法》[Administrative Measures for Charitable Trusts] (People's Republic of China) China Banking Regulatory Commission and Ministry of Civil Affairs, 10 July 2017 (n 10) art 23. According to this legislative requirement, the inclusion of commercial or private purposes that are incidental or ancillary to charitable purposes will render the whole charitable trust invalid in China. This kind of legislative arrangement is in stark contrast with those relating to Australian charitable trusts. In Australia, no charitable trust can be held to be invalid by reason that a non-charitable purpose is

attract serious administrative liabilities on the part of trustees (violators), which may include a warning, disgorgement of illegal gains, and fines.[68] Since trustees fully understand that they may be forced to pay penalties in the event of non-compliance, their motivation to breach in the first place will be greatly reduced. Moreover, punishments can very quickly become public knowledge, and it is difficult for defaulters to shelter from such controversies. Thus, the damage to a trustee's reputation is not likely to be constrained.

The perceived risk thus influences trustees' conduct; for example, they may have no incentive to take high-risk actions. Recognizing this, the next question to consider is as follows: if a settlor asks a trustee to take certain actions that violate legislative or regulatory requirements (e.g., prioritizing settlors' private interests when distributing charitable assets), what will the trustee do? A few trustee managers and lawyers were asked this question, seven of whom replied. They pointed out that one of the main reasons for detailed contractual arrangements was to guide the performance of trustees' legal duties when disagreement occurs.[69] The vagueness of the law creates a high level of uncertainty regarding trustees' management of charitable trusts. Trustees do not know how their performance could be assessed and whether their management is compliant with the requirements of regulatory measures. This uncertainty creates greater scope for settlors to interfere with the management of charitable trusts. In this regard, trust parties often incorporate a lengthy and clear clause in the contract articulating the process to be followed in the event of disputes. According to this clause, when disputes arise regarding whether settlors' private interest can be prioritized, the trustees will first communicate with the settlors, explaining that any consideration of a trust party's private interest is disallowed by regulators. If a deadlock occurs, the charitable trusts parties will agree in advance that these

included in any of the purposes to, or for which, an application of any of the trust funds is directed or allowed by the trust. See *Charitable Trusts Act 1993* (NSW) pt 5 s 23 sub-s (1); *Charities Act 1978* (Vic) pt IB s 7M sub-s (1); *Trustees Act 1962* (WA) pt VIII s 102 sub-s (3); *Variation of Trusts Act 1994* (Tas) pt 2 s 4 sub-s (2); *Trustee Act 1936* (SA) pt 4 s 69A sub-s (1); *Trusts Act 1973* (Qld) pt 8 s 104 sub-s (1). See also analysis in Section II-B of Chapter 2.

68 《慈善信托管理办法》 [Administrative Measures for Charitable Trusts] (People's Republic of China) China Banking Regulatory Commission and Ministry of Civil Affairs, 10 July 2017 (n 10) art 59.

69 See interviews with T1, T2, T3, T4, L1, L2, and L3.

disputes can be referred to regulators for resolution. This observation has been evidenced in contractual practice. Eighteen of the twenty-eight charitable trust contracts were carefully planned with one provision, namely, settlors are obliged not to require trustees to manage trust assets in illegal ways and not to seek illegal benefits through the operation of charitable trusts. In response to this contractual duty, a large group of trustees also indicated that they reserve the right to resign.[70] This right is favourable to protecting trustees' interest as it often takes the form of a contractual clause that allows trustees to terminate the contract without fault of either party. Where the appearance of a conflict between trust parties is so great and the settlors' intervention demonstrates a high possibility of non-compliance, trustees would expect to exercise this right.

Nevertheless, it is a common practice for settlors to reserve the contractual power to replace trustees. Two observations are pertinent in relation to this practice. First, the power to replace trustees can facilitate settlors' supervision of charitable trusts. Where a risk arises from trustees' misappropriation of trust assets, settlors can exercise this power to replace the trustees. Second, this power may also pose a risk to the trustees' management of charitable trusts. If the trust contract does not clearly define the content of the power and the way in which it functions, settlors may arbitrarily exercise this power, thereby creating uncertainty in the trustees' decision-making and forcing them to perform their roles inactively. Given these concerns, it is of enormous significance to strike a sensible balance between settlors' exercise of power and the protection of trustees' autonomy in managing charitable trusts. Among the twenty-eight contracts collected, ten conferred on settlors the power to replace trustees, and they uniformly incorporated the provision that 'the settlor can replace or change the trustee only if the trustee disposes of trust assets in breach of the trust purpose or causes losses to the trust assets due to violation of its management duties or improper handling of the trust affairs'.

[70] It is possible for trustees to reserve the right to resign in trust contracts as per article 39 of the Measures for Charitable Trusts – the trustees of charitable trusts may not resign on their own, unless otherwise prescribed in trust documents. In contrast, the right to resign is not reserved by trustees of Chinese public welfare trusts. Article 66 of the Chinese Trust Law prescribes that 'no trustee of a public welfare trust may resign without the approval of the public welfare administration authority'.

2 The Termination of Charitable Trusts

The second area where trust parties elect to plan in detail is the termination of charitable trusts. Two observations can be drawn from the investigation of the trust contracts collected. First, all the contracts examined required that the assets of the charitable trust and the proceeds thereof be used for charitable purposes; where trustees use trust assets and the proceeds thereof for non-charitable purposes, settlors have the power to ask the trustees to restore the assets to their former state or seek compensation.[71] Second, twenty-three contracts provided detailed descriptions of how charitable trust assets shall be dealt with in the event of termination. Interviews with regulatory officials and trustee managers suggest that this planning is closely related to the risk perceptions of both regulators and trust parties.

First, regulators have no expertise in exercising the cy-près power. Pursuant to article 43 of the Measures for Charitable Trusts, where a charitable trust is terminated and the trust assets have no owner or the owner is the unspecified general public, the CAD that processes the record-filing of the charitable trust is empowered to guide the trustee to use the trust assets for purposes similar to the original charitable purposes. This cy-près mechanism aims, to the greatest extent, to strike a balance between securing settlor autonomy and preserving charitable resources in the public domain.[72] However, charitable trusts in China are still in their infancy, and there are ambiguities regarding this mechanism. How should the cy-près use of charitable trust assets be controlled? To what extent can the purposes be considered similar to the original charitable purposes? Since no government documents or laws have been issued for reference, these two questions remain unanswerable. The government officials and scholars interviewed stated that it was still unclear how the cy-près mechanism should work in practice and what role regulators could play in the cy-près use of charitable trust assets.[73] Before clarifying these two questions, the CADs in Beijing, Shanghai, Hangzhou, Gansu, and Qinghai are disinclined to exercise their cy-près power over the operation of charitable trusts, as evidenced by the

[71] This practice is consistent with the requirement of article 23 of the Measures for Charitable Trusts.

[72] Edith L. Fisch, 'Changing Concepts and Cy Pres' (1959) 44(3) *Cornell Law Review* 382, 382; W. Barton Leach, 'Perpetuities: Cy Pres on the March' (1964) 4 *Vanderbilt Law Review* 1381, 1385–6.

[73] See interviews with R1, R2, A1, A3, A4, A5, and A6.

complete absence of cy-près work conducted in any of the five cities since the enactment of the Chinese Charity Law in 2016. Furthermore, the interview data show that regulators tend to require trust parties to incorporate detailed contractual provisions specifying how trust assets should be used when charitable trusts are terminated.[74] This practice is consistent with the regulatory strategy noted in Section III-B; namely, regulators use their regulatory powers to influence contractual planning between trust parties so as to mitigate potential risks faced by regulators in the discharge of their roles.

Second, the cy-près use of charitable assets is also of primary concern to trust parties. Aside from the cy-près scheme implemented by regulators, trustees also have the power to direct charitable asset cy-près use to a similar purpose, provided that this use is approved by relevant regulators.[75] In the eyes of trustees, how can the cy-près use of charitable trust assets be compliant with regulatory measures? Even more importantly, in what way could the cy-près use of charitable trust assets avoid public criticism? These questions significantly affect trustees' decision-making, especially considering that the public at large lacks trust in the performance of their duties, and they would face administrative liabilities in the event the improper use of trust assets is made known to relevant regulators. In view of the legal and reputational risks, the parties to charitable trusts elect to clearly describe how the trust assets should be dealt with in the trust contract and consult regulators on how the clauses concerning the cy-près use of charitable trust assets should be designed or modified. Among the twenty-eight charitable trust contracts collected, twenty incorporated a similar provision describing the cy-près use of charitable assets upon the termination of charitable trusts: where a charitable trust is terminated, upon approval by the relevant regulators, the trustee of the charitable trust should use the trust assets for purposes similar to the original charitable purposes.

3 The Defective Performance of Trust Parties

It is common for contract parties to use 'actual or potential sanctions to induce performance of the contract or to compensate for

[74] See interviews with L1, L2, T5, and T7.

[75] 《慈善信托管理办法》 [Administrative Measures for Charitable Trusts] (People's Republic of China) China Banking Regulatory Commission and Ministry of Civil Affairs, 10 July 2017 (n 10) art 43.

non-performance'.[76] Upon a careful reading of the twenty-eight charitable trust contracts, one can observe that trust parties tend to plan in detail how the defective performance of each party should be dealt with, especially those that are likely to attract the attention of regulators. In the twenty-eight charitable trust contracts, two clauses were commonly incorporated. The first relates to the unlawful creation of charitable trusts – when settlors create charitable trusts for illegal purposes.[77] This unlawful practice, pursuant to article 54 of the Measures for Charitable Trust and article 11 of the Chinese Trust Law, will strike down the legality of the whole trust scheme and attract an investigation from the relevant regulators. In the eyes of trustees, it is cumbersome and difficult to identify the source of trust assets and discern the true purpose behind the establishment of a trust. More significantly, regulatory investigations of such illegal behaviours might easily become public knowledge and attract media coverage. Because of this concern, trustees are incentivized to include a clause dealing with the illegal creation of charitable trusts. This thinking has been demonstrated in contractual practice: among the twenty-eight contracts examined, twenty-one had incorporated a clause stipulating that settlors should not create trusts for illegal purposes; if trustees suffer losses due to the illegal creation of charitable trusts, the settlors shall provide compensation for the losses in question.

A second clause commonly found in charitable trust contracts relates to the guarantee and statement made by the trust parties. In practice, the most common guarantee made by trust parties is that settlors or trustees have no direct or indirect interest in the selected beneficiaries. This guarantee is in line with the requirement of the no-interest rule stipulated in article 10 of the Measures for Charitable Trusts. There is a strong policy consideration regarding the operation of the no-interest rule: to prevent charitable trusts from becoming channels for corruption or crime.[78] Consistent with the policy rhetoric of creating a strict regulatory

[76] Macaulay (n 27) 56. See also *United Group Rail Services Ltd* v *Rail Corporation New South Wales* (2009) 74 NSWLR 618, 630, 636; *Beaton* v *McDivitt* (1987) 13 NSWLR 162, 168; Jeannie Marie Paterson, Andrew Robertson and Arlen Duke, *Principles of Contract Law* (Thomson Reuters (Professional) Australia Limited, 5th ed., 2016) 6; Roger Brownsword, 'Two Concepts of Good Faith' (1994) 7 *Journal of Contract Law* 197, 211; Geoffrey K. Flint, 'Enforce Them All: A Battle Cry for the Beleaguered Agreement to Negotiate' (1995) 13 *Australian Bar Review* 262, 270–1.

[77] 《中华人民共和国信托法》 [Trust Law of the People's Republic of China] (People's Republic of China) National People's Congress, 28 April 2001 (n 2) arts 11, 14.

[78] See interviews with R2, L3, A1, A3, A4, and A7.

environment for charitable trusts,[79] regulators tend to exercise their powers in a strict manner when dealing with violations of the no-interest rule and tend to disclose their disciplinary decisions in a timely manner to show the public that they are effectively executing their oversight roles. Trustees understand the legal consequences of violating the no-interest rule and, thus, are very cautious about distributing charitable assets to selected beneficiaries. This line of thinking has been demonstrated in contractual practice. Interviewees with experience of beneficiary selection stated that bargaining over the terms of the no-interest rule was a key part of contract negotiation between settlors and trustees.[80] Among the twenty-eight charitable trust contracts collected, twenty-four included the following clause: 'If trustees (or settlors) find that the selected beneficiaries have an interest in settlors (or trustees), trustees (or settlors) have the power to request the beneficiaries to return all benefits within the prescribed timeframe. Failing that deadline, settlors (or trustees) shall compensate these benefits to the trust assets'. For the four contracts that made no mention of the no-interest rule, I made an inquiry to the relevant trustee managers. This inquiry revealed that the trusts involved were not complicated and shared a similar fact pattern: the trust parties had agreed in advance that all trust funds should be donated to designated social organizations for the achievement of specific charitable purposes, and the trustees had already confirmed that the settlors concerned had no interest, direct or indirect, in these donee organizations.

IV Conclusion

Chapter 3 analysed the legislative regime governing the internal relationship between trust parties (i.e., settlors, trustees, and beneficiaries). The analysis showed that, while the law did set up the internal governance framework, it is incomplete and vague in terms of the role of each party and the ways in which these parties should interact. Chapter 4 analysed administrative practices and discovered that regulators in China are subject to intense policy and administrative pressures and, thus, are highly responsive to extra-legal factors in their implementation of the law. Due to the vagueness of the law and the administrative style of the regulation of charitable trusts, trust parties have perceived three types of risk in the creation and ongoing management of charitable trusts: the vagueness of

79 See analysis in Section II of Chapter 4.
80 See interviews with T1, L2, L1, and L5.

the law, public scrutiny, and regulatory scrutiny. This chapter examined these risks and how they affect the use of contractual tools by trust parties. This examination revealed that two relationship levels are generally regulated in the contractual practice of charitable trusts.

The first is the horizontal relationship between settlors and trustees. To mitigate the three types of risk, trust parties often employ contracts to plan the performance of their respective roles. Because of the vagueness of the law, settlors and trustees have a strong desire to clarify the scope of their powers and duties and the way in which trust assets are disposed of. Trustees elect to use contracts to limit the extent to which settlors interfere with the management of charitable assets. Meanwhile, settlors elect contracts that specify the types of duties for which trustees are responsible and the way in which these duties are discharged. As regards public scrutiny, the lack of clear criteria for assessing trustees' performance makes it easy for the public to criticize their management of charitable assets. This concern has forced trust parties to define the performance of their roles by virtue of contracts, especially when the relevant charitable purposes are socially and politically sensitive. Given the fact that regulators tend to deal with violations of law in a strict manner, settlors and trustees are willing to provide detailed plans of the handling of disputes, the disposition of trust assets in the event of trust termination, as well as those addressing defective performance by the various trust parties. The focus on these aspects of the contractual arrangement suggests that trust parties are willing to comply with the requirements of regulatory measures.

The second is the hierarchical relationship between regulators and trust parties. This chapter examined the role of regulators in the design of contract clauses between trust parties. It showed that regulators are willing to advise trust parties on what contract clauses are ambiguous and how they might be modified. This practice derives from regulators' own risk perceptions, a point that connects us back to the analysis presented in Chapter 4. To mitigate regulatory risk, regulators often require trust parties to incorporate or amend certain clauses in the trust contract, such as specifying how information disclosure in the contract works and what information is involved. Whether contract clauses are compliant with regulators' requirements is essential to determining whether or not a charitable trust can be recorded. These regulatory suggestions or recommendations have also been incorporated into precedent contracts in the form of standard contract clauses that are then used to guide future negotiations between trust parties on contractual arrangements.

However, in response to the risk of regulatory scrutiny, trust parties also expressed the willingness to consult regulators regarding the design and amendment of trust contract clauses. Given the role of regulators in contractual practice, it can be reasonably asserted that regulators, in representing the interest of the state, have had a systematic impact on the creation and operation of charitable trusts in China.

6

Analysis and Conclusion

I Introduction

This chapter reflects on the research questions proposed in Chapter 1, presents the key findings, and discusses avenues for future research. This book has tested the hypothesis that the governance framework for Chinese charitable trusts can only be fully understood in light of relevant law, administrative practice, and private actions undertaken by trust parties, all considered together. Testing this hypothesis has involved the examination of three inter-related factors shaping the governance framework for charitable trusts. First, according to the law, there is a governance framework for charitable trusts, but the law is vague and under-determined in various respects. Second, administrative practice is a significant part of the governance framework, as regulators in China are subject to intense administrative and policy pressures and are thus strongly responsive to extra-legal concerns. Third, private action is essential in the governance framework, as trust parties vary the governance framework of the law to mitigate the risks posed by administrative practice and the vagueness of the law. The inter-relationship between these three facets of charitable trust governance was explored through three research questions. First, how has the new charity law shaped the governance structure of Chinese charitable trusts? Second, how have regulators implemented the legal regulatory regime in practice? Third, what private actions have trust parties undertaken when engaging with the law?

II Summary of Key Findings

This book has examined the governance framework of Chinese charitable trusts from the perspectives of both law and practice. The examination resulted in three key findings. First, in contrast to the public law nature of public welfare trusts, legislators have incorporated several private law norms into the legal structure of charitable trusts. Despite the increasing autonomy of trust parties to a certain extent, the predominant role of public law norms indicates that the charitable trust model continues to privilege the state's desire to maintain control over charitable undertakings.[1] Second, the governance framework for Chinese charitable trusts comprises three aspects: law,[2] administrative practice,[3] and private actions undertaken by trust parties.[4] These three aspects are inter-related and, taken together, constitute the governance framework for Chinese charitable trusts. Third, due to the vagueness of the law and the political environment in which charitable trusts are introduced and operate, trust parties[5] and regulators[6] perceive different types of risk regarding the performance of their responsibilities. Adopting risk mitigation strategies has, accordingly, become an important driver shaping the governance framework for Chinese charitable trusts.

A *The Establishment of a Public–Private Hybrid Model*

As discussed in Chapter 2, legislators have created a public law–private law hybrid model for Chinese charitable trusts. The private law norms indicate the state's willingness to use charitable trusts to increase the participation of the general public in the development of charitable causes.[7] Under these private law norms, settlors are granted wide powers, such as the powers to change the trust management method and to appoint trust supervisors. This legislative approach allows settlors to play a proactive role in the creation and ongoing administration of charitable trusts. At the same time, the state is reluctant to relinquish its control over the use of charitable resources. Consequently, legislators have endowed regulators with wide supervisory powers to facilitate their control of the use of charitable assets.[8] Such allocation of powers and responsibilities between trust parties and regulators suggests that private law norms continue to be subordinated to public law norms in the legal structure of charitable trusts. More specifically, private parties are not

[1] See analysis in Section III of Chapter 3.
[2] Ibid.
[3] See analysis in Section III of Chapter 4.
[4] See analysis in Section III of Chapter 5.
[5] Ibid.
[6] See analysis in Section III of Chapter 4.
[7] See analysis in Section II of Chapter 2.
[8] See analysis in Section II of Chapter 4.

allowed to use charitable resources for personal purposes. They have the autonomy to determine how their management rights can be exercised, but only insofar as such exercise is in line with the state's public welfare policy.[9]

B *Three Inter-related Aspects of Charitable Trust Governance*

The second key finding relates to the three facets of Chinese charitable trust governance. As noted in Chapter 2, the charity law establishes the public law–private law divide in the governance framework for charitable trusts, but the law is vague in various respects. The vagueness of the law has motivated trust parties and regulators to adopt risk mitigation strategies in performing their legal roles and has also created a situation whereby these actors must consider extra-legal factors when determining which strategies are available and how they can be applied. Therefore, the law is only a part of the whole picture when it comes to understanding the governance of Chinese charitable trusts.

The public law aspects of charitable trust governance are related to regulation and thus connect the analysis of charitable trust governance to the role of regulators.[10] In the Chinese administrative system, regulators have long been subject to policy pressures and are, thus, strongly responsive to extra-legal concerns when implementing the law. Chapter 4 has identified three extra-legal factors that influence the decision-making of regulatory officials: the regional development agenda, the tension between regulatory capacity and regulatory objectives, and regulators' risk perceptions. The examination of regulatory practice has shown that administrative factors supplement, or even prevail over, legal rules in guiding regulators' supervisory work. Administrative practice is, therefore, a significant part of the charitable trust governance framework.

The private law aspects of charitable trust governance are related to the internal relationships between trust parties and, thus, connect the analysis of charitable trust governance to the roles of settlors, trustees, and beneficiaries.[11] The law establishes the internal relationship between trust parties, but it does not clearly elaborate how these parties should interact and perform their legal roles.[12] The vagueness of the law has resulted in a

[9] See analysis in Section II of Chapter 2.
[10] See analysis in Section III of Chapter 2.
[11] Ibid.
[12] See analysis in Section III of Chapter 3.

great deal of uncertainty in the management of charitable assets. The book has examined the areas in which the law related to trust parties is vague,[13] the types of risk perceived by trust parties,[14] and the strategies that such parties have taken to mitigate risks.[15] The examination has revealed that settlors and trustees are willing to use contract tools to mitigate the risks posed by administrative practice and the vagueness of the law. Contract practice is, thus, essential in the governance framework for charitable trusts.

C *Risk Mitigation by Trust Parties and Regulators*

The third finding, which concerns the three inter-related aspects of governance, is that adopting risk mitigation strategies is an important driver that shapes the behavioural patterns of regulators and trust parties.

In relation to the regulatory framework of charitable trusts, the charity law has established the powers and obligations of regulators. However, the law does not clearly define the scope of these powers and obligations and how they should be performed, as noted in Chapter 4. Such vagueness has posed risks to regulators when performing their oversight roles.[16] In addition to the law, regulators in the Chinese bureaucratic system suffer intense policy and administrative pressures. Regulators who fail to meet the political goals of the state are subject to severe administrative penalties.[17] Due to the vagueness of the law and the perception of administrative risks, regulators tend to consider extra-legal factors when implementing the law.[18]

In relation to the internal governance structure of charitable trusts, the law has established the checks-and-balances mechanisms between trust parties. However, the law does not clearly define the scope of settlors' powers and how such powers should be exercised, the scope of trustees' duties, and the ways in which settlors should interact with trustees. Due to the regulatory practice and the vagueness of the law, charitable trust parties have perceived various risks, as discussed in Chapter 5. Such a perception of risk has considerably influenced the distribution of powers

[13] Ibid.
[14] See analysis in Section III of Chapter 5.
[15] Ibid.
[16] See analysis in Section III of Chapter 4.
[17] Ibid.
[18] Ibid.

and duties of trust parties. To mitigate the risks associated with the management of charitable trusts, settlors and trustees have incentives to use contract tools to allocate their powers and obligations and to define the ways in which they should interact.[19]

III Answers to the Research Questions

A How Has the Charity Law Shaped the Governance Structure of Charitable Trusts?

This book has analysed the legal governance framework for Chinese charitable trusts and its distinctive characteristics. The analysis produced five key observations. First, legislators introduced a public law–private law hybrid model for Chinese charitable trusts, which continues to privilege state control over the autonomy of private parties.[20] This hybridity permeates and informs the governance structure of charitable trusts, as discussed in Chapter 2. Second, the law established checks-and-balances mechanisms between settlors and trustees.[21] The legal framework allows settlors to be proactive in the use and management of charitable assets, as discussed in Chapter 3. Third, legislators did not envisage beneficiaries playing a role in the governance of charitable trusts. The law does not define the legal status of beneficiaries in the Chinese charitable trust setting, nor does the law mention the rights or powers that the beneficiaries of a charitable trust may have.[22] Fourth, the law grants regulators wide powers in overseeing whether charitable assets are used in alignment with the state's public welfare goals.[23] This approach demonstrates the state's willingness to maintain strict control over the use of charitable resources, as noted in Chapter 4. Fifth, the law is vague in defining the relationship between and the responsibilities of trust parties and regulators; consequently, this vagueness has created substantive risks for both parties. The perceived risks have incentivized regulators to use administrative mechanisms when exercising their supervisory roles (as discussed under the second research question) and have motivated trust parties to undertake private actions when managing charitable assets (as discussed under the third research question).

[19] See analysis in Section III of Chapter 5.
[20] See analysis in Section III of Chapter 2.
[21] See analysis in Section III of Chapter 3.
[22] See analysis in Section IV of Chapter 3.
[23] See analysis in Section II of Chapter 4.

1 The Internal Relationship between Trust Parties

In contrast to the public law model of public welfare trusts, the hybrid model of charitable trusts emphasizes the autonomy of trust parties and, in theory, limits the extent to which the creation and ongoing operations of a charitable trust are subject to state intervention.[24] In the post-2016 legal framework, this legislative change is reflected by the fact that wide supervisory powers have been granted to settlors, along with the capacity to appoint trust supervisors.

As discussed in Chapter 3, a settlor in a charitable trust is granted wide powers by law, including the powers to change the management method of charitable assets and to appoint trust supervisors. This legislative approach is in stark contrast to the approach used in common law jurisdictions, as, according to common law, settlors generally drop out of the picture when charitable trusts are legally established.[25] In the Chinese charitable trust setting, the possession of wide powers enables settlors to not only define the way in which charitable assets are managed but to also be proactive in supervising the performance of trustees' duties.[26] However, the law is incomplete, which has resulted in a number of ambiguities in the relationship between settlors and trustees. For example, the vagueness of the law in defining the scope of settlors' powers has produced a great deal of uncertainty in the exercise of trustees' autonomous management powers and in the interactions between settlors and trustees in the day-to-day governance of charitable trusts.[27] In addition, the law is vague in defining the ways in which trustees should perform their duties. In the absence of clear criteria for the discharge of trustees' obligations, it is difficult for trustees to assess whether their management of charitable assets complies with the requirements of the law and the state's public welfare goals.[28] Such vagueness has created risks for both settlors and trustees and has motivated them to undertake private actions when performing their legal roles in practice (as discussed under the third research question).

The second aspect that illustrates private law norms in the governance of charitable trusts is the settlors' power to appoint trust supervisors, as discussed in Chapter 2. In contrast to public welfare trusts, the appointment of a

24 See analysis in Section III of Chapter 3.
25 See analysis in Section II of Chapter 2.
26 See analysis in Section III of Chapter 3.
27 Ibid.
28 Ibid.

trust supervisor is not mandatory in the charitable trust setting: settlors in a charitable trust have the discretion to determine whether a trust supervisor should be appointed. This legislative approach demonstrates the state's willingness to grant benevolent property owners greater autonomy in deciding how charitable trusts should be managed.[29] At the same time, the law is vague because it fails to provide clear criteria for the determination of a trust supervisor's powers and obligations.[30] Therefore, it is unclear how trust supervisors should discharge their obligations and to what extent trust supervisors can fulfil their duty of supervising trustees' actions.[31]

Aside from the vagueness of the law regarding the relationship between settlors, trustees, and trust supervisors, the law is also vague regarding beneficiaries' role in the governance framework. As analysed in Chapter 3, the new charity law adopted the term 'beneficiary' but made no mention of what powers or rights a beneficiary has in the governance setting. In the Chinese literature, there are two arguments regarding the nature of charitable trust beneficiaries: the beneficiary argument and the recipient argument. Chapter 3 has examined the way in which and the extent to which beneficiaries may play a monitoring role according to each argument. The beneficiary argument states that objects with the beneficiary title are entitled to sue when trustees cause losses to trust assets due to duty violations or the improper handling of trust affairs. However, this argument limits the situations under which objects of a charitable trust can initiate proceedings.[32] By contrast, drawing an analogy with the interpretation of 'direct interest' in the Civil Procedure Law and EPIL, an object can sue if they can demonstrate that their direct interests were harmed under the recipient argument. However, as the rules or principles regarding the role and nature of objects have not been conclusively settled, it is unclear whether the theoretical standing of objects in a charitable trust is upheld in practice, and if so, in what way and to what extent.[33]

2 The Establishment of a New Regulatory Framework

Before the introduction of charitable trusts, legislators attempted to use the model of public welfare trusts to encourage the public to participate

[29] Ibid.
[30] Ibid.
[31] Ibid.
[32] See analysis in Section IV of Chapter 3.
[33] Ibid.

in charitable undertakings.[34] However, as discussed in Chapter 3, public welfare trusts did not work very well, and the experience of the last twenty years has shown that there has been a considerable gap between the advantages that public welfare trusts were supposed to offer in developing charitable causes and the limited role that they played in reality. The fragmented regulation system has been responsible for the failure of public welfare trusts, particularly by discouraging the establishment of public welfare trusts.[35] Two issues illustrate this point. The first issue is the difficulty that benevolent property owners have had in identifying relevant administration authorities (regulators) for the establishment of public welfare trusts. The law requires private actors to submit documents to regulators for registration but makes no mention of who these regulators are and how they can be identified. Therefore, it has been difficult for private actors to know whom a registration application can be submitted to.[36] The second issue is related to regulators' unwillingness to approve the establishment of public welfare trusts. Regulators have exhibited a conservative attitude towards public welfare trusts and have been concerned about the risks related to the supervision of public welfare trusts.[37]

Due to the failure of public welfare trusts, legislators established a new regulatory framework for charitable trusts. The design of this new regulatory framework incorporated two policy objectives formulated by the central government: to control the use of charitable resources for public welfare purposes and to encourage the public's participation in the development of charitable causes.[38] Under this new regulatory framework, two specialized regulators (i.e., the BRAs and CADs) are tasked with regulating the creation and day-to-day administration of charitable

[34] See analysis in Section I of Chapter 1.

[35] See analysis in Section II of Chapter 4.

[36] See analysis in Section II of Chapter 3.

[37] See analysis in Section I of Chapter 1.

[38] See《中国慈善事业发展指导纲要（2011–2015年）》 [Guidelines for the Development of China's Charitable Causes (2011–2015)] (People's Republic of China) Ministry of Civil Affairs, 15 July 2011, chs 2–3; 《国务院关于促进慈善事业健康发展的指导意见》 [Guiding Opinions of the State Council on Promoting Healthy Development of Charitable Causes] (People's Republic of China) State Council, 24 November 2014, chs 2–5; 《民政部关于贯彻落实<国务院关于促进慈善事业健康发展的指导意见>的通知》 [Notice of the Ministry of Civil Affairs on Implementing the 'Guiding Opinions of the State Council on Promoting the Healthy Development of Charitable Causes'] (People's Republic of China) Ministry of Civil Affairs of People's Republic of China, 15 December 2014, ch 2.

trusts.[39] They represent the interests of the state and are granted wide supervisory powers to control the use of charitable assets.

As observed in Chapter 4, regulators can determine whether a charitable trust is recorded. When a charitable trust is legally established, regulators can ask trustees to submit annual reports, revoke trustees' registration licenses, and conduct supervisory conversations. This legislative arrangement allows regulators to maintain a high degree of control over the use of charitable trust resources.[40] In addition to granting regulatory powers, the law also requires regulators to take educative and consultative measures when performing their oversight roles. The law gives regulators broad authority in determining what forms these educative measures should take and how often the relevant consultative programmes or training efforts should be carried out. This regulatory approach involving public education reflects the public law norms in the legal structure of charitable trusts.[41]

At the same time, the regulatory framework for charitable trusts also contains several ambiguities. As noted in Chapter 4, the charity law does not clearly define the relationship between the two regulators. It is unclear how the two kinds of regulators should cooperate with each other in the exercise of their overlapping powers, such as the powers to assess charitable trusts and to conduct supervisory conversations. Nor does the charity law clearly define regulators' role in the creation and administration of charitable trusts.[42] There exists considerable uncertainty regarding the recording of new charitable trusts, the scope of regulators' powers and responsibilities, and the ways in which regulators should interact with trustees.[43] These ambiguities have created substantive risks for regulators and have incentivized them to adopt administrative mechanisms when discharging their supervisory duties. The use of administrative mechanisms has been discussed in more detail under the second research question.

3 The Predominant Role of Public Law Norms

The hybrid nature of charitable trusts indicates that the implementation of the policies concerning charitable trusts involves contradictions and

[39] See analysis in Section II of Chapter 4.
[40] See analysis in Section II of Chapter 2.
[41] Ibid.
[42] See analysis in Section II of Chapter 4.
[43] Ibid.

conflicts between the various interests of trust parties and the broader interests of the state. These contradictions include giving trust parties broad control over the exercise of their management rights while ensuring that charitable resources are used in a way that benefits the legitimate interests of society as defined by the state. The distribution of rights and responsibilities between trust parties and regulators in the creation and administration of charitable trusts shows that the private interests of trust parties continue to be subordinated to the interests of the community and, ultimately, to the interests of the state.[44]

In this public–private hybrid model, trust parties are granted broad autonomy in determining the ways in which charitable assets are managed. However, this autonomy can only take effect when the management of charitable trusts is in line with the state's public welfare goals.[45] As illustrated in Chapter 2, the state defines the scope of charitable purposes, and trust parties are not allowed to consider different purposes that might, for example, promote political advocacy in areas not approved by the state or to consider ancillary or subsidiary private benefits when handling charitable assets. The subordination of trust parties is ensured through the application of the public benefit doctrine (as discussed in Chapter 2), the granting of broad powers to regulators to control the use of charitable resources (as discussed in Chapter 4), and the establishment of the legal requirement that charitable trust assets and the proceeds thereof will all be used for charitable purposes (as discussed in Chapter 2). In China, the legislative reforms pertaining to charitable trusts reflect the historical tension between private individuals and state control and the ongoing tension between the social welfare goals that charitable trusts pursue and the autonomy of private actors in deciding how their assets can be used for charitable purposes.[46]

B *How Have Regulators Implemented the Legal Regulatory Regime in Practice?*

This book has studied regulatory practices by interviewing persons with experience in the establishment and regulation of charitable trusts. The study has shown that an examination of regulatory practices must consider both the legal framework and the political environment in which

44 See analysis in Section II of Chapter 2.
45 Ibid.
46 See analysis in Section I of Chapter 1.

laws are implemented as well as the interactions between the two. First, the law sets up a regulatory framework for charitable trusts that is vague and under-determined in various respects.[47] This vagueness has created risks for regulators in discharging their supervisory duties and has motivated them to adopt risk mitigation strategies. Second, political objectives have dictated the development of the charitable sector in China. Consequently, ensuring conformity with overarching policy objectives is an important driver shaping the function and scope of the regulatory framework for charitable trusts.[48] The vagueness of the law and the political objectives underlying the regulation of charitable trusts have prompted regulators to consider extra-legal factors when performing their responsibilities.[49]

Chapter 4 has provided a detailed analysis of the extra-legal factors that influence regulatory practices and regulators' risk mitigation strategies. Chapter 5 has discussed how regulators impact trust parties' use of contractual tools and the reasons behind this regulatory approach. This analysis enables the governance of charitable trusts to be understood not only in terms of what the regulators say they are doing but also by what they actually do in the day-to-day governance of charitable trusts.

1 The Vagueness of the Legal Regulatory Framework

With the promulgation of the Chinese Charity Law in 2016, legislators established a new regulatory framework for the charitable trust model. The law governing charitable trusts expressly requires CADs and BRAs to oversee whether charitable assets are used in compliance with the state's public welfare policy. Although the two regulators are granted extensive powers to strictly control the use of charitable trusts, the legal governance framework is vague about their actual roles. The law does not clearly define the relationship between the two regulators, what their regulatory powers entail in substance, or how they should be exercised.[50]

The wording of the charity law suggests that there is, or should be, a cooperative relationship between the CADs and BRAs.[51] Both regulators are empowered to inspect the discharge of trustees' duties and to entrust

47 See analysis in Section II of Chapter 4.
48 See analysis in Section III of Chapter 4.
49 Ibid.
50 See analysis in Section II of Chapter 4.
51 Ibid.

third-party agencies to assess the management of charitable assets.[52] However, the law makes no mention of how the two regulators should cooperate with each other in exercising their overlapping powers. It is unclear whether they should communicate and reach consensus before making regulatory decisions, or whether they should exercise powers individually without any communication.[53] Confronted with the vagueness of the law, the CADs and BRAs have adopted different approaches in performing their supervisory roles.

In China, the CADs have long been subject to policy and administrative pressures in the regulation of charitable trusts. Therefore, they are willing to take positive measures to specify what the law says and what they should do. As shown in Chapter 4, in practice, the CADs tend to exercise substantive examinations of trust documents and to issue letters or notices to inspect whether trust assets are used in alignment with charitable purposes. Chapter 5 has highlighted the active role of CADs in the design of contract clauses between trust parties. To direct the use of charitable assets, the CADs advise trust parties on which clauses should be incorporated into trust documents and which clauses are ambiguous and how to modify them. The information disclosure clause is a case in point. The CADs often require trust parties to specify how information disclosure works in contracts and what information is involved.[54] By requiring trustees to disclose the required information in a timely and adequate manner, the CADs can learn whether trust assets are used appropriately and whether beneficiaries are selected in line with the criteria specified in the trust documents.

By contrast, the BRAs have not played a proactive role in supervising the day-to-day governance of charitable trusts. There are two reasons for this. First, it is questionable whether BRAs are the appropriate kind of regulator for charitable trusts, as discussed in Chapter 4. The BRAs have gained extensive experience in supervising commercial trust business over the past twenty years. Commercial trust business involves achieving private benefits for individuals such as settlors and trust companies, whose objectives are substantively different from those of charitable trust business. The regulatory experience concerning commercial trusts has prompted the BRAs to focus their work on the supervision of trustee companies themselves – for example, by examining whether trustee

52 Ibid.
53 Ibid.
54 See analysis in Section III of Chapter 5.

companies have good corporate governance structures, sound risk management systems, and effective internal control mechanisms. Second, in contrast to the CADs, the BRAs do not suffer intense policy and administrative pressures in monitoring the management of charitable trust assets.[55] As charitable trusts are outside the focus of their supervisory work, the BRAs lack strong motivation to clarify the scope and content of their powers as well as the procedures they should adopt when interacting with the CADs. Over the past five years, the BRAs have not yet conducted any assessment work or regulatory conversations. If the risks related to the oversight of charitable trusts arise in practice, the BRAs consult the relevant CADs to determine the measures to be taken and whether administrative penalties should be imposed on the trustees.[56]

2 Extra-Legal Factors in Regulatory Practice

Apart from the law, China's policy and social environments in which charitable trusts exist and operate are vital in shaping the decision-making of regulatory officials.[57] As noted in Chapter 2, regulators in China have long been subject to policy and administrative pressures. Regulators represent state interests and are obliged to strictly follow the directives of the central government. Therefore, the two regulators of charitable trusts have strong incentives to consider extra-legal factors in their implementation of the law. This approach can help them align their supervisory work with the state's public welfare policy and minimize the risks that may arise when performing their supervisory roles.[58] Chapter 4 has identified three extra-legal factors that influence regulatory practice: the regional development agenda, the tension between regulatory capacity and regulatory objectives, and regulators' risk perceptions.[59] These three factors are inter-related and strongly affect the ways in which regulatory officials implement the law.[60]

The regional development agenda differs between the eastern developed areas and the western undeveloped areas. As shown in Chapter 1, the central government has formulated a substantial number of policies pertaining to charitable trusts. Nevertheless, these policies are,

[55] See analysis in Section II of Chapter 4.
[56] Ibid.
[57] See analysis in Section III of Chapter 2.
[58] See analysis in Section III of Chapter 4.
[59] Ibid.
[60] Ibid.

in most cases, vague, poorly defined, abstract, and hard to measure in an objective and fair manner.[61] Due to the rapid rate of economic development, the CADs in the eastern areas face greater policy pressures in the development of charitable trusts. In response to this national policy, the CADs created a favourable environment for charitable trusts, developed guidelines to remedy the vagueness of charity policies, and encouraged the public to create charitable trusts for diverse purposes. By contrast, the central government's policy in western China is that of poverty alleviation; therefore, local regulators focus their limited resources on alleviating poverty or helping the needy. In fact, almost 90 percent of charitable trusts registered in the western undeveloped areas are related to poverty alleviation.[62]

The second extra-legal factor is the tension between regulatory capacity and regulatory objectives. Regulators in eastern China can handle the number of charitable trusts that require inspection. Moreover, the regulators in these areas are willing to maintain consistent communication and interaction with the regulated trustees. By comparison, regulators in the western undeveloped areas do not have sufficient budgets and personnel to carry out supervisory work. In response to the lack of regulatory resources, the regulators in these areas have adopted a conservative attitude towards the recording of charitable trusts.[63]

The final extra-legal factor concerns regulators' risk perceptions. Over the past twenty years, regulators have witnessed a large number of scandals involving the misuse of charity funds, as discussed in Chapter 1. Regulators in both areas are thus clearly aware of the legal and reputational risks that may arise from the day-to-day supervision of charitable trusts. They know that any regulatory failure or scandal would lead to irrevocable reputational damage and serious administrative punishments on their part. Therefore, regulators in eastern China are willing to exercise their powers strictly in dealing with violations and to disclose their disciplinary decisions to show the public that they are performing their job properly.[64] By contrast, in the western undeveloped areas, risk perception coupled with the shortage of regulatory resources dissuades regulators from playing a proactive supervisory role. The CADs in western China rarely take educative measures to promote public

[61] See analysis in Section II of Chapter 1.

[62] See analysis in Section III of Chapter 4.

[63] Ibid.

[64] Ibid.

awareness of charitable trusts. Instead, they strongly prefer to decline the recording of charitable trusts whose purposes are not directly related to poverty alleviation.[65]

C *What Private Actions Have Trust Parties Undertaken When Engaging with the Law?*

This book has examined contract practices, discovering that contracts are widely used in two ways in the charitable trust setting. First, due to problems with legislative and administrative practices, trust parties perceive three kinds of risk in the creation and management of charitable trusts: the risk of vagueness of the law, the risk of public scrutiny, and the risk of regulatory scrutiny.[66] To mitigate risks, charitable trust parties are willing to use contracts to clarify their powers and duties as well as the ways in which charitable assets are managed.[67] Second, contracts are an important tool using which regulators can entrench their regulatory preferences, as discussed in Chapter 5. Charitable trust practice showed that regulators have incentives to advise trust parties on which contractual clauses should be incorporated and how they should be modified. This approach enables regulators to incorporate their preferences into the contractual arrangements between trust parties so that charitable trusts can be managed in alignment with regulators' expectations.[68]

1 Trust Parties' Risk Perceptions

Trust parties perceive three kinds of risk regarding the management of charitable trusts: the vagueness of the law, public scrutiny, and regulatory scrutiny (as discussed in Chapter 5). The first risk concerns the vagueness of the law. The law governs the internal relationship between trust parties. However, the law is incomplete, which has created multifaceted uncertainty regarding the scope of settlors' powers and how these powers should be exercised, the scope of trustees' duties, and beneficiaries' legal nature and role in charitable trusts.[69] The vagueness of the law enables settlors to intervene intensively in the daily management of charitable

[65] Ibid.
[66] See analysis in Section II of Chapter 5.
[67] See analysis in Section III of Chapter 5.
[68] Ibid.
[69] See analysis in Section III of Chapter 3.

trusts, which produces a great deal of uncertainty for trustees when exercising their powers or responsibilities.

The second type of risk concerns public scrutiny. As noted in Chapter 1, due to a large number of scandals involving the misuse of charity funds over the last two decades, the general public lacks trust and confidence in trustees and how the latter perform their duties. Accordingly, the general public has a strong interest in ensuring that charitable trusts are managed properly and charitable assets are distributed in alignment with trusts' charitable purposes. Moreover, the lack of clear criteria when it comes to assessing the performance of trustees makes it easy for the public to criticise the management of charitable trusts. Such criticism can lead to trustees suffering reputational damage; more importantly, the career advancement of trustee managers may be threatened.[70]

The third type of risk concerns regulatory scrutiny. As discussed in Chapter 4, the law does not clearly define the relationship between the two regulators, the ways in which the regulators should exercise their powers and the content of regulatory measures. Charitable trust parties are, therefore, uncertain whether their administration of charitable trusts complies with regulatory requirements, and, if not, what they should do.[71] At the same time, to show the public that they are performing their supervisory roles properly and to minimize the risks associated with the discharge of their regulatory duties, regulators tend to severely interfere with the management of charitable trusts. This administrative practice, in turn, poses risks to trustees' management of charitable trusts.[72]

2 The Use of Contractual Tools for Risk Mitigation

It is widely acknowledged by contract theorists that contracts are used as tools to guide the actions of parties and to allocate powers and divide risks between them. Driven by the imperative of risk allocation, settlors and trustees are inclined to use contractual tools to vary the legal framework in relation to charitable trusts. In response to the vagueness of the law, trust parties use contracts to clarify how they should interact when managing charitable trust affairs, how the performance of their duties can be assessed, and how disputes between them are to be resolved.[73] For example, when settlors wish to participate in the

[70] See analysis in Section II of Chapter 5.
[71] See analysis in Section III of Chapter 5.
[72] See analysis in Section II of Chapter 5.
[73] See analysis in Section III of Chapter 5.

management of trust affairs, trustees may have incentives to specify by way of a contract how exactly settlors can intervene. However, the extent to which trustees' wishes can be implemented depends on the intensity of the perceived risk associated with a settlor's intervention and how powerful trustees are when trying to impose constraints on the settlor. Likewise, when trustees wish to minimize legal or reputational risks related to the use of charitable assets, they may wish to employ collective decision-making mechanisms. An illustrative example is the wide use of charitable trust committees, as discussed in Chapter 5. By allowing settlors and trust supervisors to participate in the decision-making process, the responsibilities related to the administration of charitable trusts can be shared and diluted between different parties.[74]

When there is a high risk of public scrutiny, settlors may wish to play a proactive role in the ongoing management of charitable trusts.[75] In charity practice, the extent to which settlors intervene in trusts varies considerably and depends on the balancing and weighing of multiple factors, including the settlor's wishes and identity, the scale of trust assets, the nature of charitable purposes, and the duration of charitable trusts, as discussed in Chapter 5. The nature of charitable purposes is the most important factor in determining whether settlors will actively participate in the management of trust assets. The more politically or socially sensitive the charitable trust purpose, the greater the likelihood that a settlor will play an active role in the trust.[76] When charitable purposes are related to poverty alleviation, stakeholders are willing to play an active supervisory role because the fulfilment of these purposes is closely related to their interests.[77] In this case, settlors will be motivated to keep a close eye on how trustees perform their duties. Accordingly, trustees want to clearly define the scope of settlors' powers and the ways in which trustees' performance can be assessed.[78]

3 The Role of Regulators in Contract Practice

In addition to the interaction between settlors and trustees, regulators have also played an important role in contract practices. In the recording stage, regulators tend to advise trust parties regarding ambiguous

[74] Ibid.
[75] Ibid.
[76] Ibid.
[77] Ibid.
[78] Ibid.

contract clauses and how such clauses may be modified.[79] This practice stems from regulators' risk perceptions, discussed in Chapter 4. Over the last two decades, regulators have witnessed a large number of scandals involving the misuse of charity funds. Therefore, regulators can easily identify the risks related to the day-to-day operations of charitable trusts.[80] To mitigate risks, regulators often ask trust parties to include or amend certain clauses in the trust contract – for example, clauses to do with handling disputes between trust parties, using trust assets at the time of termination and dealing with the poor performance of each party. The primary purpose of this approach is to make it easier for regulators to learn about the administration of charitable trusts to identify risks and implement corresponding measures in a timely manner.[81]

An illustrative example is the design of information disclosure clauses by trust parties, as discussed in Chapter 5. When trust parties submit documents for recording, regulators often require them to specify how information disclosure will work and what information will be involved. The degree of specificity of the information disclosure clause is essential in determining whether a charitable trust will be successfully recorded.[82] These regulatory suggestions or recommendations have also been incorporated into precedent contracts in the form of standard contract clauses, which are then used to guide future negotiations between trust parties on contractual arrangements. At the same time, given the risk of regulatory scrutiny, trust parties are also willing to consult with regulators regarding ambiguous contract clauses and how to modify them. By closely reviewing the clauses of trust contracts and advising trust parties on how they can be amended, regulators systematically impact the ways in which charitable trusts are constructed and operate in China.[83]

IV Future Research

This book has focused on the importance of policy and social contexts in the implementation of laws related to charitable trusts. The book has identified the norms of public and private law in the legal structure of charitable trusts and has examined the ways in which China's policy and

79 Ibid.
80 See analysis in Section III of Chapter 4.
81 See analysis in Section III of Chapter 5.
82 Ibid.
83 Ibid.

social conditions influence the interactions of these two types of norms. However, the book does not propose a detailed pathway for the reform of governance rules concerning Chinese charitable trusts, as this would require an examination of the gaps in the current legal framework from a more comprehensive perspective that encompasses law, sociology, and politics. In this regard, future research should examine the relationships between China's particular institutional structures, politics, economy, and society to consider potential reform models for the governance of charitable trusts.

As analysed in Chapters 3 and 4, the current legal framework has several deficiencies, and it is not difficult to identify the legal uncertainties that these deficiencies have created. More specifically, four problems can be distilled regarding the governance practices of charitable trusts in China. First, the law does not clearly define the scope of settlors' powers and how such powers should be exercised, the scope of trustees' duties, the relationship between settlors and trustees,[84] and beneficiaries' legal nature and role in charitable trusts.[85] Second, the law does not clearly establish the role of regulators, the scope of regulators' powers and how such powers should be exercised, and the relationship between regulators and trust parties.[86] Third, the law does not clarify the ways in which the two types of norms (i.e., public and private) should interact in relation to charitable trusts. It is unclear whether a balance can be struck between the social welfare goals that charitable trusts must pursue and the autonomy that private actors should have in deciding how their assets can be used for charitable purposes.[87] Fourth, with respect to the accounting and reporting system, the law does not perform well in promoting the relevance, comparability, and understandability of information concerning financial reports and annual work reports, which is important in satisfying the information needs of the general public and trust parties.[88]

In view of these four problems, future research can be conducted in at least three areas. First, to address the problems or deficiencies in the current legislative framework, future research should investigate the reform of governance rules concerning Chinese charitable trusts. China

[84] See analysis in Section III of Chapter 3.
[85] See analysis in Section IV of Chapter 3.
[86] See analysis in Section II of Chapter 4.
[87] See analysis in Section II of Chapter 2.
[88] See analysis in Section II of Chapter 4.

needs a charitable trust governance model and supplementary governance mechanisms that suit the social and particular political conditions under which Chinese charitable trusts are established and operate. Government control of charitable trusts and the charitable sector is not going to change any time soon. Therefore, any future reforms of the governance framework for charitable trusts must be developed with this reality in mind. Second, besides charitable trusts, there are three other institutional forms related to charitable causes in China: foundations, social associations, and privately-operated non-enterprise organizations.[89] These institutional forms follow a similar legislated objective (i.e., promoting charitable undertakings) as charitable trusts, and their development also bears the marks of China's political and social environmental norms. In this regard, future research should consider the impact of charitable trust reforms on a broader area. For example, to what extent and in what way can research on charitable trust governance provide insights into the management of charitable organizations more generally? In what way can the governance of charitable trusts illuminate the relationship between the state and the charity sector in the delivery of public welfare services? Third, the charitable trust model has been part of the Chinese legal system for only five years. It is unclear whether the charitable trust model can fulfil the state's mission to encourage the development of charitable undertakings. As more charitable trusts are established in the coming years, empirical evidence can be marshalled to explore this question.

[89] See analysis in Section I of Chapter 1.

Appendix

Translation of Important Terms Used in This Book

English	Chinese characters
planned economy	计划经济
reform and opening up	改革开放
annual work report	年度工作报告
charitable organization	慈善组织
social organization	社会组织
charitable purpose	慈善目的
charitable sector	慈善行业
governance	治理
agency	代理
governance mechanism	治理机制
governance rule	治理规则
governance goal	治理目标
private law norm	私法规范
public law norm	公法规范
regulation	规章
notice	通知
opinion	意见
department of civil affairs	民政部门
banking regulatory authority	银保监部门
Ministry of Civil Affairs	民政部
foundation	基金会
social association	社会团体
privately-operated non-enterprise organization	民办非企业单位
public welfare trust	公益信托
charitable trust	慈善信托
commercial trust	商事信托
public benefit	公共利益/公益
social welfare	社会福利
public welfare	公共福利
charitable undertaking	慈善事业
public benefit activity	公益活动
trust supervisor	信托监察人

(*cont.*)

English	Chinese characters
trust asset	信托财产
check-and-balance mechanism	监督与制约机制
registration	登记
recording	备案
assess	评估
supervisory conversation	监管谈话
administrative investigation	行政调查
registration license	登记许可
administrative punishment	行政处罚
regulatory measure	监管措施
charity-promoting measure	慈善促进措施
interview	访谈
performance target	绩效目标
performance appraisal system	绩效考核机制
poverty alleviation	扶贫
cy-près doctrine	近似原则
belong to	属于
standing	诉讼地位
public scrutiny	公众监督
charitable trust committee	慈善委员会
China Trustee Association	中国信托业协会

BIBLIOGRAPHY

Articles/Books/Reports

Alexander, Gregory S., 'Trust Protectors: Who Will Watch the Watchmen' (2006) 27 *Cardozo Law Review* 2807

Arai, Makoto, 'Trust Law in Japan: Inspiring Changes in Asia, 1922 and 2006' in Lusina Ho and Rebecca Lee (eds.), *Trust Law in Asian Civil Law Jurisdiction: A Comparative Analysis* (Cambridge University Press, 2013)

Ausness, Richard C., 'The Role of Trust Protectors in American Trust Law' (2010) 45(2) *Real Property, Trust and Estate Law Journal* 319

Australian Charities and Not-for-profits Commission, *Governance for Good: The ACNC's Guide for Charity Board Members* (July 2013)

Strengthening for Purpose: Australian Charities and Not-for-profits Commission Legislative Review (2018)

何宝玉 [Baoyu He],《信托法原理研究》[*Research on the Jurisprudence of Trust Law*] (中国政法大学出版社 [China University of Political Science and Law Press], 2005)

[Baoyu He],《信托法原理研究第二版》[*Research on the Jurisprudence of Trust Law, 2nd ed.*] (中国法制出版社 [China Legal Publishing House], 2015)

Bebchuk, Lucian, Alma Cohen and Allen Ferrell, 'What Matters in Corporate Governance?' (2009) 22(2) *The Review of Financial Studies* 783

Beever, Allan and Charles Rickett, 'Interpretive Legal Theory and the Academic Lawyer' (2005) 68(2) *Modern Law Review* 320

Bernstein, Lisa, 'Opting out of the Legal System: Extralegal Contractual Relations in the Diamond Industry' (1992) 21(1) *Journal of Legal Studies* 115

卞耀武 [Bian Yaowu],《中华人民共和国信托法释义》[*Interpretation of the Trust Law of the People's Republic of China*] (法律出版社 [Law Press], 2002)

Biddulph, Sarah, *Legal Reform and Administrative Detention Powers in China* (Cambridge University Press, 2007)

'The Production of Legal Norms: A Case Study of Administrative Detention in China' (2003) 20 *UCLA Pacific Basin Law Journal* 217

Biddulph, Sarah, Sean Cooney and Ying Zhu, 'Rule of Law with Chinese Characteristics: The Role of Campaigns in Lawmaking' (2012) 34(4) *Law & Policy* 373

Bove, Alexander A. Jr, 'The Letter of Wishes: Can We Influence Discretion in Discretionary Trusts' (2009) 35 *ACTEC Journal* 38

Brady, David, Jason Beckfield and Wei Zhao, 'The Consequences of Economic Globalization for Affluent Democracies' (2007) 33 *Annual Review of Sociology* 313

Brody, Evelyn, 'Charity Governance: What's Trust Law Got to Do with It?' (2005) 80 *Chicago-Kent Law Review* 641

Brown, Lesley (ed.), *The New Shorter Oxford English Dictionary on Historical Principles (Volume 1 A–M)*, vol 2 (Clarendon Press, 4th ed., 1993)

(ed.), *The New Shorter Oxford English Dictionary on Historical Principles (Volume 2 N–Z)* (Clarendon Press, 4th ed., 1993)

Brown, Philip, Wendy Beekes and Peter Verhoeven, 'Corporate Governance, Accounting and Finance: A Review' (2011) 51(1) *Accounting & Finance* 96

Brownsword, Roger, 'Two Concepts of Good Faith' (1994) 7 *Journal of Contract Law* 197

Bryan, Michael, Simone Degeling, Scott Donald and Vicki Vann, *A Sourcebook on Equity and Trusts in Australia* (Cambridge University Press, 2016)

Bu, Yuanshi (ed.), *Chinese Civil Law* (Hart Publishing, 2013)

Butler, Susan (ed.), *Macquarie Dictionary* (Macquarie Dictionary Publishers, 5th ed., 2009)

Cappiello, Antonio, 'Using Trusts to Manage Private and Charitable Patrimony: An Overview and Comparison of U.S., EU, and Chinese Law' (2014) 22 *National Italian American Bar Association Law Journal* 13

Cartwright, John, *Contract Law: An Introduction to the English Law of Contract for the Civil Lawyer*, 3rd ed. (Hart, 2016)

Chan, Hon S. and Jie Gao, 'Performance Measurement in Chinese Local Governments' (2008) 41 *Chinese Law & Government* 4

Chan, Kathryn, *The Public–Private Nature of Charity Law* (Hart Publishing, 2016)

Chau, Ruby C. M. and Sam W. K. Yu, 'Social Welfare and Economic Development in China and Hong Kong' (1999) 19(1) *Critical Social Policy* 87

Chen, Lincoln C., Jennifer Ryan and Tony Saich, 'Introduction: Philanthropy for Health in China: Distinctive Roots and Future Prospects' in Jennifer Ryan, Lincoln C. Chen and Tony Saich (eds.), *Philanthropy for Health in China* (Indiana University Press, 2014)

陈向聪 [Chen Xiangcong],《信托法律制度研究》 [Research on Trust Law System] (中国检察出版社 [China People's Procuratorate Press], 2007)

陈先红 [Chen Xianhong],《郭美美事件: 微博江湖"真""假"困局》[Guo Meimei Scandal: Dilemmas of 'True' and 'False' in Weibo] (2011) 21 人民论坛 *People's Forum* 60

Chen, Xiufeng and Li Li, 'The Rise of Corporate Social Responsibility and Charitable Foundations in China' in Chien-Chung Huang, Guosheng

Deng, Zhenyao Wang and Richard L. Edwards (eds.), *China's Nonprofit Sector: Progress and Challenges* (Transaction Publishers, 2014)

Chevalier-Watts, Juliet, *Charity Law: International Perspectives* (Routledge, 2018)

Chia, Joyce, Matthew Harding and Ann O'Connell, 'Navigating the Politics of Charity: Reflections on Aid/Watch Inc v Federal Commissioner of Taxation' (2011) 35 *Melbourne University Law Review* 353

中国信托业协会 [China Trustee Association] (ed.),《慈善信托研究》[*Research on the Charitable Trust*] (中国金融出版社 [China Financial Publishing House], 2016)

Cho, Young Nam, 'The Politics of Lawmaking in Chinese Local People's Congresses' (2006) 187 *China Quarterly* 592

Chodorow, Adam S, 'Charity with Chinese Characteristics' (2012) 30 *UCLA Pacific Basin Law Journal* 1

Choi, Albert and George Triantis, 'The Effect of Bargaining Power on Contract Design' (2012) 98(8) *Virginia Law Review* 1665, 1670

Clarke, Donald C., 'Corporate Governance in China: An Overview' (2003) 14(4) *China Economic Review* 494

Conaglen, Matthew, *Fiduciary Loyalty: Protecting the Due Performance of Non-Fiduciary Duties* (Hart, 2010)

'The Nature and Function of Fiduciary Loyalty' (2005) 121 *Law Quarterly Review* 452

Cooney, Sean, 'Making Chinese Labor Law Work: The Prospects for Regulatory Innovation in the People's Republic of China' (2007) 30 *Fordham International Law Journal* 1050

Coplan, Karl S., 'Citizen Litigants Citizen Regulators: Four Cases Where Citizen Suits Drove Development of Clean Water Law' (2014) 25 *Colorado Natural Resources, Energy & Environmental Law Review* 61

Cotterrell, Roger, 'Seeking Similarity, Appreciating Difference: Comparative Law and Communities' in Andrew Harding and Esin Örücü (eds.), *Comparative Law in the 21st Century* (Kluwer Academic Publishers, 2002)

Cotterrell, Roger and Austin D. Sarat, *Law, Culture and Society: Legal Ideas in the Mirror of Social Theory* (Ashgate Publishing Ltd, 2006)

Dagan, Hanoch, 'Doctrinal Categories, Legal Realism, and the Rule of Law' (2015) 163 *University of Pennsylvania Law Review* 1889

Dagan, Ḥanoch, *Reconstructing American Legal Realism & Rethinking Private Law Theory* (Oxford University Press, 2013)

Dal Pont, G. E., *Charity Law in Australia and New Zealand* (Oxford University Press, 1999)

Davis, Deborah, 'Chinese Social Welfare: Policies and Outcomes' (1989) 119 *China Quarterly* 577

Delany, Hilary, 'The Law Relating to Charitable Trusts: Judicial Guidance and Statutory Intervention' (2011) 33 *Dublin University Law Journal* 196

Deng, Guosheng, Shuang Lu and Chien-Chung Huang, 'Transparency of Grassroots Human Service Organizations in China: Does Transparency Affect Donation and Grants?' (2015) 39(5) *Human Service Organizations: Management, Leadership & Governance* 475

邓禾 [Deng He], 鲁颖然 [Lu Yingran], and 孙凌佼 [Sun Lingjiao],《环境行政约谈的实践考察及制度完善》 [The Practice and Perfection of Environmental Administrative Interview System] (2018) 4 重庆大学学报(社会科学版) *Journal of Chongqing University (Social Sciences)* 156

董蕾红 [Dong Leihong] and 李宝军 [Li Baojun],《论慈善组织的政府监管》[On the Government Supervision over Charitable Organizations] (2015) 6 山东大学学报(哲学社会科学版) *Journal of Shandong University (Philosophy and Social Sciences)* 77

杜健荣 [Du Jianrong],《法律与社会的共同演化 – 基于卢曼的社会系统理论反思转型时期法律与社会的关系》 [Co-Evolution of Law and Society Reflection – On the Relationship between Law and Society in Transition Period by Luhmann's Social System Theory] (2009) 2 法制与社会发展 *Law and Social Development* 109

Dubois, Thomas David, 'Before the NGO: China Charities in Historical Perspective' (2015) 39(4) *Asian Studies Review* 541

Dunn, Alison, 'As Cold as Charity: Poverty, Equity and the Charitable Trust' (2000) 20 *Legal Studies* 222

Edin, Maria, 'State Capacity and Local Agent Control in China: CCP Cadre Management from a Township Perspective' (2003) 173 *China Quarterly* 35

樊小玲 [Fan Xiaoling],《机构形象传播中主体意识的缺失与重建 – "郭美美"事件引发的"红会"危机案例分析》[Absence of Subject Consciousness in the Communication of Institutional Image and Its Reconstruction – A Case Study on the 'Red Cross' Crisis in the 'Guo Meimei Scandal'] (2013) 5 华东师范大学学报 (哲学社会科学版) *Journal of East China Normal University (Humanities and Social Sciences)* 118

范愉 [Fan Yu],《新法律现实主义的勃兴与当代中国法学反思》 [The Rise of New Legal Realism and Reflections on Current Chinese Law] (2006) 4 中国法学 *China Legal Science* 38

Farrar, John H., 'Developing Corporate Governance in Greater China' (2002) 25(2) *University of New South Wales Law Journal* 462

Feld, Harold, 'Saving the Citizen Suit: The Effect of Lujan v Defenders of Wildlife and the Role of Citizen Suits in Environmental Enforcement' (1994) 19 *Columbia Journal of Environmental Law* 141

冯果 [Feng Guo],《"禁止篡夺公司机会"规则探究》[Research on the Doctrine of Prohibiting the Usurpation of Corporate Opportunities] (2010) 1 中国法学 *China Legal Science* 96

Feng, Xiaoming, 'China's Charitable Foundations: Development and Policy-Related Issues' (2015) 48(2) *Chinese Economy* 130

Feng, Yuqing and Xin He, 'From Law to Politics: Petitioners' Framing of Disputes in Chinese Courts' (2018) 80 *China Journal* 130

Finkelstein, Ray, P. J. Butt, Rod Howie and David Hamer (eds.), *LexisNexis Concise Australian Legal Dictionary* (LexisNexis Butterworths, 5th ed., 2015)

Finkelstein, Raymond, David Hamer, R. N. Howie, Margaret Allars, R. C. D. McCallum and J. C. Gibson (eds.), *LexisNexis Australian Legal Dictionary*, 2nd ed. (LexisNexis Butterworths, 2016)

Fisch, Edith L., 'Changing Concepts and Cy Pres' (1959) 44(3) *Cornell Law Review* 382

Flint, Geoffrey K., 'Enforce Them All: A Battle Cry for the Beleaguered Agreement to Negotiate' (1995) 13 *Australian Bar Review* 262

Foster, Frances H., 'American Trust Law in a Chinese Mirror' (2010) 94 *Minnesota Law Review* 602

Freeman, Jody, 'Extending Public Law Norms through Privatization' (2003) 116(5) *Harvard Law Review* 1285

'The Private Role in the Public Governance' (2000) 75 *New York University Law Review* 543

Friedman, Lawrence M., 'Legal Culture and Social Development' (1969) 4(1) *Law & Society Review* 29

甘培忠 [Gan Peizhong],《企业与公司法学》[*Enterprise and Company Law*] (北京大学出版社 [Peking University Press], 2014)

Gao, Jie, 'Governing by Goals and Numbers: A Case Study in the Use of Performance Measurement to Build State Capacity in China' (2009) 29(1) *Public Administration and Development* 21

高静华 [Gao Jinghua], 《慈善透明的困境与治理策略》[Dilemmas of the Transparency of Charities and Governance Strategies] (2018) 15 中国社会组织 *China Social Organization* 53

Gao, Lingyun, 'The Development of Private Trusts in Mainland China: Legal Obstacles and Solutions' (2014) 20(4) *Trusts & Trustees* 350

高凌云 [Gao Lingyun],《被误读的信托–信托法原论》[*A Misreading of Trust: Discussion on the Origin of Trust*] (复旦大学出版社 [Fudan University Press], 2010)

Gardner, Simon, *An Introduction to The Law of Trusts* (Oxford University Press, 2011)

Garton, Jonathan, *Public Benefit in Charity Law* (Oxford University Press, 2013)

Gilmore, Grant, 'Legal Realism: Its Cause and Cure' (1961) 70(7) *Yale Law Journal* 1037

Glenn, H. Patrick, 'Against Method' in Maurice Adams and Dirk Heirbaut (eds.), *The Method and Culture of Comparative Law: Essays in Honour of Mark Van Hoecke* (Oxford University Press, 2014)

Goetsch, Charles C., 'The Future of Legal Formalism' (1980) 24(3) *American Journal of Legal History* 221

巩固 [Gong Gu],《2015年中国环境民事公益诉讼的实证分析》[An Empirical Analysis of China's Environmental Civil Public Interest Litigation in 2015] (2016) 9 法学 *Law Science* 16

《大同小异抑或貌合神离？中美环境公益诉讼比较研究》 [Looking Like Twins: Comparative Research on Environmental Public Interest Litigation between China and United States] (2017) 2 比较法研究 *Journal of Comparative Law* 105

Gonzalez, Carlos E., 'Statutory Interpretation: Looking Back – Looking Forward' (2006) 58(3) *Rutgers Law Review* 703

Gordon, Deborah S., 'Letters Non-Testamentary' (2013) 62 *University of Kansas Law Review* 585

Gray, John Chipman, 'Gifts for a Non-Charitable Purpose' (1902) 15(7) *Harvard Law Review* 509

Grayson-Morison, Reegan and Ian Ramsay, 'An Analysis of Companies' Business Objectives' (2014) 32(6) *Company and Security Law Journal* 438

Green, Alexander, 'Expanding Law's Empire: Interpretivism, Morality and the Value of Legality' (2011) 4(1) *European Journal of Legal Studies* 122

Greenberg, Daniel (ed.), *Jowitt's Dictionary of English Law (Volume 1: A–I)* (Sweet & Maxwell, 4th ed., 2015)

Hage, Jaap, 'Comparative Law as Method and the Method of Comparative Law' in Maurice Adams and Dirk Heirbaut (eds.), *The Method and Culture of Comparative Law: Essays in Honor of Mark Van Hoecke* (Hart, 2014)

韩丽欣 [Han Lixin],《中国慈善组织治理法治化研究》[*Research on the Governance of Chinese Charities*] (法律出版社 [Law Press], 2015)

Harding, Matthew, *Charity Law and the Liberal State* (Cambridge University Press, 2014)

Harpur, Paul, 'Charity Law's Public Benefit Test: Is Legislative Reform in the Public Interest' (2003) 3(2) *Queensland University of Technology Law and Justice Journal* 1

Harrington, Christine B. and Barbara Yngvesson, 'Interpretive Sociolegal Research' (1990) 15(1) *Law & Social Inquiry* 135

Hayton, David, 'English Fiduciary Standards and Trust Law' (1999) 32 *Vanderbilt Journal of Transnational Law* 555

He, Xin, 'Administrative Reconsideration's Erosion of Administrative Litigation in China' (2014) 2(2) *Chinese Journal of Comparative Law* 252

'No Malicious Incidents: The Concern for Stability in China's Divorce Law Practice' (2017) 26(4) *Social & Legal Studies* 467

He, Xin and Fen Lin, 'The Losing Media? An Empirical Study of Defamation Litigation in China' (2017) 230 *China Quarterly* 371

He, Xin and Kwai Hang Ng, 'Inquisitorial Adjudication and Institutional Constraints in Chinese Civil Justice' (2013) 35(4) *Law & Policy* 290

'In the Name of Harmony: The Erasure of Domestic Violence in China's Judicial Mediation' (2013) 27(1) *International Journal of Law, Policy and the Family* 97

Hecker, James M., 'The Citizen's Role in Environmental Enforcement: Private Attorney General, Private Citizen, or Both' (1994) 8(4) *Natural Resources & Environment* 31

High, Anna Jane, 'Grassroots NGO Regulations and China's Local Legal Culture' (2013) 9 *Socio-Legal Review* 1

Hirsch, Adam J., 'Bequests for Purposes: A Unified Theory' (1999) 56 *Washington and Lee Law Review* 33

'Trusts for Purposes: Policy, Ambiguity, and Anomaly in the Uniform Laws' (1998) 26 *Florida State University Law Review* 913

Ho, Lusina, 'Business Trusts in China: A Reality Check' (2020) 88(3) *University of Cincinnati Law Review* 767

'The Reception of Trust in Asia: Emerging Asian Principles of Trust?' (2004) 2004(2) *Singapore Journal of Legal Studies* 287

Trust Law in China (Sweet & Maxell Asia, 2003)

'Trust Laws in China: History, Ambiguity and Beneficiary's Rights' in Lionel Smith (ed.), *Re-Imaging the Trust: Trusts in Civil Law* (Cambridge University Press, 2012)

Ho, Lusina and Rebecca Lee, 'Case 3: Protecting Ring-Fenced Assets against Disloyalty of the Asset Manager' in Lusina Ho and Rebecca Lee (eds.), *Trust Law in Asian Civil Law Jurisdiction: A Comparative Analysis* (Cambridge University Press, 2013) 163

(eds.), *Trust Law in Asian Civil Law Jurisdiction: A Comparative Analysis* (Cambridge University Press, 2013)

Ho, Lusina, Rebecca Lee and Jinping Jin, 'Trust Law in China: A Critical Evaluation of Its Conceptual Foundation' in Lusina Ho and Rebecca Lee (eds.), *Trust Law in Asian Civil Law Jurisdiction: A Comparative Analysis* (Cambridge University Press, 2013)

Ho, Virginia E. Harper, 'Beyond Regulation: A Comparative Look at State-Centric Corporate Social Responsibility and the Law in China' (2013) 46 *Vanderbilt Journal of Transnational Law* 375

'Corporate Governance as Risk Regulation in China: A Comparative View of Risk Oversight, Risk Management, and Accountability' (2012) 3(4) *European Journal of Risk Regulation* 463

'From Contracts to Compliance: An Early Look at Implementation under China's New Labor Legislation' (2009) 23 *Columbia Journal of Asian Law* 35

Holmes, Oliver Wendell, 'The Path of the Law' (1997) 110(5) *Harvard Law Review* 991

Huang, Xian, 'The Politics of Social Welfare Reform in Urban China: Social Welfare Preferences and Reform Policies' (2013) 18 *Journal of Chinese Political Science* 61

Husa, Jaakko, 'Research Designs of Comparative Law: Methodology or Heuristics?' in Maurice Adams and Dirk Heirbaut (eds.), *The Method and Culture of Comparative Law: Essays in Honour of Mark Van Hoecke* (Oxford University Press, 2014)

中国社会科学院语言研究所 [Institute of Language Studies, Chinese Academy of Social Sciences],《现代汉语词典》[*Modern Chinese Dictionary*] (商务印书馆 [The Commercial Press], 7th ed., 2016)

中国人民大学信托与基金研究所 [Institute of Trust and Fund of Renmin University of China],《中国信托业发展报告 2016 》[*The Development Report of Chinese Trust Business (2016)*] (中国经济出版社 [China Economic Publishing House], 2018)

中国人民大学信托与基金研究所 [Institute of Trust and Fund of Renmin University of China], 《中国信托业发展报告 2018 》 [*The Development Report of Chinese Trust Business (2018)*] (中国经济出版社 [China Economic Publishing House], 2018)

Jamieson, Philip, 'Trusts for the Maintenance of Particular Animals' (1985) 14(2) *The University of Queensland Law Journal* 175

季卫东 [Ji Weidong],《法律议论的社会科学研究新范式》[New Method of Social Scientific Study in Legal Discussion] (2015) 6 中国法学 *China Legal Science* 25

江平 [Jiang Ping] and 周小明 [Zhou Xiaoming],《建构大陆的信托法制的若干设想》[Several Thoughts on the Construction of Trust System in Mainland China] (1993) 6 政法论坛 *Tribune of Political Science and Law* 5

《论中国的信托立法》[Research on the Legislation of Chinese Trust Law] (1994) 6 中国法学 *China Legal Science* 53

金锦萍 [Jin Jinping],《慈善信托的规制之道 – 兼评<慈善信托管理办法>》[Regulation of Charitable Trusts: Comment on 'Administrative Measures for Charitable Trusts'] (2017) 16 中国社会组织 *China Social Organization* 23

《论公益信托之界定及其规范意义》[Research on the Definition of the Public Welfare Trust and Its Normative Significance] (2015) 6 华东政法大学学报 *Journal of Peking University (Philosophy & Social Sciences)* 72

金晓文 [Jin Xiaowen],《中国公司法原理与适用》[*Principles and Application of Chinese Corporation Law*] (中国法制出版社 [China Legal Publishing House], 2017)

Jing, Hui, 'The Legal Nature of the Chinese Charitable Trust' in Matthew Harding and Ying Khai Liew (eds.), *Asia-Pacific Trusts Law: Theory and Practice in Context* (Hart, 2021)

Jing, Yijia and E. S. Savas, 'Managing Collaborative Service Delivery: Comparing China and the United States' (2009) 69 *Public Administration Review* 101

Khaitan, Tarunabh, *A Theory of Discrimination Law* (Oxford University Press, 2015)

孔祥俊 [Kong Xiangjun],《公司法要论》[*Key Discussions on Chinese Company Law*] (最高人民法院出版社 [Supreme People's Court Press], 1997)

Krahe, Justin Friedrich, 'The Impact of Public Law Norms on Private Law Relationships' (2015) 2 *European Journal of Comparative Law and Governance* 124

Kutner, Luis and Henry H. Koven, 'Charitable Trust Legislation in the Several States' (1966) 61 *Northwestern University Law Review* 411

Lang, Elizabeth Z., 'Some Reflections on Charity Law in the People's Republic of China' (2003) 15(2) *Bond Law Review* 358

Langbein, John H., 'Mandatory Rules in the Law of Trusts' (2004) 98(3) *Northwestern University Law Review* 1105

'The Secret Life of the Trust: The Trust as an Instrument of Commerce' (1997) 107 *Yale Law Journal* 165

Langford, Rosemary Teele, 'High Court of Australia on Fiduciary Theory' in Ken Coghill, Charles Sampford, and Tim Smith (eds.), *Fiduciary Duty and the Atmospheric Trust* (Routledge, 2016)

Leach, W. Barton, 'Perpetuities: Cy Pres on the March' (1964) 4 *Vanderbilt Law Review* 1381

Lee, C. David, 'Legal Reform in China: A Role for Nongovernmental Organizations' (2000) 25 *Yale Journal of International Law* 363

Lee, Rebecca, 'Conceptualizing the Chinese Trust' (2009) 58(3) *International & Comparative Law Quarterly* 655

'Convergence and Divergence in the Worlds of the Trust: Duties and Liabilities of Trustees under the Chinese Trust' in Lionel D. Smith (ed.), *The Worlds of the Trust* (Cambridge University Press, 2013)

'Modernize Charity Law in China' (2009) 18 *Pacific Rim Law & Policy Journal* 347

Leiter, Brian, 'Legal Formalism and Legal Realism: What Is the Issue' (2010) 16(2) *Legal Theory* 111

'Legal Realism and Legal Positivism Reconsidered' (2001) 111(2) *Ethics* 278

'Rethinking Legal Realism: Toward a Naturalized Jurisprudence' (1997) 76(2) *Texas Law Review* 267

李德健 [Li Dejian],《公共利益与法人自治的平衡 – 中国慈善法人制度变革的进路选择》[The Balance of Public Interest and Legal Person Autonomy – Selection of Approaches for Reform of the Chinese Charity Legal Person System] (2016) 31(163) 法学论坛 *Legal Forum* 54

李文华 [Li Wenhua],《完善我国慈善信托制度若干问题的思考》[Thoughts on Several Issues of Perfecting the Charitable Trust System in China] (2017) 7 法学杂志 *Law Science Magazine* 89

李子顺 [Li Zishun],《公益信托的性质与税收优惠》[The Nature of the Public Welfare Trust and Its Tax Privileges] (2009) 2 法律适用 *Journal of Law Application* 91

Liew, Ying Khai, 'Justifying Anglo-American Trusts Law' (2021) 12 *William & Mary Business Law Review* 685

LIN, SEN, 'A New Pattern of Decentralization in China: The Increase of Provincial Powers in Economic Legislation' (1992) 7(3) *China Information* 27

Lin, Siyi, 'China's New Charity Law: A New Era of Charitable Trusts' (2018) 24(8) *Trusts & Trustees* 768

刘迎霜 [Liu Yingshuang],《我国公益信托法律移植及其本土化：一种正本清源与直面当下的思考》[The Transplantation and Localization of Charitable Trusts in China: A Thought of Radical Reform and Facing up to the Present] (2015) 27(1) 中外法学 *Peking University Law Journal* 151

Lo, Carlos Wing-Hung, Gerald E. Fryxell, Benjamin van Rooij, Wei Wang and Pansy Honying Li, 'Explaining the Enforcement Gap in China: Local Government Support and Internal Agency Obstacles as Predictors of Enforcement Actions in Guangzhou' (2012) 111 *Journal of Environmental Management* 227

Löhnig, Martin, 'Comparative Law and Legal History: A Few Words about Comparative Legal History' in *The Method and Culture of Comparative Law: Essays in Honour of Mark Van Hoecke* (Oxford University Press, 2014)

楼秋然 [Lou Qiuran],《理解慈善信托中的"近似原则"：美国经验与中国借鉴》[Understanding Cy Pres in Charitable Trusts: American Experience and Its Adoption in China] (2019) 3 中国政法大学学报 *Journal of China University of Political Science and Law* 49

Lyu, Kai, 'Re-Clarifying China's Trust Law: Characteristics and New Conceptual Basis' (2015) 36 *Loyola of Los Angeles International and Comparative Law Review* 447

吕鑫 [Lyu Xin],《从公益信托到慈善信托：跨国移植及其本土建构》[From Public Welfare Trusts to Charitable Trusts: Transnational Transplantation and Local Construction] (2019) 10 社会科学战线 *Social Science Front* 199

马剑银 [Ma Jianyin],《中国慈善法立法观察》[Legislative Observations on the Chinese Charity Law] in 杨团 [Yang Tuan] (ed.),《中国慈善发展报告 2016》[*Annual Report on China's Philanthropy Development (2016)*] (社会科学文献出版社 [Social Science Academic Press], 2016)

马金芳 [Ma Jinfang],《我国社会组织立法的困境与出路》[The Dilemma and Outlet of the Social Organization Legislation in China] (2016) 6 法商研究 *Study of Law and Business* 3

Ma, Qiusha, 'The Governance of NGOs in China since 1978: How Much Autonomy?' (2002) 31(3) *Nonprofit and Voluntary Sector Quarterly* 305

Macaulay, Stewart, 'An Empirical View of Contract Law' (1985) 1985 *Wisconsin Law Review* 465

'Non-Contractual Relations in Business: A Preliminary Study' (1963) 28(1) *American Sociological Review* 55

Mann, Trischa (ed.), *Australian Law Dictionary*, 2nd ed. (Oxford University Press, 2013)

Mcallister, Lesley K., 'Dimensions of Enforcement Style: Factoring in Regulatory Autonomy and Capacity' (2010) 32(1) *Law & Policy* 61

McLean, Janet, 'Convergence in Public and Private Law Doctrines: The Case of Public Contracts' (2016) 2016(1) *New Zealand Law Review* 5

McMeel, Gerard, 'What Kind of Jurist Was Peter Binks' (2011) 19 *Restitution Law Review* 15

孟强龙 [Meng Qianglong],《行政约谈法治化研究》[Study on Legalization of Administrative Interviews] (2015) 6 行政法学研究 *Administrative Law Review* 99

Minzner, Carl F., 'Riots and Cover-Ups: Counterproductive Control of Local Agents in China' (2014) 31 *University of Pennsylvania Journal of International Law* 53

Miu, Chung Yan, Huang Xin, Kenneth W. Foster and Frank Tester, 'Charity Development in China: An Overview' (2007) 17(1) *Asia Pacific Journal of Social Work and Development* 79

Moore, Sally Falk, 'Law and Social Change: The Semi-Autonomous Social Field as an Appropriate Subject of Study' (1973) 4(4) *Law & Society Review* 719

Morley, John D. and Robert H. Sitkoff, 'Making Directed Trusts Work: The Uniform Directed Trust Act' (2019) 44(1) *ACTEC Law Journal* 3

Nagel, Ilene H., 'The Legal/Extra-Legal Controversy: Judicial Decisions in Pretrial Release' (1983) 17(3) *Law & Society Review* 481

Nelken, David, 'Legal Transplants and Beyond: Of Disciplines and Metaphors' in Andrew Harding and Esin Örücü (eds.), *Comparative Law in the 21st Century* (Kluwer Academic Publishers, 2002)

Newark, F. H., 'Public Benefit and Religious Trusts' (1946) 62(3) *Law Quarterly Review* 284

Ng, Kwai Hang and Xin He, *Embedded Courts: Judicial Decision-Making in China* (Cambridge University Press, 2017)

'The Institutional and Cultural Logics of Legal Commensuration: Blood Money and Negotiated Justice in China' (2017) 122(4) *American Journal of Sociology* 1104

倪受彬 [Ni Shoubin],《现代慈善信托的组织法特征及其功能优势 – 与慈善基金会法人的比较》[The Advantage and Character of Modern Charitable

Trusts as Organizations: Compared to Charity Foundations] (2014) 46(7) 学术月刊 *Academic Monthly* 86

Nie, Lin, Helen K. Liu and Wenhao Cheng, 'Exploring Factors That Influence Voluntary Disclosure by Chinese Foundations' (2016) 27(5) *International Journal of Voluntary and Nonprofit Organizations* 2374

Nolan, Richard, 'Invoking the Administrative Jurisdiction: The Enforcement of Modern Trust Structures' in Paul S. Davies and James Penner (eds.), *Equity, Trusts, and Commerce* (Hart, 2017)

汉语大字典编纂处 [Office of Chinese Dictionary Compilation],《现代汉语词典》[Modern Chinese Dictionary] (四川辞书出版社 [Sichuan Dictionary Press], 2014)

Örücü, Esin, 'Unde Venit, Quo Tendit Comparative Law' in Andrew Harding and Esin Örücü (eds.), *Comparative Law in the 21st Century* (Kluwer Academic Publishers, 2002)

Parker, David B. and Anthony R. Mellows, *The Modern Law of Trusts*, 5th ed. (Sweet and Maxwell, 1983)

Paterson, Jeannie Marie, Andrew Robertson and Arlen Duke, *Contract: Cases and Materials* (Thomson Reuters, 2016)

Principles of Contract Law, 5th ed. (Thomson Reuters (Professional) Australia Limited, 2016)

Pawlowski, Mark, 'Confidentiality or Disclosure?' (2008) 96 *Trusts and Estates Law & Tax Journal* 12

北京大学非营利法组织研究中心 [Peking University Law School Nonprofit Organization Law Research Center],《中国非营利组织法的基本问题》[*Fundamental Issues of the Non-Profit Organization Law in China*] (中国方正出版社 [China Fangzheng Press], 2006)

Picarda, Hubert, *The Law and Practice Relating to Charities*, 4th ed. (Bloomsbury Professional, 2010)

Pont, G. E. Dal and Stefan Petrow, *Law of Charity* (LexisNexis Butterworths, 2010)

Potter, Pitman B., 'Belief in Control: Regulation of Religion in China' (2003) 174 *China Quarterly* 317

Qu, Charles Zhen, 'The Doctrinal Basis of the Trust Principles in China's Trust Law' (2003) 38 *Real Property, Probate and Trust Journal* 345

Rainer, J. Michael, *Introduction to Comparative Law* (Manz, 2010)

Ramsay, Ian M., 'The Corporate Governance Debate and the Role of Directors' Duties' in Ian M. Ramsay (ed.), *Corporate Governance and the Duties of Company Directors* (Centre for Corporate Law and Securities Regulation, 1997)

Reimann, Mathias, 'The Progress and Failure of Comparative Law in the Second Half of the Twentieth Century' (2002) 50(4) *American Journal of Comparative Law* 671

Renz, David O. and Fredrik O. Andersson, 'Nonprofit Governance: A Review of the Field' in Chris Cornforth and William A. Brown (eds.), *Nonprofit Governance: Innovative Perspectives and Approaches* (Routledge, 2014) 18

van Rooij, Benjamin, 'China's War on Graft: Politico-Legal Campaigns against Corruption in China and Their Similarities to the Legal Reactions to Crisis in the US' (2005) 14(2) *Pacific Rim Law & Political Journal* 289

'Implementation of Chinese Environmental Law: Regular Enforcement and Political Campaigns' (2006) 37(1) *Development and Change* 57

van Rooij, Benjamin, Gerald E. Fryxell, Carlos Wing-Hung Lo and Wei Wang, 'From Support to Pressure: The Dynamics of Social and Governmental Influences on Environmental Law Enforcement in Guangzhou City, China' (2013) 7(3) *Regulation & Governance* 321

van Rooij, Benjamin, Rachel E. Stern and Kathinka Fürst, 'The Authoritarian Logic of Regulatory Pluralism: Understanding China's New Environmental Actors' (2016) 10(1) *Regulation & Governance* 1

阮建芳 [Ruan Jianfang],《慈善与公益》[*Charity and Public Welfare*] (同心出版社 [Tongxin Publishing House], 2013)

Ruce, Philip J., 'The Trustee and the Trust Protector: A Question of Fiduciary Power: Should a Trust Protector Be Held to a Fiduciary Standard?' (2011) 59 *Drake Law Review* 67

Rundle, Kristen, *Forms Liberate: Reclaiming the Jurisprudence of Lon L Fuller* (Hart, 2012)

'Opening the Doors of Inquiry: Lon Fuller and the Natural Law Tradition' in George Duke and Robert P. George (eds.), *The Cambridge Companion to Natural Law Jurisprudence* (Cambridge University Press, 2017)

Saidov, A. Kh, *Comparative Law*, trans William Elliott Butler (Wildy, Simmonds & Hill, 2003)

Salter, Michael and Julie Mason, *Writing Law Dissertations: An Introduction and Guide to the Conduct of Legal Research* (Pearson Education Limited, 2007)

Samuels, Alec, 'Disclosure of Trust Documents' (1965) 28(2) *Modern Law Review* 220

Schwartz, Alan and Robert E. Scott, 'Contract Theory and the Limits of Contract Law' (2003) 113(3) *Yale Law Journal* 541

Seidenfeld, Mark and Janna Satz Nugent, 'The Friendship of the People: Citizen Participation in Environmental Enforcement' (2005) 73 *George Washington Law Review* 269

Shi, Chenxia, *Political Determinants of Corporate Governance in China* (Routledge, 2012)

Shleifer, Andrei and Robert W. Vishny, 'A Survey of Corporate Governance' (1997) 52(2) *Journal of Finance* 737

Simon, Karla W., *Civil Society in China: The Legal Framework from Ancient Times to the 'New Reform Era'* (Oxford University Press, 2013)

'Regulation of Civil Society in China: Necessary Changes after the Olympic Games and the Sichuan Earthquake' (2008) 32 *Fordham International Law Journal* 943

Simpson, J. A. and E. S. C. Weiner (eds.), *The Oxford English Dictionary (VI)*, 2nd ed. (Clarendon Press, 1989)

(eds.), *The Oxford English Dictionary (XIII)*, 2nd ed. (Clarendon Press, 1989)

Sites, William, 'Primitive Globalization? State and Locale in Neoliberal Global Engagement' (2000) 18(1) *Sociological Theory* 121

Sitkoff, Robert H., 'Trusts and Estates: Implementing Freedom of Disposition' (2014) 58 *Saint Louis University Law Journal* 643

Sloan, Richard G., 'Financial Accounting and Corporate Governance: A Discussion' (2001) 32(1) *Journal of Accounting and Economics* 335

Smith, Lionel, 'Massively Discretionary Trusts' in Richard C. Nolan, Kelvin F. K. Low and Tang Hang Wu (eds.), *Trusts and Modern Wealth Management* (Cambridge University Press, 2018)

Smith, Stephen A., *Contract Theory* (Oxford University Press, 2004)

Spires, Anthony J., 'Contingent Symbiosis and Civil Society in an Authoritarian State: Understanding the Survival of China's Grassroots NGOs' (2011) 117 (1) *American Journal of Sociology* 1

Stake, Jeffrey Evans, 'A Brief Comment on Trust Protectors' (2006) 27 *Cardozo Law Review* 2813

Steele, David A., 'Disclosure of Trust Documents Revisited' (1995) 15 *Estates and Trusts Journal* 218

Sterk, Stewart E., 'Trust Protectors, Agency Costs, and Fiduciary Duty' (2005) 27 *Cardozo Law Review* 2761

Stern, Rachel E., *Environmental Litigation in China: A Study in Political Ambivalence* (Cambridge University Press, 2013)

Sugin, Linda, 'Rhetoric and Reality in the Tax Law of Charity' (2016) 84(6) *Fordham Law Review* 2607

Synge, Mary, *The 'New' Public Benefit Requirement: Making Sense of Charity Law?* (Hart Publishing, 2015)

Tamanaha, Brian Z., *Beyond the Formalist–Realist Divide: The Role of Politics in Judging* (Princeton University Press, 2010)

Tamaruya, Masayuki, 'Japanese Law and the Global Diffusion of Trust and Fiduciary Law' (2017) 103 *Iowa Law Review* 2229

Tan, Zhenting, 'The Chinese Law of Trusts: A Compromise between Two Legal Systems' (2001) 13(1) *Bond Law Review* 224

谭振亭 [Tan Zhenting],《信托法》[*Trust Law*] (中国政法大学出版社 [China University of Political Science and Law Press], 2010)

Tanner, Murray Scot, 'State Coercion and the Balance of Awe: The 1983–1986 "Stern Blows" Anti-Crime Campaign' (2000) 44 *China Journal* 93

Tey, Tsun Hang, 'Letters of Wishes' (2009) 21 *Singapore Academy of Law Journal* 193

'Reservation of Settlor's Powers' (2009) 21(2) *Singapore Academy of Law Journal* 517

'Trustee's Duty of Disclosure' (2012) 24 *Singapore Academy of Law Journal* 191

Thompson, Barton H., 'The Continuing Innovations of Citizen Enforcement' (2000) 2000 *University of Illinois Law Review* 185

Tomasic, Roman, 'Good Corporate Governance: The International Challenge' (2000) 12 *Australian Journal of Corporate Law* 142

Trevaskes, Susan, 'Yanda 2001: Form and Strategy in a Chinese Anti-Crime Campaign' (2003) 36(3) *Australian & New Zealand Journal of Criminology* 272

Tucker, Lynton, Nicholas Le Poidevin, James Brightwell, Thomas Fletcher and Aidan Briggs (eds.), *Lewin on Trusts*, 20th ed. (Sweet & Maxwell, 2020)

Turner, P. G., 'The Entitlements of Objects as Defining Features of Discretionary Trusts' in Richard C. Nolan, Kelvin F. K. Low and Tang Hang Wu (eds.), *Trusts and Modern Wealth Management* (Cambridge University Press, 2018)

Underhill, Arthur, David J. Hayton, Paul Matthews and Charles Mitchell, *Underhill and Hayton Law Relating to Trusts and Trustees*, 17th ed. (LexisNexis Butterworths, 2007)

Vestal, Allan D., 'Critical Evaluation of the Charitable Trust as a Giving Device' (1957) 1957(3) *Washington University Law Review* 195

Wallace, Jude and John Fiocco, 'Recent Criticisms of Formalism in Legal Theory and Legal Education' (1980) 7(3) *Adelaide Law Review* 309

Wang, Alex L., 'The Search for Sustainable Legitimacy: Environmental Law and Bureaucracy in China' (2013) 37 *Harvard Environmental Law Review* 365

王虎 [Wang Hu],《风险社会中的行政约谈制度: 因应、反思与完善》 [The System of Administrative Interviews in Risk Society: Response, Reflection, and Improvement] (2018) 1 法商研究 *Study of Law and Business* 22

王建军 [Wang Jianjun], 燕翀 [Yan Chong] and 张时飞 [Zhang Shifei],《慈善信托法律制度运行机理及其在我国发展的障碍》[The Operational Mechanism and Theories Related to the Charitable Trust and Its Development Obstacles in Mainland China] (2011) 4 环球法律评论 *Global Law Review* 108

王军 [Wang Jun],《中国公司法》[*Corporation Law of China*] (高等教育出版社 [Higher Education Press], 2015)

王丽萍 [Wang Liping],《突破环境公益诉讼启动的瓶颈: 适格原告扩张与激励机制构建》 [Breaking the Bottleneck of Initiating Environmental Public Interest Litigation: Expansion of Standing and Construction of Incentive Mechanisms] (2017) 3 法学论坛 *Legal Forum* 89

王萍 [Wang Ping],《大陆法代理制度与英美法信托制度之比较》[Comparison between the Agency System of Mainland Law and Anglo-American Trust Law System] (1998) 3 甘肃政法学院学报 *Journal of Gansu Political Science and Law Institute* 49

王涛 [Wang Tao],《慈善法的立法理念、制度创新和完善路径》[Research on the Legislative Idea, System Innovation and Development Path of the Chinese Charity Law] (2018) 33(1) 法学论坛 *Legal Forum* 143

Wang, Wen-Yeu, Chih-Cheng Wang, and Shieh Jer-Sheng, 'Trust Law in Taiwan: History, Current Features and Future Prospects' in Lusina Ho and Rebecca Lee (eds.), *Trust Law in Asian Civil Law Jurisdiction: A Comparative Analysis* (Cambridge University Press, 2013)

王锡三 [Wang Xisan],《近代诉权理论的探讨》[On the Theory of Modern Appealing Right] (1989) 6 现代法学 *Modern Law Science* 16

王振耀 [Wang Zhenyao],《现代慈善与社会治理：2013 年度中国公益事业发展报告》[Modern Charity and Social Governance: 2013 Annual Report of the Charity Sector in China] (社会科学文献出版社 [Social Science Academic Press], 2014)

Wang, Zhenyao and Yanhui Zhao, 'The Collapse and Reemergence of Private Philanthropy in China, 1949–2012' in Jennifer Ryan, Lincoln C. Chen and Tony Saich (eds.), *Philanthropy for Health in China* (Indiana University Press, 2014)

王众 [Wang Zhong],《中国信托法原理与实例精要》[*Principles and Examples of the Chinese Trust Law*] (中国政法大学出版社 [China University of Political Science and Law Press], 2017)

魏艳 [Wei Yan],《慈善信托政府监管权配置研究》[Research on Allocation of Administrative Regulatory Powers for Charitable Trusts] (2018) 6 国家行政学院学报 *Journal of Chinese Academy of Governance* 103

White, G. Edward, 'From Sociological Jurisprudence to Realism: Jurisprudence and Social Change in Early Twentieth-Century America' (1972) 58(6) *Virginia Law Review* 999

Williamson, Oliver E., 'Corporate Finance and Corporate Governance' (1988) 43 (3) *Journal of Finance* 567

Wu, Ying-Chieh, 'Trust Law in South Korea: Developments and Challenges' in Lusina Ho and Rebecca Lee (eds.), *Trust Law in Asian Civil Law Jurisdiction: A Comparative Analysis* (Cambridge University Press, 2013)

'Trusts Reimagined: The Transplantation and Evolution of Trust Law in Northeast Asia' (2020) 68(2) *American Journal of Comparative Law* 441

谢琼 [Xie Qiong],《立体监管：我国慈善事业发展的理性选择》[Stereoscopic Supervision: Rational Choice for the Development of Charitable Causes in China] (2015) 4 国家行政学院学报 *Journal of Chinese Academy of Governance* 73

谢哲胜 [Xie Zhesheng],《信托法》[*Trust Law*] (元照出版公司 [Angle Publishing], 2009)

徐卫 [Xu Wei],《慈善宣言信托制度构建研究》[*Research on the Construction of Charitable Declaration Trusts*] (法律出版社 [Law Press], 2012)

Xu, Ying and Ngan-Pun Ngai, 'Moral Resources and Political Capital: Theorizing the Relationship between Voluntary Service Organizations and the Development of Civil Society in China' (2011) 40(2) *Nonprofit and Voluntary Sector Quarterly* 247

薛宁兰 [Xue Ninglan] and 邓丽 [Deng Li],《中国慈善法研究与立法建议稿》[*Research on Chinese Charity Law and Relevant Legislative Proposals*] (中国社会科学出版社 [China Social Science Press], 2014)

薛智胜 [Xue Zhisheng] and 王海涛 [Wang Haitao],《论我国公益信托监察人法律制度的完善》[Perfecting the Institution of the Trust Supervisor in the Chinese Charitable Trust System] (2009) 11(2) 天津大学学报　社会科学版　*Journal of Tianjin University (Social Science)* 123

闫荣涛 [Yan Rongtao],《中国信托财产所有权归属分析与建构》[Analysis and Reconstruction on the Internal Structure of Trust Ownership in China] (2009) 9 昆明理工大学学报 (社会科学版) *Journal of Kunming University of Science and Technology (Social Sciences)* 60

杨春桃 [Yang Chuntao],《论自然人提起环境公益诉讼》[Research on Natural Person to Bring Environmental Public Interest Litigation] (2014) 6 北京航空航天大学学报 (社会科学版) *Journal of Beijing University of Aeronautics and Astronautics (Social Sciences Edition)* 50

张淳 [Zhang Chun],《<中华人民共和国信托法>中的创造性规定及其评析》[The Creative Provisions in the Trust Law of the People's Republic of China and Its Evaluation] (2002) 2 法律科学 *Law Science* 110

张家慧 [Zhang Jiahui],《诉权意义的回复 – 诉讼法与实体法关系的理论基点》[Responses to the Meaning of Appealing Right: Theoretical Basis of the Relationship between Procedural Law and Substantive Law] (2000) 2 法律评论 *Law Review* 58

Zhang, Ruiqiao, 'Trust Law of China and Its Uncertainties: Examination of the Rights and Obligations of Trust and Ownership of Trust Property' (2015) 10 *National Taiwan University Law Review* 45

赵廉慧 [Zhao Lianhui],《信托法解释论》[*Interpretative Theory of Trust Law*] (中国法制出版社 [China Legal Publishing House], 2015)

周小明 [Zhou Xiaoming],《信托制度：法理与实务》[*Trust System: Theory and Practice*] (中国法制出版社 [China Legal Publishing House], 2012)

朱锦清 [Zhu Jinqing],《公司法学　下　》[*Company Law (II)*] (清华大学出版社 [Tsinghua University Press], 2017)

朱庆育 [Zhu Qingyu],《民法总论》[*The General Theory of Civil Law*] (北京大学出版社 [Peking University Press], 2016)

朱新力 [Zhu Xinli] and 李芹 [Li Qin],《行政约谈的功能定位与制度建构》[The Functional Orientation and Institutional Design of Administrative Interviews] (2018) 4 国家行政学院学报 *Journal of Chinese Academy of Governance* 91

朱志峰 [Zhu Zhifeng], 《公益信托的法律特征及我国模式的探索》[Legal Nature of the Charitable Trust and Exploration of a Chinese Model] (2008) 22(6) 当代法学 *Contemporary Law Review* 112

Zinn, Matthew D, 'Policing Environmental Regulatory Enforcement: Cooperation, Capture, and Citizen Suits' (2002) 21 *Stanford Environmental Law Journal* 81

Cases

Aid/Watch Inc v *Federal Commissioner of Taxation* (2010) 272 ALR 417

Attorney General (NSW) v *Homeland Community Ltd* [2015] NSWCA 15 (16 February 2015)

Attorney-General for New South Wales v *Perpetual Trustee Co (Ltd)* (1940) 63 CLR 209

Bateman's Bay Local Aboriginal Land Council v *The Aboriginal Community Benefit Fund Pty Limited* [1998] HCA 49 (6 August 1998)

Bath and North East Somerset Council v *HM Attorney General* (2002) EWHC 1623 (Ch)

Bathurst City Council v *PWC Properties Pty Ltd* [1998] HCA 59 (30 September 1998)

Beaton v *McDivitt* (1987) 13 NSWLR 162

Blenkinsop v *Blenkinsop Nominees Pty Ltd (as trustee for Blenkinsop Family Trust (No 2))* [2016] WASC 61 (4 March 2016)

Blenkinsop v *Herbert* [2017] WASCA 87 (8 June 2017)

Bourne v *Keane* (1919) AC 815

Bowman v *Secular Society Ltd* (1917) AC 406

Bradshaw v *University College of Wales* (1988) 1 WLR 190

Breakspear v *Ackland* (2008) 3 WLR 698

Bropho v *City of Perth* [2016] FCA 1098 (8 September 2016)

BSH Holding Pty Ltd v Commissioner of State Revenue [2000] VSC 302 (2 August 2000)

Carson v *Presbyterian Church of Queensland* [1956] St R Qd 466 (15 December 1955)

Chesterman v *Mitchell* (1923) 24 SR (NSW) 108

Clay v *Clay* (2001) 202 ALR 410

Edge v *Pensions Ombudsman* (2000) Ch 602

Farah Construction Pty Ltd v *Say-Dee Pty Ltd* (2007) 236 ALR 209

Gartside v *Inland Revenue Commissioners* (1968) AC 553, 617
Hartigan Nominees Pty Ltd v *Rydge* (1992) 29 NSWLR 405
Haslemere Estates Ltd v *Baker* (1982) 1 WLR 1109
Investors Compensation Scheme Ltd v *West Bromwich Building Society* (1998) 1 WLR 896
James Cook University v *Townsville City Council & Anor* [2011] QSC 209 (23 June 2011)
Kambouris v *Tahmazis* (2012) VSC 432
Knudsen v *Kara Kar Holdings Pty Ltd* [2000] NSWSC 715 (21 July 2000)
Laura & Alfred West Cottage Homes Inc v *Attorney-General (SA)* [2018] SASA 19 (26 February 2018)
LGSS v *Egan* [2002] NSWSC 1171 (12 April 2002)
《林承恩、李江山、涂雅雅侵占公司机会纠纷案》 [*Lin Chengen and Li Jiangshen* v *Tu Yaya* – Company Opportunity Dispute] [2012] 最高人民法院 [Supreme People's Court] (2012) 民四终字第15号 [Civil Fourth Division, Appealing Ruling, Case No 15]
Lygon Nominees Pty Ltd v *Commissioner of State Revenue* (2005) VSC 247
McPhail v *Doulton* (1971) AC 424, 441
Melbourne Jewish Orphan and Children's Aid Society Inc & Anor v *ANZ Executors and Trustee Company Ltd & Anor* [2007] VSC 26 (20 February 2007)
Metropolitan Petar v *Mitreski* [2001] NSWSC 976 (31 October 2001)
National Anti-vivisection Society v *Inland Revenue Commissioners* (1948) AC 31
Ngarluma Aboriginal Corp RNTBC v *Attorney General (WA)* [2014] WASC 245 (7 July 2014)
Ofrex (George Drexler) Foundation (Trustees) v *IRC* (1965) 3 All ER 529
Pedulla v *Nasti* (1990) 20 NSWLR 720
Perpetual Trustees Victoria Limited v *Barns & Anor* [2012] VSCA 77 (2 May 2012)
Pope v *Drp Nominees Pty Ltd* (1999) 337 SASC
Public Trustee v *Attorney-General (NSW)* (1997) 42 NSWLR 600
Radmanovich v *Nedeljkovic* [2001] NSWSC 492 (15 June 2001)
Re Astor's Settlement Trusts (1952) 1 All ER 1067
Re Cooper Street Property Trust (2016) VSC 756
Re Cooper Street Property Trust (No 2) [2017] VSC 291 (26 May 2017)
Re Denley's Trust Deed (1969) 1 Ch 373
Re Hampton Fuel Allotment Charity (1988) 3 WLR 513
Re Hummeltenberg (1923) All ER Rep 49
Re Londonderry's Settlement (1965) Ch 918
Re Pearce [1946] SASR 118 (24 October 1946)
Re Rabaiott's Settlement (2000) WTLR 953
Re Thompson (1934) Ch 342
Re Wood (1949) Ch 498
Regal (Hastings) Ltd v *Gulliver* (1967) 2 AC 134

Richstar Enterprises Pty Ltd v *Carey (No 6)* (2006) 233 ALR 475

Royal Society for the Prevention of Cruelty to Animals v *Attorney General* (2001) 3 All ER 530

The Salvation Army (New South Wales) Property Trust v *Chief Commissioner of State Revenue* [2018] NSWSC 128 (16 February 2018)

Scott v *National Trust for Places of Historical Interest or Natural Beauty* (1998) 2 All ER 705

Sharp v *Maritime Super Pty Ltd* [2012] NSWSC 1350 (7 November 2012)

Thorn v *Bettens* [2006] SASC 59 (3 March 2006)

Trustees Executors & Agency Co Ltd v *Zelman Memorial Symphony Orchestra Ltd* (1958) VR 523

United Group Rail Services Ltd v *Rail Corporation New South Wales* (2009) 74 NSWLR 618

Walter v *Registrar of Titles* [2003] VSCA 122

Warman International Ltd v *Dwyer* (1995) 128 ALR 201

Waubra Foundation and Commissioner of Australian Charities and Not-for-profits Commission [2017] AATA 2424 (4 December 2017)

Wills v *Solicitor-General for New Zealand* (1903) AC 173

Wright v *Stevens* [2018] NSWSC 548 (3 May 2018)

Legislation/Policy Documents

《"十三五"脱贫攻坚规划》 ['13th Five-Year Plan' for Poverty Alleviation] (People's Republic of China) State Council, 23 November 2016

《慈善信托管理办法》[Administrative Measures for Charitable Trusts] (People's Republic of China) China Banking Regulatory Commission and Ministry of Civil Affairs, 10 July 2017

《信托公司集合资金信托计划管理办法》 [Administrative Measures for Collective Investment Trust Schemes of Trust Companies] (People's Republic of China) China Banking Regulatory Commission, 4 February 2009

《广州市社会组织评估管理办法》[Administrative Measures for the Assessment and Management of Social Organizations in Guangzhou] (People's Republic of China) Guangzhou Civil Affairs Bureau, 2 December 2013

《深圳市社会组织评估管理办法 试行 》 [Administrative Measures for the Assessment and Management of Social Organizations in Shenzhen (Trial)] (People's Republic of China) Shenzhen Civil Affairs Bureau, 21 September 2011

《天津市社会组织评估管理办法》[Administrative Measures for the Assessment and Management of Social Organizations in Tianjin] (People's Republic of China) Tianjin Civil Affairs Bureau, 28 May 2012

《社会组织评估管理办法》[Administrative Measures for the Assessment of Social Organizations] (People's Republic of China) Ministry of Civil Affairs, 20 December 2010

Australian Charities and Not-for-Profits Commission Act 2012 (Cth)

《北京慈善信托管理办法》 [Beijing Administrative Measures for Charitable Trusts] (People's Republic of China) Beijing Bureau of Civil Affairs, 21 September 2016

《北京海淀科技发展有限公司诉深圳市新华锦源投资发展有限公司财产权属纠纷案》 [*Beijing Haidian Technology Development Co Ltd* v *Shenzhen Xinhua Jinyuan Investment Development Co Ltd* – Dispute over the Plaintiff's Property Ownership], 重庆市高级人民法院 [Chongqing High People's Court], 渝高法民初字第14号 [Civil Division, Initial Ruling, Case No 14], 19 March 2007

《上海交通大学中国公益发展研究院<中国社会组织评估发展报告(2018)>蓝皮书发布》 [The Blue Book of 'China Social Organization Evaluation and Development Report (2018)' Released by China Philanthropy Development Institute of Shanghai Jiaotong University] (29 December 2018) <https://Dzb.Sjtu.Edu.Cn/Data/View/3309>

Charitable Trusts Act 1993 (NSW)

Charities Act 1978 (Vic)

Charities Act 2011 (England and Wales)

Charities Act 2013 (Cth)

《中华人民共和国慈善法》 [Charity Law of the People's Republic of China] (People's Republic of China) National People's Congress, 16 March 2016

《中华人民共和国民法典》 [Civil Code of the People's Republic of China] (People's Republic of China) National People's Congress, 28 May 2020

《杭州市西湖区西湖家园业主委员会与杭州安泰西湖房地产有限公司清算委员会房屋买卖合同纠纷申诉民事裁定书》 [Civil Order of the Appeal of the Housing Sales Contract Dispute between West Lake Home Owners Committee and the Liquidation Committee of Hangzhou Antai West Lake Real Estate Co Ltd], 最高人民法院 [Supreme People's Court], 民提字第100号 [Supreme People's Court, Civil Division, Case No 100], 29 October 2014

《中银投资有限公司与太原市北晨综合开发有限责任公司一般借款合同纠纷二审民事裁定书》 [Civil Order of the Second Instance of the General Loan Contract Dispute between Bank of China Investment Co Ltd and Taiyuan Beichen Comprehensive Development Co Ltd], 最高人民法院 [Supreme People's Court], 民二终字第38号 [Civil Division, Appeal Ruling, Case No 38], 15 June 2014

《胡云河与云南鑫潮融和置业有限公司民间借贷纠纷二审民事裁定书》 [Civil Order of the Second Instance of the Private Lending Dispute between Hu Yunhe and Yunnan Xinchao Ronghe Real Estate Co Ltd], 最高人民法院

[Supreme People's Court], 民一终字第139号 [Civil Division, Appeal Ruling, Case No 139], 16 October 2013

《河北省直纪元房地产开发有限公司、河北省西山迎宾馆有限公司物权保护纠纷二审民事裁定书》 [Civil Order of the Second Instance of the Property Protection Dispute between Hebei Province Zhijiyuan Real Estate Development Co Ltd and Hebei Province Xi Shanying Hotel Co Ltd], 最高人民法院 [Supreme People's Court], 最高法民终764号 [Civil Division, Appeal Ruling, Case No 764], 16 December 2016

《吴振庆与哈尔滨现代房地产开发有限公司不当得利纠纷二审民事裁定书》 [Civil Order of the Second Instance of the Unjust Enrichment Dispute between Wu Zhenqing and Harbin Modern Real Estate Development Co Ltd], 最高人民法院 [Supreme People's Court], 最高法民终149号 [Civil Division, Appeal Ruling, Case No 149], 1 March 2017

《中华人民共和国民事诉讼法》[Civil Procedure Law of the People's Republic of China] (People's Republic of China) Standing Committee of the National People's Congress, 24 December 2021

《中华人民共和国公司法》[Company Law of the People's Republic of China] (People's Republic of China) National People's Congress, 26 October 2018

《中共中央、国务院关于打赢脱贫攻坚战的决定》 [Decision of the Central Committee of the Communist Party of China and the State Council on Winning the Battle Against Poverty] (People's Republic of China) Central Committee of the Communist Party of China and the State Council, 29 November 2015

《中共中央关于全面深化改革若干重大问题的决定》[Decision of the Central Committee of the Communist Party of China on Several Major Issues on Comprehensively Deepening Reforms] (People's Republic of China) Central Committee of the Communist Party of China, 12 November 2018

《民政部关于表彰第十届"中华慈善奖"获得者的决定》 [Decision of the Ministry of Civil Affairs on Commending the Winners of the 10th China Charity Award] (People's Republic of China) Ministry of Civil Affairs, 10 September 2018

《中华人民共和国环境保护法》[Environmental Protection Law of the People's Republic of China] (People's Republic of China) Standing Committee of the National People's Congress, 24 April 2014

《关于<中华人民共和国慈善法 （草案） >的说明》 [Explanations on the Charity Law of the People's Republic of China (Draft)] (People's Republic of China) Standing Committee of the People's Congress, 9 March 2016

《关于<中华人民共和国信托法 （草案） >的说明》 [Explanations on the Trust Law of the People's Republic of China (Draft)] (People's Republic of China) Standing Committee of the People's Congress, 24 December 1996

《冯锦等诉高育新公司利益纠纷案》[*Feng Jin* v *Gao Yuxin* – Company Interest Dispute], 北京市第一中级人民法院 [Beijing First Intermediate Court], 民

终字第7378号 [Civil Division, Appealing Ruling, Case No 7378], 31 October 2017

《上市公司治理准则》 [Governance Codes for Listed Companies in China] (People's Republic of China) China Security Regulatory Commission, 30 September 2018

《信托公司行业评级指引（试行）》[Guidelines for Industry Rating of Trust Companies (Trial)] (People's Republic of China) China Trustee Association, 14 September 2017

《中国慈善事业发展指导纲要（2011–2015年）》 [Guidelines for the Development of China's Charitable Causes (2011–2015)] (People's Republic of China) Ministry of Civil Affairs, 15 July 2011

《国务院关于促进慈善事业健康发展的指导意见》[Guiding Opinions of the State Council on Promoting Healthy Development of Charitable Causes] (People's Republic of China) State Council, 24 November 2014

《潮州市全市性社会组织评估实施办法》 [Implementation Measures for the Assessment of Social Organizations in Chaozhou] (People's Republic of China) Chaozhou Civil Affairs Bureau, 8 July 2011

《惠州市民政局关于社会组织评估管理的实施办法》[Implementation Measures of Huizhou Civil Affairs Bureau on the Assessment and Management of Social Organizations] (People's Republic of China) Huizhou Civil Affairs Bureau, 12 October 2011

《北京市海淀区关于促进慈善事业发展的实施方案》[Implementation Plan for Promoting the Development of Charitable Causes in Haidian District of Beijing] (People's Republic of China) Haidian District Government of Beijing, 14 March 2017

《宝鸡市慈善爱心基金管理暂行办法》 [Interim Measures for the Administration of Charity Love Fund in Baoji City] (People's Republic of China) The People's Government of Baoji City, 10 January 2008

《信托投资公司信息披露管理暂行办法》 [Interim Measures for the Administration of Information Disclosure by Trust Companies] (People's Republic of China) China Banking Regulatory Commission, 18 January 2015

《江苏省慈善信托备案管理暂行实施办法》 [Interim Measures for the Administration of Recording of Charitable Trusts in Jiangsu Province] (People's Republic of China) Jiangsu Provincial Civil Affairs Department and Jiangsu Office of the China Banking Regulatory Commission, 23 October 2017

《慈善组织保值增值投资活动管理暂行办法》 [Interim Measures for the Administration of the Investment Activities for Value Preservation and Appreciation of Charitable Organizations] (People's Republic of China) Ministry of Civil Affairs, 30 October 2018

《民办非企业单位登记管理暂行条例》 [Interim Regulations on the Administration of the Registration of Privately-Operated Non-Enterprise Organizations] (People's Republic of China) State Council, 25 October 1998

《最高人民法院关于审理环境民事公益诉讼案件适用法律若干问题的解释》 [Interpretations of the Supreme People's Court on Several Issues Concerning the Application of Law in the Hearing of Environmental Civil Public Interest Lawsuits] (People's Republic of China) Supreme People's Court, 7 January 2015

《健桥证券股份有限公司与宝鸡钛业股份有限公司委托理财合同纠纷上诉案》 [*Jianqiao Securities Co Ltd* v *Baoji Titanium Industry Co Ltd* – Dispute over Entrusted Financial Management Contract], 最高人民法院 [Supreme People's Court], 民二终字第29号 [Civil Division, Appeal Ruling, Case No 29], 29 April 2005

最高人民法院审判委员会 [Judicial Committee of the Supreme People's Court],《最高法发布十起环境公益诉讼典型案例之二: 中国生物多样性保护与绿色发展基金会诉宁夏瑞泰科技股份有限公司环境污染公益诉讼案》 (2016年12月28日) [No 2 of Ten Guiding Cases regarding Environmental Public Interest Litigations Published by the Supreme People's Court: *China Biodiversity Conservation and Green Development Foundation* v *Ningxia Ruitai Science and Technology Co Ltd*] (28 December 2016)

最高人民法院审判委员会 [Judicial Committee of the Supreme People's Court], 《最高法发布十起环境公益诉讼典型案例之九: 贵州省六盘水市六枝特区人民检察院诉贵州省镇宁布依族苗族自治县丁旗镇人民政府环境行政公益诉讼案》 (2016年12月28日) [No 9 of Ten Guiding Cases regarding Environmental Public Interest Litigations Published by the Supreme People's Court: *People's Procuratorate of Liuzhi Special District of Liupanshui City, Guizhou Province* v *People's Government of Dingqi Township, Zhenning Buyi and Miao Autonomous County, Guizhou Province* – Environmental Administrative Public Interest Litigation] (28 December 2016)

《2019年江苏省民政工作要点》 [Key Points of Civil Affairs Work in Jiangsu Province in 2019] (People's Republic of China) Jiangsu Civil Affairs Department, 19 February 2019

《2020年上海慈善事业促进工作要点》 [Key Work Points of Shanghai Charity Promotion Work in 2019] (People's Republic of China) Shanghai Civil Affairs Bureau, 20 March 2020

《刘彬与李占军监事损害公司利益纠纷上诉案》 [*Lin Bin* v *Li Zhanjun* – Company Interest Dispute], 北京市第一中级人民法院 [Beijing First Intermediate Court], 民终字第1099号 [Civil Division, Appealing Ruling, Case No 1099], 9 March 2010

《信托公司管理办法》 [Measures for Administration of Trust Companies] (People's Republic of China) China Banking Regulatory Commission, 23 January 2007

《信托公司净资本管理办法》[Measures for the Administration of Net Capital of Trust Companies] (People's Republic of China) China Banking Regulatory Commission, 24 August 2010

《浙江省实施<中华人民共和国慈善法>办法》 [Measures for the Implementation of the Chinese Charity Law in Zhejiang Province] (People's Republic of China) Standing Committee of Zhejiang Provincial People's Congress, 30 November 2018

《甘肃省慈善捐助管理办法》 [Measures for the Management of Charitable Donations in Gansu Province] (People's Republic of China) The People's Government in Gansu Province, 1 May 2006

《北京市社会组织行政约谈办法》[Measures of Administrative Interviews for Social Organizations in Beijing] (People's Republic of China) Beijing Civil Affairs Bureau, 25 October 2015

《无锡市社会组织评估管理办法》 [Measures for the Assessment and Management of Social Organizations in Wuxi] (People's Republic of China) Wuxi Civil Affairs Bureau, 28 April 2013

《"中华慈善奖"评选表彰办法》[Method for the Selection and Commendation of 'China Charity Award'] (People's Republic of China) Ministry of Civil Affairs, 3 June 2014

《中国银监会办公厅关于进一步明确信托公司风险监管责任的通知》 [Notice by the General Office of the China Insurance Regulatory Commission of Further Clarifying the Risk Supervision Responsibilities of Trust Companies] China Banking Regulatory Commission, 25 June 2013

《关于公益性捐赠税前扣除有关问题的通知》[Notice Concerning the Relevant Issues of Pre-Tax Deduction of Public Welfare Donations] (People's Republic of China) Ministry of Finance; State Administration of Taxation; Ministry of Civil Affairs, 31 December 2018

《民政部、中国银行业监督管理委员会关于做好慈善信托备案有关工作的通知》[Notice of Civil Affairs Department and China Banking Regulatory Commission on the Recordation Work for Charitable Trusts] (People's Republic of China) Civil Affairs Department and China Banking Regulatory Commission, 25 August 2016

《中国银监会办公厅关于鼓励信托公司开展公益信托业务支持灾后重建工作的通知》 [Notice of the General Office of China Banking Regulatory Commission on the Encouragement of Charitable Trust Business of Trust Companies to Support Post-Earthquake Reconstruction] (People's Republic of China) General Office of China Banking Regulatory Commission, 6 February 2008

《中国银行业监督管理委员会办公厅关于信托公司房地产信托业务风险提示的通知》[Notice of the General Office of the China Banking Regulatory

Commission on Risk Reminders for the Real Estate Trust Business of Trust Companies] (People's Republic of China) General Office of the China Banking Regulatory Commission, 12 November 2010

《民政部关于印发各类社会组织评估指标的通知》[Notice of the Ministry of Civil Affairs on Printing and Distributing the Assessment Indicators of Various Social Organizations] (People's Republic of China) Ministry of Civil Affairs, 23 August 2011

《民政部关于贯彻落实<国务院关于促进慈善事业健康发展的指导意见>的通知》[Notice of the Ministry of Civil Affairs on Implementing the 'Guiding Opinions of the State Council on Promoting the Healthy Development of Charitable Causes'] (People's Republic of China) Ministry of Civil Affairs of People's Republic of China, 15 December 2014

《上海市民政局关于贯彻落实<中华人民共和国慈善法>的通知》 [Notice of the Shanghai Bureau of Civil Affairs on the Implementation of the Charity Law of the People's Republic of China] (People's Republic of China) Shanghai Bureau of Civil Affairs, 26 August 2016

《中国银监会办公厅关于进一步加强信托公司风险监管工作的意见》[Opinions of the General Office of the China Banking Regulatory Commission on Further Strengthening the Work of Supervising the Risks of Trust Companies] China Banking Regulatory Commission, 18 March 2016

《民政部、国资委关于支持中央企业积极投身公益慈善事业的意见》[Opinions of the Ministry of Civil Affairs and the State-Owned Assets Supervision and Administration Commission on Supporting the Central Enterprises to Actively Participate in Charitable Causes] (People's Republic of China) Ministry of Civil Affairs and State-Owned Assets Supervision and Administration Commission, 19 May 2015

《民政部关于推进深度贫困地区民政领域脱贫攻坚工作的意见》[Opinions of the Ministry of Civil Affairs on Promoting Poverty Alleviation in the Field of Civil Affairs in Deep Poverty Stricken Areas] (People's Republic of China) Ministry of Civil Affairs, 7 April 2018

《民政部关于加强和创新慈善超市建设的意见》[Opinions of the Ministry of Civil Affairs on Strengthening and Innovating the Construction of Charity Supermarkets] (People's Republic of China) Ministry of Civil Affairs, 31 December 2013

《中国农村扶贫开发纲要 (2011–2020年) 》[Outline of Poverty Alleviation and Development in China Rural Areas (2011–2020)] (People's Republic of China) Central Committee of the Communist Party of China and State Council, 27 May 2011

《最高人民法院关于审理企业破产案件若干问题的规定》 [Provisions of the Supreme People's Court on Certain Issues Concerning the Trial of

Enterprise Bankruptcy Cases] (People's Republic of China) Supreme People's Court, 9 January 2002

《社会组织登记管理机关行政执法约谈工作规定 (试行) 》 [Provisions on the Interview Works in the Administrative Law Enforcement by Social Organization Registration and Administration Organs: for Trail Implementation] (People's Republic of China) Ministry of Civil Affairs, 16 March 2016

《长沙市慈善事业促进条例》 [Regulations of Charity Promotion in Changsha City] (People's Republic of China) Standing Committee of the People's Congress of Changsha City, 1 September 2012

《江苏省慈善事业促进条例》 [Regulations of Charity Promotion in Jiangsu Province] (People's Republic of China) Standing Committee of the People's Congress of Jiangsu Province, 1 May 2010

《宁波市慈善事业促进条例》 [Regulations of Charity Promotion in Ningbo City] (People's Republic of China) Standing Committee of the People's Congress of Ningbo City, 1 October 2011

《宁夏回族自治区慈善事业促进条例》 [Regulations of Charity Promotion in Ningxia Hui Autonomous Region] (People's Republic of China) Standing Committee of the People's Congress of Ningxia Hui Autonomous Region, 1 November 2011

《基金会管理条例》 [Regulations on Administration of Foundations] (People's Republic of China) State Council, 3 August 2004

《社会团体登记管理条例》 [Regulations on Registration Administration of Associations] (People's Republic of China) State Council, 6 February 2016

《关于慈善信托管理工作的实施细则》 [Regulations on the Management of Charitable Trusts] (People's Republic of China) Guangdong Provincial Civil Affairs Department and Guangdong Office of the China Banking Insurance Regulatory Commission, 21 February 2019

《全国人大法律委员会关于<中华人民共和国信托法(草案)>修改情况的汇报》 [Report of the Law Committee of the National People's Congress on the Revision of Trust Law of the People's Republic of China (Draft)] (People's Republic of China) National People's Congress, 3 July 2000

《全国人民代表大会关于国民经济和社会发展第十三个五年规划纲要的决议》 [Resolution of the National People's Congress on the Outline of the Thirteenth Five-Year Plan for National Economic and Social Development] (People's Republic of China) National People's Congress, 16 March 2016

《全国人民代表大会关于国民经济和社会发展第十二个五年规划纲要的决议》 [Resolution of the National People's Congress on the Outline of the Twelfth Five-Year Plan for National Economic and Social Development] (People's Republic of China) National People's Congress, 14 March 2011

《北京市促进慈善事业若干规定》[Several Regulations for Developing Charity in Beijing] (People's Republic of China) Beijing Municipal People's Government, 1 January 2014

《上海岩鑫实业投资有限公司诉华宝信托投资有限责任公司信托合同纠纷案》[*Shanghai Yanxin Industrial Investment Co Ltd* v *Huabao Trust Investment Co Ltd* – Dispute over Trust Contract], 上海市第一中级人民法院 [Shanghai First Intermediate Court], 沪一中民三 商 初字第201号[Civil Division, Initial Ruling, Case No 201], 25 August 2004

Supreme Court Civil Procedure Act 1932 (Tas)

《吉林省建苑设计集团有限公司与四川信托有限公司信托纠纷案》 [Trust Dispute between Jilin Jianyuan Design Company and Sichuan Trust Company], 四川省成都市中级人民法院 [Chengdu Intermediate People's Court of Sichuan Province], 成民初字第2449号 [Civil Division, Initial Ruling, Case No 2449], 20 October 2016

《中华人民共和国信托法》 [Trust Law of the People's Republic of China] (People's Republic of China) National People's Congress, 28 April 2001

Trustee Act 1925 (ACT)

Trustee Act 1936 (SA)

Trustees Act 1962 (WA)

Trusts Act 1973 (Qld)

Variation of Trusts Act 1994 (Tas)

《杭州市民政系统2017年工作总结和2018年工作要点》 [Work Summary of Hangzhou Civil Affair System in 2017 and Key Work Points in 2018] (People's Republic of China) Hangzhou Civil Affairs Bureau, 13 February 2018

《江苏省慈善信托备案管理暂行实施办法》 [Interim Measures for the Administration of Recording of Charitable Trusts in Jiangsu Province] (People's Republic of China) Jiangsu Provincial Civil Affairs Department and Jiangsu Office of the China Banking Regulatory Commission, 23 October 2017

Others

'Former Executive Vice President of Sichuan Provincial Red Cross Was Sued for Corruption', *Best China News* (20 August 2016), available at: <www.bestchinanews.com/Domestic/7092.html> (last accessed 1 June 2020).

Hanlon, Fiona, 'An Analysis of the Office of Attorney General in Australia and Directions for the Future' (PhD Thesis, Faculty of Law, The University of Melbourne, 2007)

Li, Dejian, 'Reform of Charity Governance in China: From Economic and Comparative Perspectives' (PhD Thesis, Faculty of Law, The University of Liverpool, 2017)

Li, Raymond, 'Unexplained Destruction of Statue in Henan Raises Suspicion', *South China Morning Post* (7 July 2013), available at: <www.scmp.com/comment/insight-opinion/article/1276973/unexplained-destruction-statue-henan-raises-suspicion> (last accessed 18 June 2020)

Tan, Zhenting, 'Perfecting the Chinese Law of Trusts: A Critical and Comparative Study of the Australian and the Chinese Law of Trusts' (PhD Thesis, Bond University, 2005)

The Treasury, The Australian Government, *Development of Governance Standards-Consultation Paper* (December 2012)

Review of Not-for-Profit Governance Arrangement-Consultation Paper (2011)

Tsu, Yu-Yue, 'The Spirit of Chinese Philanthropy: A Study in Mutual Aid' (PhD Thesis, The Faculty of Political Science, Columbia University, 1912)

相庆梅 [Xiang Qingmei],《民事诉权论》[Research on the Right of Civil Suits] (PhD Thesis, China University of Political Science and Law, 2006)

INDEX

www.ingramcontent.com/pod-product-compliance
Lightning Source LLC
LaVergne TN
LVHW011813200926
848484LV00005B/1175
9781009327909